# WHAT YOU DON'T KNOW

# ABOUT DISASTERS

# CAN HURT YOU

## PREPARE TO PROTECT

*by*

**L.G. Wellington**

**Copyright through United States Copyright Office - 2012 by L.G. Wellington**

**ISBN-13: 978-1973773405**
**ISBN-10: 1973773406**

# Hello there!

In this book, I will provide a wealth of information on how to protect family members from natural disasters as well as manmade disasters and dangerous events that can occur during the present time as well as in the future.  These events can happen within a short period of time or over a longer period of time.  And as a consequence, vital elements we count on for ultimate survival would certainly be affected.  For example, with the failure of the electrical grid in the country, there would be no electric lights, no water, no heat, no sewer, no communication, no transportation systems, no medical facilities or supplies, no banks or other financial institutions, and no stores or commercial markets.  And everyone would need to fend for themselves.

In our unpredictable and volatile world, we never know *when* or *where* a dangerous event will occur and how it will adversely affect the *physical, mental, emotional, spiritual* and *psychological* <u>health</u> of an individual, a family, a community or the entire country.

Thus, it is critical for individuals to recognize the importance of *planning and preparing in advance* for emergencies, and as we begin our journey into learning survival strategies, techniques and guidelines, a family should evaluate your own unique circumstances and based on where you live, current lifestyle and other factors affecting individual situations, review the information and make a *realistic* and *smart* decision on what would be good choices for you.

As we learn strategies on how to **PREPARE AND PROTECT** *before*, *during* and *after* dangerous events, it is important families recognize we cannot control natural events. However, families *can* implement a plan and be *proactive* in creating an environment that reduces or eliminates a dangerous event and perhaps lessens the consequences of the disaster.  For example, although we can not stop an earthquake, we *can* take steps in our home to reduce possible injuries by inspecting the home and surroundings for possible hazards and then take action to lessen those hazards.

We can also eliminate manmade dangerous events such as a home invasion by making sure the home is armed with high quality dead bolts on all outer doors and has an alarm system.

As an integral part of **PREPARE AND PROTECT** against dangerous events, we need to become <u>self sufficient</u> and vigilant in stocking emergency supplies - a continual and on-going process.  It is now time to learn about *specific* types of emergencies and disasters that can occur in regions around the world and in your area, and what steps family members can take *in advance* to prepare for these dangerous events.

## <u>STUDY - LEARN - PONDER - THINK - ANALYZE - DISCUSS</u>

# TABLE OF CONTENTS

**PREFACE**

During peaceful as well as disaster times, our own protection and the protection of loved ones against *dangerous events* is a continual and persistent mission and must be aggressively pursued at all times. What is a dangerous event? Simply stated, a *dangerous event* is any <u>incident</u> that happens to an individual, a group of individuals, an entire population of a country, an entire civilization or everyone on earth. This dangerous event could be created by a natural force such as an earthquake, volcano eruption, flood or tsunami. The event could also be created by humans such as a home invasion, robbery, riot, chemical or biological warfare, terrorist attack on the electrical grid or even nuclear war.

For example: A single person could experience a home invasion - a group of individuals could be caught up in a mudslide - an entire country could be experiencing a serious drought - an entire civilization could be wiped out by a plague - or the population of the entire world could look up in the sky one morning and see a comet heading straight for earth. As a world in crisis, it becomes even more important to take steps to protect the lives and well being of family members, our homes and its contents and the health and safety of pets and livestock who count on us for their health and well being.

When studying the various agencies and organizations responsible for protecting us in a crisis, there are several interesting facts about assumptions regarding the occurrence of these events. Obviously, these perceptions are derived from past experiences, mathematical analyses and projections and observing actual disaster occurrences. As a result, overall disaster plans are created based on what has been learned from past events and conclusions of what *might* occur in the future. For example, an emergency or disaster will:

- Only occur in a **specific area** or **region** of a city or state, country or continent, e.g. the west end of New York City; the northern part of Washington; the entire state of California; the entire east coast of the United States; the entire United States; or the entire African continent

- Have a **finite time period** in which it will be destructive based on the type of disaster, e.g. an earthquake generally lasts less than 5-10 minutes; a tornado starts and finishes in less than an hour; a drought lasts for several years

- Have a **finite amount of property damage, destruction and loss of life** based on the type of disaster, e.g. a wildfire that damages and destroys 1,000 acres of forest, six homes and kills ten people

- Generally not include more than **two disaster types at a time**, e.g. earthquake and the resulting tsunami

- **Not create such a cataclysmic disaster** that it cannot be "handled". Emergency personnel and government agencies, charitable organizations, medical personnel and other responders will be able to respond to the crisis and effectively perform their duties so a "normal" environment can be restored in the foreseeable future

Frankly, as I have studied various disasters that have occurred in my lifetime and over the past several millenniums, I can think of only two disasters that were so catastrophic - the affects were felt around the entire globe. The first one supposedly occurred sixty-five million years ago when a comet hit the earth and took out all the dinosaurs, and the second one occurred about 4,500 years ago when a man by the name of Noah was warned about a pending rain storm. With the exception of these two events, all other manmade and natural disasters seem to fall in line with the above conclusions.

Therefore, based on past disasters, it would seem realistic and logical to assume future dangerous events and disasters would also mimic the behavior of their predecessors. Since those agencies responsible for the safety and security of the overall population *before*, *during* and *after* a disaster relies on the fact that it is highly unlikely another comet or great big rain storm will happen again, there would be no reason they could not jump in and save us all from certain death and destruction.

Let's review specific areas or regions around the world where a dangerous event could happen and how others outside of the disaster region can easily come to their aid:

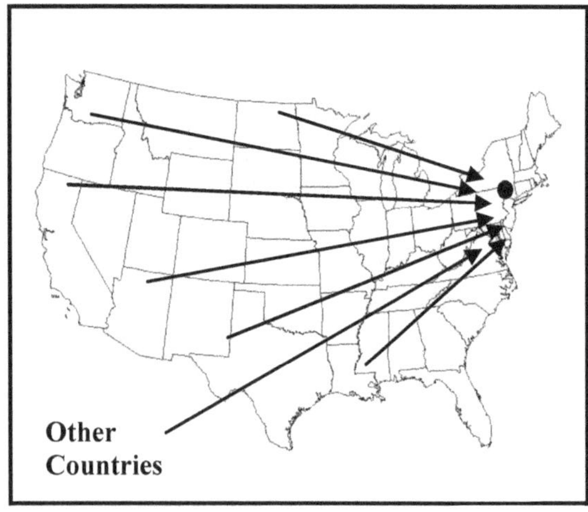


**West Side of New York City**

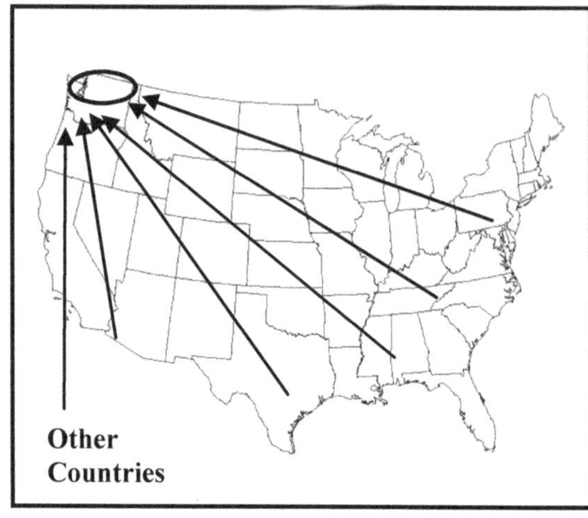


**Northern Region of the State of Washington**

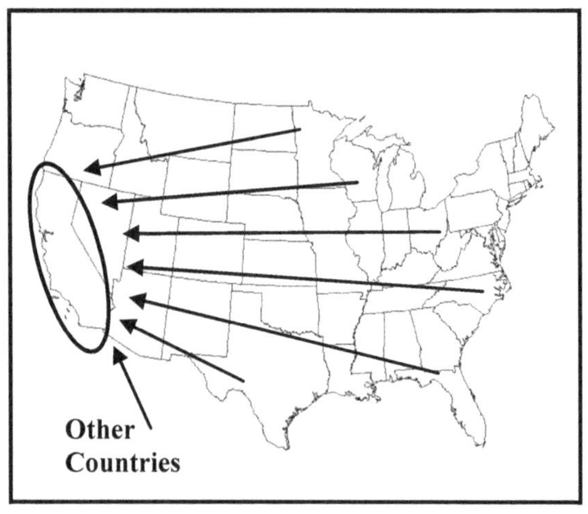


**Entire State of California**

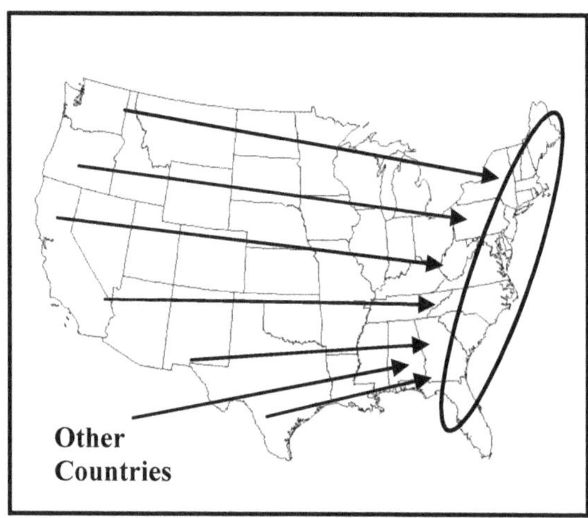


**Entire East Coast of the United States**

**Entire United States**

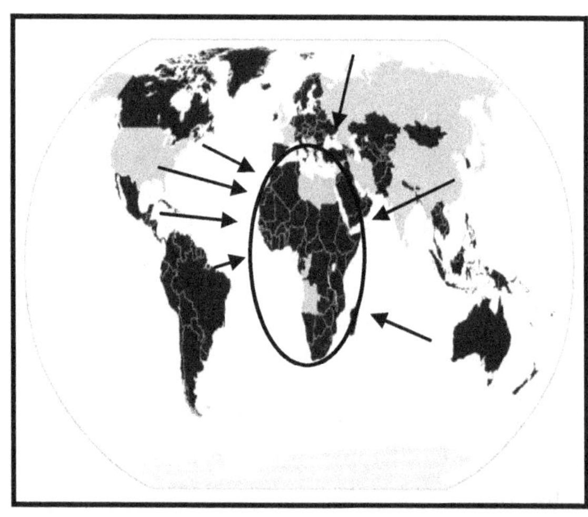

**Entire Continent of Africa**

As you can plainly see from the above maps, it doesn't matter what type of dangerous event, when it happens, how long it lasts or where it occurs - **IN ALL CASES** - government, religious, charitable and the scientific communities (as demonstrated by the arrows on the maps) come to the rescue and support the troubled area or region. There will be shelter, food, water, money, medical and pharmaceutical supplies, clothing, building materials, generators, toilet paper and all other possible supplies brought to the disaster site. Corporations would also provide financial assistance and citizens bring donations and/or travel to the area to help with rebuilding and cleanup.

**WORST CASE SCENARIO**

But what happens if there actually WAS such a cataclysmic disaster affecting the entire planet again? Could such a disaster _really_ happen during these current times? This type of serious and long-term disaster would more than likely include both manmade disasters such as nuclear war, nuclear meltdowns, electrical grid failure, terrorist attacks and chemical and biological attacks and natural disaster scenarios such as drought, famine, pestilence, earthquakes, volcanoes, flooding, heat waves and cold temperatures.

These types of events can occur - within a short period of time or over a longer period of time. And as a consequence, **all** vital elements we count on for ultimate survival would certainly be affected. For example, with the failure of the electrical grid in the country - caused be either/or a manmade or natural disaster, there would be no electric lights, no water, no heat, no sewer, no communication, no transportation systems, no medical facilities or supplies, no banks or other financial institutions, and no stores or commercial markets. And everyone would need to fend for themselves.

As we learn strategies on how to prepare and protect _before_, _during_ and _after_ dangerous events that can happen in our lives, it is important for families to assume the ***worst case scenario.*** In most cases, we cannot control natural events. A Higher Power determines _why_, _when_, _where_ and _how_ an earthquake, tsunami, volcanic eruption or hurricane will affect our lives.

However, families can implement a plan and be _proactive_ in creating an environment to reduce or eliminate a dangerous event or lessen the consequences of the disaster. For example, although we can not stop an earthquake, we can at least take steps in our home to reduce possible injuries by inspecting the home and surroundings for possible hazards and then take action to lessen those hazards.

We have much more control over dangerous events created by humans. For example, we can take preemptive steps to secure our home from robberies, fires, and hazardous materials by installing deadbolts on outer doors, clearing brush and dead trees from around the house and properly storing household chemicals.

As an integral part of **prepare and protect** against dangerous events, we need to prepare to be <u>self sufficient</u> and vigilant in stocking emergency supplies to maintain our health and keep us alive. And as part of that preparation, it is vital to incorporate protection into the plan - to protect not only family members, but emergency supplies as well.

**PROTECTIONISM**

In the world today, a 'normal' environment is loosely defined as a day without the occurrence of a dangerous event. Unfortunately, over the years, our world has become more violent, vicious and aggressive. There has been a radical change in the attitudes of people (and those in Washington) and a decline in morals, values, standards and principles. As a result, we see more and more people willing to take what they want at any price – money, television sets, shoes, virtue, lives or the family dog.

There also appears to be a promiscuous sense of self gratification and lust for control – especially with young adults - leading to explosions of rape, theft and drug-related crimes. Young children are killing their friends in order to get their shoes. Teenagers are killing innocent bystanders just to find out what it feels like to kill another person. Husbands are killing their wives, wives are killing their husbands and children are killing their parents.

During these troubling but 'normal' times, we must all try to do our best to extend a hand of friendship, charity and service towards those individuals in need – wherever possible – and whenever safe to do so. We must also try to live each day to the fullest and enjoy the simple pleasures of life - a rising sun, a field of wildflowers, a babbling brook, a child chasing a butterfly or a glorious sunset. Unfortunately – at the same time we are extending a helping hand, it is also essential for us to use caution with every stranger – every circumstance – and every situation in our daily lives. We still have to be vigilant in protecting our homes as well as our personal property, emergency supplies, pets and livestock, and of course – ourselves!  We must always remember it only takes one time – one mistake – to be a victim in the wrong place at the wrong time.

As one ponders the many possibilities of serious and dangerous events, we begin to recognize the consequences of manmade or natural disasters and visualize severe shortages of food, water, fuel, transportation, communication, sanitation and medical supplies.

We may be faced with a decision of how we will protect our families, personal property and even emergency supplies. Some will choose to rely on the power of God and others will choose to rely on manmade weapons and still others will choose to rely on both spiritual and temporal weapons.  It will be during these extremely difficult times we may – for the first time – have to make hard choices on what we are willing to do to protect ourselves from a dangerous event.

It is relatively simple <u>at this moment in time</u> to trust we would be on our best behavior – even during a long-term disaster.  It is easy to believe because at this moment - we are not hungry, thirsty, cold, hot, wet or parched.  More importantly - our families are safe and secure.  But if a day comes when we no longer have the means to shelter and feed our families, we may have to ask ourselves some extremely hard questions.

I refer to these questions as the "**DREADFUL DRAGON DILEMMA**" scenarios:

## KILLING

### <u>Human Beings</u>

1.      Are you willing to kill someone in order to protect <u>yourself</u>

2.      Are you willing to kill someone in order to protect <u>family members</u>

3.      Are you willing to kill someone in order to protect <u>immediate family members</u>

4.      Are you willing to kill someone in order to protect other family members (<u>relatives</u>)

5.      Are you willing to kill someone in order to protect a <u>friend</u>

6.      Are you willing to kill someone in order to protect a <u>neighbor</u>

7.      Are you willing to kill someone in order to protect an <u>acquaintance</u>

8.      Are you willing to kill someone in order to protect a <u>stranger</u>

**<u>Property</u>** (tangible personal assets such as car, money, furniture, computers, video games etc.)

1.      Are you willing to kill an <u>immediate family member</u> in order to protect your property

2.      Are you willing to kill other family members (<u>relatives</u>) in order to protect your property

3.      Are you willing to kill a <u>friend</u> in order to protect your property

4.      Are you willing to kill a <u>neighbor</u> in order to protect your property

5.      Are you willing to kill an <u>acquaintance</u> in order to protect your property

6.      Are you willing to kill a <u>stranger</u> in order to protect your property

**<u>Survival Items</u>** (food, water, medicines, sanitary supplies, clothing, equipment, machinery, etc.)

1.      Are you willing to kill an <u>immediate family member</u> in order to protect your survival items

2.      Are you willing to kill other family members (<u>relatives</u>) in order to protect your survival items

3.      Are you willing to kill a <u>friend</u> in order to protect your survival items

4.      Are you willing to kill a <u>neighbor</u> in order to protect your survival items

5.      Are you willing to kill an <u>acquaintance</u> in order to protect your survival items

6.      Are you willing to kill a <u>stranger</u> in order to protect your survival items

**DYING**

1.      Are you willing to die in order to protect your <u>immediate family members</u>

2.      Are you willing to die in order to protect your other family members (<u>relatives</u>)

3.      Are you willing to die in order to protect a <u>friend</u>

4.      Are you willing to die in order to protect a <u>neighbor</u>

5.      Are you willing to die in order to protect an <u>acquaintance</u>

6.      Are you willing to die in order to protect a <u>stranger</u>

<u>**Property**</u> (tangible personal assets such as car, money, furniture, computers, video games etc.)

1.      Are you willing to die in order to protect your <u>own</u> personal property

2.      Are you willing to die in order to protect the property of <u>immediate family members</u>

3.      Are you willing to die in order to protect the property of other family members (<u>relatives</u>)

4.      Are you willing to die in order to protect the property of a <u>friend</u>

5.      Are you willing to die in order to protect the property of a <u>neighbor</u>

6.      Are you willing to die in order to protect the property of an <u>acquaintance</u>

7.      Are you willing to die in order to protect the property of a <u>stranger</u>

<u>**Survival Items**</u>

1.      Are you willing to die in order to protect your <u>own</u> personal survival items

2.      Are you willing to die in order to protect the survival items of <u>immediate family members</u>

3.      Are you willing to die in order to protect the survival items of other family members (<u>relatives</u>)

4.      Are you willing to die in order to protect the survival items of a <u>friend</u>

5.      Are you willing to die in order to protect the survival items of a <u>neighbor</u>

6.      Are you willing to die in order to protect the survival items of an <u>acquaintance</u>

7.      Are you willing to die in order to protect the survival items of a <u>stranger</u>

**SHARING**

1.  Are you willing to share your survival items with <u>immediate family members</u>

2.  Are you willing to share your survival items with other family members (<u>relatives</u>)

3.  Are you willing to share your survival items with a <u>friend</u>

4.  Are you willing to share your survival items with a <u>neighbor</u>

5.  Are you willing to share your survival items with an <u>acquaintance</u>

6.  Are you willing to share your survival items with a <u>stranger</u>

7.  Are you willing to share your survival items with a <u>group</u>

As you recover from shock and distress after reviewing these scenarios, I would venture a guess a mother would have very quickly found the dragon if she believed her children were in danger. A dragon in my father would have come thundering out to defend my mother, my brothers, myself and the grandchildren. It may also have been easier to take drastic action against a stranger versus a close family member or a neighbor. If you were hungry while reading the list, did it affect how you answered the questions? Were you willing to share emergency supplies with your best friend, but stopped short of supplying his/her entire family with survival items? How long and how much was you willing to share with others? Was there anyone or any group that you were not willing to share your supplies?

A dangerous event may take place in the future where you may actually face the dragon dilemma. But, there is one fact all family members must know and accept:

**THERE ARE COUNTLESS HUMAN BEINGS WHO WOULD NOT HESITATE TO STEAL THE PROPERTY OF OTHERS AND KILL ANOTHER HUMAN BEING TO DEFEND THEMSELVES OR THEIR FAMILIES OR TO TAKE WHAT THEY WANT OR NEED DURING DANGEROUS TIMES.**

Now is the time to scrutinize your belief system and analyze your own principles and values and TRY to figure out what you would be willing to do to protect your own life, the lives of family members, friends, relatives, neighbors and strangers - and your possessions. By taking preemptive steps <u>now</u> to protect our families, home and belongings during "good times" – we can prepare our household and family members for the "bad times" when safety and security would become so important.

# MANMADE DANGEROUS EVENTS

Now, let's take a look at some *manmade* dangerous events that can happen to any of us *now* and in the *future*. As you learn about each scenario, plan and prepare preventive steps to avoid the situation and ponder how you might respond if the disaster were to happen to you or family members. Remember, a manmade disaster can happen to just one individual, one family, an entire neighborhood or a large population.

## HOME INVASION

Home invasion is the act of an unauthorized, forceful and illegal entry into a private and occupied dwelling for the purpose of committing a crime against the occupants such as robbery, burglary, assault, rape, murder or kidnapping. The best defense against home invasion is *education* and *planning in advance* **to reduce or eliminate the possibility of any type of home invasion**. The same tactics and practices used to prevent daytime burglaries will also support the prevention of forced entry home robberies.

> **The weakest home security link is a family member who fails to lock doors or windows or who will open the door without question at the sound of the doorbell.**

All family members should remember these important preemptive steps in helping to reduce home invasion:

- Install solid core or metal doors on all entrance points into the residence.

- Use high quality Grade-1/Grade-2 locks on exterior doors to resist twisting, prying, and lock-picking attempts.

- Install heavy-duty deadbolt locks on all outside doors with a one-inch throw bolt and a beveled casing to inhibit the use of channel-lock pliers used to shear off lock cylinder pins.

- Use high quality, heavy-duty, knob-in-lock sets with a dead-latch mechanism to prevent slipping the lock with a shim or credit card.

- Use heavy-duty, four-screw, strike plates with three-inch screws to penetrate into a wooden door frame.

- Install a peephole and use it **BEFORE** opening the door. Use wide-angle 160° peepholes mounted no higher than fifty-eight inches. Never rely on a chain-latch as a barrier to partially opening the door.

- Install window security devices on all windows, including basement windows.

- Intruders break glass and open doors from the inside so use a double-key lock. For the patio, use a pin or key lock with a steel rod, and install bolt locks on the garage door.

- Seriously consider installing metal security doors on all entrance doors and metal bars on all windows in the home and especially on any basement windows. I cannot emphasize strongly enough the importance of securing basement windows and outside entrances into the basement. A thief can easily break a basement window or door without being detected, come into the basement and up to the main level of the house.

- Install burglar alarms and attach alarm decals on all windows and doors. If you choose not to install an alarm, purchase fake alarm stickers when visibly placed in a window can act as a solid deterrent.

- A dog is good for preventing burglaries since thieves don't want to deal with barks and bites. Large dogs are best but even a small dog can be adequate protection if its bark has the necessary volume to wake family members or neighbors. If you don't want a dog, purchase a "Beware of Dog" sign or a barking-dog alarm that growls and yelps on its own.

- Lights should be used for entryways and parking areas whenever possible. Motion-sensor lights are a good choice for the front and back yards but keep them at least ten feet high to stop burglars from disabling them. Make sure they shine close to doors and windows to give full visibility of the area.

**THE TOP PRIORITY FOR ELIMINATING OR REDUCING THE POSSIBILITY OF HOME INVASION IS TO <u>STOP THE CRIMINAL FROM ENTERING THE PREMISES IN THE FIRST PLACE</u>.**

As part of the overall home security plan, families must also evaluate the appropriate <u>reaction</u> family members would take in the event a criminal breaks into the home. There are four reactions that can be taken by families upon discovering an intruder entering or already in the premises:

- *Escape from the house and call 9-1-1*
- *Prepare to defend family members and property*
- *Hide from detection*
- *Submit to the demands of the intruder*

> **Always lock outside doors, garage doors and windows when away or while at home. ALWAYS.**

Although escape from the house and calling 9-1-1 would appear to be the best reaction in most cases – especially during a normal environment – it may not always be possible to do so in a realistic or timely manner. *Plan in advance* and attempt to analyze and discuss scenarios that could occur in the event an intruder enters the home while occupied by family members – at any time or under any circumstance – including a disaster situation. There are several factors to consider when making the analyses:

- **TIME OF DAY.** The time of day an intruder breaks into the house can significantly affect the reaction of family members and the ability to escape from the house or defend each other. For example, if the villain breaks into the house in the morning, more than likely, family members will be sitting in the kitchen eating breakfast or taking a shower in the bathroom. If the scoundrel breaks in at noon, chances are good everyone will be at school or work. Later in the afternoon could find family members sitting in the family room playing games, watching television or studying their lessons. And of course, if there is a late night intrusion, family members could be asleep in the bedrooms.

- **LOCATION.** The appropriate reaction will depend on the location of family members in the house at the time of intrusion, the placement of windows and doors offering escape routes and locations that provide hiding places.

- **HABITS.** The regular habits of family members could affect the outcome of survival in the event of an intrusion. A teenager very seldom is more than one inch away from a cell phone. These young adults prefer to staple the phone to their forehead so it is readily available to take calls or text their friends. It may be the habit of the kids to spend most of their time downstairs after coming home from school. The college student is continually practicing his judo in the family room. Perhaps dad always carries a pocketknife in his pants. The cell phone and an immediate call to 9-1-1 could be the weapon that saves lives. Since the basement may offer no escape routes, hiding places may need to be found. A judo expert and a pocketknife may provide a form of defense in some cases – but neither judo nor a pocketknife can stop a bullet if the intruder is armed with a gun.

- **IMPORTANCE OF LOSS.** During a "normal" environment, it is agreed the theft of any property, including emergency supplies <u>may</u> be an acceptable loss providing family members were not injured or killed. The home owners insurance would probably cover a majority of the loss including emergency supplies. However, during a disaster when emergency supplies become life-saving staples, the willingness of family members to accept this loss becomes less clear and especially if the replacement of essential food, water, medicines and other supplies may not be possible.

- **HEALTH.** Depending on the overall condition of each person, the reaction to a home invasion may be different for each family member. Consider the abilities of family members who are physically or mentally handicapped, senior citizens, infants and children, or individuals who are obese, weak or inhibited in any way to perform reactionary tasks.

- **WEAPONS.** Every family must decide whether to purchase and use guns as a means of defense. If the decision is to utilize guns as a means to defend the house, members and property against intrusion, ALL adult family members should be trained on proper safety practices, federal, state and local laws that apply to the use of guns, and how to correctly use these weapons.

Depending on the state, young adults may use guns for hunting and target practice under adult supervision and after the appropriate safety course has been completed. If guns or any other type of lethal weapon, e.g. bow and arrow, knives, swords, baseball bats, pepper spray are stored in the home for purposes of defense, they **MUST** be placed in locations where infants, children or teenagers can not access them – period. It is obvious infants and children are not capable of using a weapon. However, many teens feel confident in their ability to use a weapon but teenagers are simply not mature or experienced enough to handle weapons without adult supervision – and especially during an intrusion by a criminal into the home.

As additional precautionary measures, family members should complete the following tasks in order to further secure the home from possible intrusion and to provide *alternatives* or *layers* of protective measures – depending on the circumstances surrounding the invasion.

- Walk through each room in the home and determine possible escape routes to be utilized, e.g. doors and windows.

- Inspect all doors and windows for ease of escape e.g. windows are not painted shut, keys accessible for doors and metal bar latches work.

- Scrutinize and locate any <u>practical</u> hiding places to avoid detection, e.g. under a bed, in an attic, in a safe room, in a closet, behind the furniture or inside a cabinet. If using this survival technique, understand the importance of keeping quiet and unobtrusive the entire time the intruder is in the home.

> The entire family decided to take a vacation to Florida over the Christmas holidays. My younger brother chose not to join us. While we were gone, a gang of thieves were systematically robbing homes in the community. While my brother was visiting his friend, they broke into his house and stole all of the Christmas presents and other valuables. He immediately checked my home to see if I had also been a victim. He discovered foot prints in the snow around my entire house. But alas! The thieves found something they didn't expect – when building my home, I had chosen to install metal bars on all my windows and doors. Surprise Scumbags!

- If choosing to use lethal weapons, secure them in locations that can be <u>easily accessed and used</u> by adult family members in the event of a home intrusion but inaccessible and undetectable to children, teenagers and thieves. If using a gun, it will do no good to have an unloaded weapon. Imagine the shock of an intruder as he enters the house and you tell him he will have to wait until you get the gun out of the safe, locate the bullets and load the gun before you can defend yourself.

## ROBBERY

A **robbery** is taking or attempting to take valuables from the care, custody, or control of a person(s) by force, threat of force or violence and/or putting the victim in fear for his life. The necessary element of the crime is *specific intent* - the theft from a person by use of force or fear.

In order for a robbery to occur, all that is necessary is a motivated robber and an unwilling victim at the wrong place at the wrong time. Robberies can occur in private or public places. Robbers and their victims can be friends, relatives or total strangers. Most robberies involve one robber and one victim and the crime lasts less than a minute. It is interesting to learn most robberies occur against a citizen <u>on the street</u>. The weapon of choice for robbers is a firearm followed by knives or cutting instruments. Strong-arm tactics such as punching, pushing, kicking or threats are mainly used on the street due to the opportunistic nature of most street robberies.

Robbers prefer to use surprise on victims to force compliance with their demands. Statistics show over 61% of all robbers are under twenty-five years of age – and 90% are males. This crime is mainly a nighttime crime, increasing after 8:00 PM and subsiding after 3:00 AM in most areas of the country. Robberies often increase during the winter months because of extended periods of darkness. Dozens of robbery studies have shown robbers prefer isolation, lone victims, good escape routes, few witnesses and a cash reward for their efforts.

> Thieves respect property. They merely wish the property to become their property so they may more perfectly respect it.
>
> - Gilbert K. Chesterton

In the business of theft and burglary, the thief is interested in stealing <u>property</u> that can be easily and discretely sold to others including electronic and electrical equipment, jewelry, paintings, weapons, furs, prescription drugs and pain killers, precious metals, cash and other high-end items.  As a result, it is not only professional thieves waiting to invade the home, but it is also <u>local</u> gangs, drug addicts, the local fire or police chief, neighbors, relatives and even children and teenagers who are not willing to work but instead choose an easy way to get what they want – stealing it from others.

It is hard to stop a professional thief – and in most cases, if they want to get into your home – they will do so.  These criminals have experience, knowledge, skill and tools to break into most houses.  The professional thief generally targets homes in affluent neighborhoods looking for high-end items.  Only homes with highly sophisticated alarm systems and barriers could deter a professional burglar – and even then, I would put my money on the criminal.  Although it may be extremely difficult to stop the professional thief, it is *definitely* possible to deter, stop and barricade a *novice* burglar, drug addict or teenager from entering your premises.

In the fight against crime, and as a means of defense and protection – it is good to know your enemy.  To reduce your risks and protect family members and property, here are some facts you should know about the common every-day criminal:

- Most criminals are looking to commit a crime with little risk to them and if the home or the homes of family members appear to create unnecessary risk, they will seek another victim.

- Time is the enemy of criminals.  The longer it takes a criminal to commit a crime, the higher the risk of getting arrested or killed.  If the time to execute a crime takes too long, a criminal will abandon the effort.

- Criminals will study neighborhoods, homes, individuals and vehicles <u>prior</u> to committing the crime.

- Common burglars will generally target middle-income neighborhoods with an eye open for single households, isolated houses or senior citizens.

- Criminals try to avoid areas with Neighborhood Watch programs.

- Professional criminals have very low self-esteem and do not consider their lives to be valuable.

Most burglaries and theft are crimes of opportunity. For example, a car is left unlocked with valuables in plain sight, packages are left on the front doorstep, a bicycle or lawnmower is left out on the front lawn, a garage is left open or a door or window is left unlocked. Burglars and thieves take advantage of these opportunities to seize property that is easily and readily accessible.

> **The number one rule of thieves is that nothing is too small to steal.**
>
> **- Jimmy Breslin**

There are several guidelines that can be followed to eliminate or reduce theft in the home <u>and</u> vehicle:

- Always keep valuables out of sight
- Do not leave doors or windows in the home or vehicle open or unlocked
- Do not leave anything of value unattended e.g. idling car, lawnmower
- Do not leave an automatic garage door open more than four inches from the ground
- Keep hedges and bushes manicured around the house
- Avoid excessive landscaping and lawn ornaments around the house
- Avoid wearing expensive jewelry, furs, shoes and clothing during every day activities
- Place key locking gasoline caps on all vehicles
- Always flatten and separate boxes for television, computer and video equipment before disposal
- Avoid advertising or boasting about recent high-end purchases <u>including emergency supplies</u>
- Stay unpredictable and never make it obvious when you're home
- When away from home, keep landline phone ringer volume down and use 'call forwarding'
- Consider not publishing landline phone number and address listed in the local phone directory
- Keep expensive recreational toys in the garage or back yard
- Never open the door to strangers or solicitors and call police if a stranger acts suspicious
- Prepare a list of your most prized possessions and keep all receipts in a safe place
- Purchase home owners insurance and include a "one-hundred percent replacement" clause in the policy

<u>**Home Invasion Robbers**</u>

One of the more frightening and potentially dangerous crimes that can occur to a family is a **home invasion robbery**. A home invasion is when criminals force their way into an *occupied* home, apartment or hotel room to commit a robbery, rape or other crimes. *Plan in advance* in order to eliminate even the <u>possibility</u> of these thugs gaining entrance to the premises. Many years ago, this criminal was interested in only stealing the valuables in the home but not any more! The attitude and disposition of these lunatics has become savage and they are truly capable of anything including torture, arson, rape and homicide of the victims and their property – just for the thrill of the game.

These criminals expect privacy once inside the home and will try to increase escape time by disabling phones and leaving their victims bound or incapacitated. Once the offenders take control of a residence, they can force the occupants to open safes, locate hidden valuables, supply keys to the family car, and provide PIN numbers to ATM cards.

Home invasion robbers work more often at night and on weekends when homes are more likely to be occupied. The home invader will also target the resident as well as the dwelling and the selection process may include a woman living alone, a wealthy senior citizen or a known drug dealer. These robbers may also follow *you* home based on the value of the car you are driving or the jewelry you are wearing.

Some home invaders may have previously been in your home as a delivery person, installer or repair vendor. Home robbers rarely work alone and rely on physical confrontation, intimidation, domination and violence to gain control. The greatest violence usually occurs during the initial sixty seconds of the confrontation and home invaders often come prepared with knives, handcuffs, rope, duct tape and firearms.

> **My friend was riding a bus and was sitting next to a group of men in South America. When the bus stopped to pick up passengers, several boys were on the street asking if anyone on the bus would like to buy a bottle of water. The water bottles appeared to be sealed, so my friend bought a bottle of water, opened it, and began drinking the contents. The next thing she remembers was waking up in a jail cell without her passport, camera or money. The police told her she was found lying unconscious on the street so they brought her to the police station and were waiting for her to wake up. The men sitting next to her on the bus and the boys selling the water were part of a clever scheme to drug tourists, take their belongings and then leave the person asleep on the street.**

The most common method to enter the home is <u>through the front door or garage</u>. The home invader may simply kick open the door and confront the occupants inside the home. They have become so brazen in their crimes they have been known to spend hours ransacking a residence while the home owners are bound nearby watching in terror. Some robbers have been known to eat meals, watch television, use the toilet and even take a nap. It is not uncommon for these thugs to sexually assault or even murder their victims.

Another common approach to gain entry is when the criminals first knock on the door or ring the doorbell. The occupant opens the door without question in response to the knock and the invaders push their way through the door and into the house.

Home invaders may use a ruse or impersonation to seduce the occupant into opening the door by pretending to deliver a package or lie about having a stalled car or hitting your parked vehicle. In the world today, it is very doubtful an individual would not have a cell phone. Under no circumstances should a family member <u>ever</u> allow a stranger into the house to use the telephone. If a stranger asks to use your phone, make sure the security door is locked and inform the stranger you will make the call on their behalf – <u>including a call to the police to notify law enforcement of the situation.</u>

<u>**Pick Pockets**</u>

Pick pocketing is a form of larceny that involves stealing money or other valuables from the victim without the person noticing the theft at the time. It requires considerable dexterity and misdirection. Pickpockets and other thieves, especially those working in teams, apply a distraction such as asking a question or bumping into the victim.

A pickpocket can be found in any environment, including crowded areas such as bus or train stations, open markets, areas where victims have a different look or dress, near ATM machines and in areas where the pocket money of a tourist may be more than the local monthly income. A skilled pickpocket can hit almost any pocket but all pickpockets prefer easy targets not close to the victims' body and where the victim will not feel the touch of the thief including:

- Open bags, especially shopping bags with an interesting store label
- Outside pockets on a man's jacket or other loose-fitting outer garments
- Outside pockets of a backpack or shoulder bag
- A bag or pack sitting away from you or in an adjoining booth while at a restaurant or Internet café
- Pockets out of the victim's field of vision including rear and thigh pockets of trousers
- Items hanging on a belt, including cell phones or fanny packs

To avoid the possibility of a pickpocket, *do not* carry your wallet, phone or other valuables in any of these places. Pickpockets routinely carry razors for slitting pockets and cutting the strap on a purse, shoulder bag or camera and tongs for reaching into purses or pockets.

A majority of pickpockets employ distraction on the streets in popular tourist areas including:

- A prostitute (male or female) offers services and often keeps touching you
- A drunk and unwashed person grabs your arm and tries to talk to you
- Street musicians and magicians
- Insistent begging from women and children
- Someone passes by you and "accidentally" drops money
- A group of locals begin a loud argument or fight
- A "Beware of Pickpockets" sign prominently displayed (person checks wallet and pickpocket observes)
- A street child flashes something in your face
- A man "tackles" you asking if you play football
- Someone sprays you with ketchup or some other substance
- A fake drowning at the beach to get people away from their valuables

<u>Pickpockets often work in teams and include men, women and children.</u>  For example, getting on a crowded bus, one ahead of you may create a delay so the one behind you can get your wallet.  One may distract the victim's attention while the other reaches into a pocket on the other side.

The basics for protecting yourself from pick pockets are as follows:

- Always hold on tightly to a purse and keep the purse in front of you and not on the side
- Attach your wallet to a chain
- Be alert - especially in crowded spaces or when people invade your personal space
- Carry a cheap wallet with a few small bills in your hip pocket to serve as a decoy
- Carry money and passport in separate places so losing one doesn't mean losing the other as well
- Deep-front trouser pockets or inside and zippered jacket pockets offer better protection
- Do not advertise valuables and money in public
- **DON'T LOOK LIKE A TOURIST – BLEND IN!**
- Dress inconspicuously and avoid wearing expensive jewelry - do not draw attention to yourself
- Know and avoid the most dangerous areas
- Leave unneeded valuables and money at the hotel room in the safe
- Place cash and even credit or debit cards in your shoes instead of in any type of carrier
- Purchase underwear specially designed with zippered closed pockets
- Remove unnecessary items from the wallet such as local identification cards and driver's licenses
- Stash valuables in hard-to-reach places
- Wear a money clip in the bra or underneath the clothes
- Wear a money pouch around the neck and <u>underneath</u> your clothes
- Wear backpacks in front of you and not at the rear or side

As I have travelled around the world, I have observed countless examples of pickpockets in action.  The most glaring illustration is in areas where gypsies collect as teams to steal from tourists.  The children are taught how to approach a tourist with their hands out pretending to beg for money.

Several years ago, I took my niece to Europe as a graduation present.  We watched as a woman became inundated with several children aggressively touching and grabbing at her until they were finally kicked at and beaten off by the woman and other tourist members of the group.  Although it may appear to be brutal and abusive to kick and hit at children in order to get them away from you – remember these gypsy children are professional thieves.  You are definitely within your rights to protect yourself and your valuables from being stolen.

## Residential Burglars

Burglary is defined as a <u>non-confrontational</u> property crime that occurs when occupants are <u>not</u> at home.  According to statistics, a burglary occurs somewhere in the United States every fifteen seconds.  Residential burglars work mostly during the day when a residence is likely to be unoccupied.  These burglars work alone and tend to probe a neighborhood looking for the right opportunity and the right residence.  Alarm signs and decals, bars on windows, strong locks on doors, big dogs and alert neighbors can sometimes deter residential burglars.  Most residential burglars will avoid confrontation and will usually flee when approached.  Most burglaries do not result in violence unless the criminal is cornered and uses force to escape.

The summer months of July and August have the most burglaries (since most families are on vacation) with February having the fewest crimes.  Burglaries are most often committed by young males less than 25 years of age looking for small and expensive items that can easily be converted into cash such as jewelry, prescription medications, cell phones, guns, watches, laptop computers and other small electronic devices.  The cash is used for living expenses or to support a drug habit.  Many burglars will use force to enter a dwelling using screwdrivers, pliers, pry bars and hammers but their preference is to gain easy access through an open door or window.

Although home burglaries may seem random, they actually involve a simple selection process of choosing an unoccupied home with the easiest access, the greatest amount of cover and with the best escape routes.  The first step in securing the home is to *harden the target* by making it more difficult to enter the premises.  The burglar will bypass your home if it requires too much effort or requires excessive skill and tools.

I thought it might be a good idea for you to personally meet a burglar so he can share some interesting thoughts about his profession with you.  Again - it's important to know your enemy.

- Of course I look familiar to you!  I was cleaning your carpets, painting your house, delivering that new entertainment system and fixing that clogged drain.

- Thanks for letting me use the bathroom when I was installing that rain gutter last week.  I unlatched the back window so my return to rob your house will be easy.

- I just love those beautiful and expensive flowers in the front yard and those lawn ornaments are sensational!  That tells me you have good taste and there are nice and expensive things inside the home.

- Those expensive toys your kids leave out in the yard makes me wonder what type of entertainment and gaming system they have in the house.

- I have especially admired your motor home, the ATV, the boat and the snowmobiles surrounding your house – not only could I use all of them for myself, but their appearance leads me to believe there may be hunting and fishing equipment – and weapons in the house.

- I really do look for newspapers piled up on the driveway and mail stashed in the mailbox and I may even leave an advertisement flyer in your front door to see how long it takes you to remove it.

- If it snows while you're out of town, virgin drifts in the driveway are a dead giveaway so ask a friend or neighbor to create car and foot tracks into the house.

- If decorative glass is part of your front entrance, ask the alarm company to install the control pad where I can see if it's set.  That makes it so easy!

- I hate most loud dogs and nosy neighbors.

- A good security company will alarm the window over the sink and the windows on the second floor that access the master bedroom and your jewelry. It's not a bad idea to put motion detectors up there too.

- It's raining, you're fumbling with your umbrella, and you forget to lock your door which is understandable. But understand this: <u>I don't take a day off because of bad weather</u>.

- I always knock first and if you answer, I'll ask for directions or offer to make repairs on your house.

- I always check dresser drawers, the bedside table and the medicine cabinet.

- I almost never go into young children's rooms but will visit a teenager's room - plenty of good electronics!

- I won't have enough time to break into the safe where you keep valuables but if it's not bolted down, I will definitely try to take it with me.

- A loud television or radio can be a better deterrent than the best alarm system.

- Sometimes I carry a clipboard or may dress like a maintenance guy and carry a set of tools. I do my best to never look like a villain.

- I'll break a window to get into your house - even if it makes a little noise. If your neighbor hears one loud sound, he'll stop what he's doing and wait to hear it again. If he doesn't hear it again, he'll just go back to what he was doing. It's human nature.

- There are lots of people who pay for a fancy alarm system and then leave the house without setting it!

- I look in windows for signs that you're home, for flat screen television sets or fancy gaming systems. I'll drive or walk through your neighborhood in the evening before you close the blinds just to pick my targets.

- Announce the upcoming vacation on Facebook because it's easier than you think to look up your address.

- Leaving a window open during the day is a way to let in a little fresh air but to me, it's an invitation.

- I look to see if any basement window offers an easy access to the home so I can enter through the basement and come up through to the main level of the house.

- I especially like to target senior citizens or persons with serious diseases such as cancer and arthritis. I know there is a good chance prescription drugs are available in the house – including pain killers.

- Hide an outside key in an easily accessible location e.g. under the doormat, above the door, under the flowerpot or attached to some metal object near the home. I consider it to be a silent ticket into your home.

- I probably have an electronic device that can easily locate the code for your garage door and open it. If you want to keep me out, turn off the garage door opener when away from the house and at night. <u>Physically</u> turn off power to the lifting motor by using a computer power strip.

- If you don't answer when I knock, I'll try the door. Occasionally, I hit the jackpot and walk right in.

- You have a big mouth. I was nearby when I heard you brag about all the expensive and high tech equipment you have in your home and how your wife has such expensive jewelry.

To avoid a residential burglar from entering the premises, family members must *plan in advance* to prevent the criminal from entering the home in the first place. When attempting to protect the home and homes of family members from criminals, one of the best methods is to think like a thief! Imagine you are outside of your home and are looking for something that would be quick and easy to steal.  What would it be?  How would you do it?  Correct the obvious ways you can avoid having your possessions stolen.  A home is only as secure as its weakest entry point.  Walk around the house - think like an intruder, and ask yourself this question:  **If you had no key**:

# HOW WOULD <u>YOU</u> GET INTO THE HOUSE?

### Doors and Locks

Most burglars enter the home using the front, back or garage doors.  The garage and back doors provide the most cover and experienced burglars recognize garage doors are generally the weakest point of entry followed closely by the back door into the home.  Once inside the garage, a burglar will look inside the car for keys and other valuables even when parked inside the garage.

The most important goal of family members is to keep the burglar **OUT** of the house – period.  Do not underestimate the power and strength of a two-hundred pound young male who has just finished working out at the gym before coming to break into your home!

> **An effective measure to prevent home invasion is the installation of metal security doors on all sliding glass patio doors.**

To stop the burglar from gaining access through any <u>outside</u> door in the home, family members must *plan in advance* by using vigilance in securing outside entrances into the premises.  The most common method used by a burglar to force entry through a door with a wooden jam is to simply kick it open.  The weakest point is almost always the lock strike plate holding the latch or lock bolt in place followed by a glass paneled door.  The average door strike plate is secured only by the soft-wood door jam molding.  These lightweight moldings are often tacked on to the door frame and can be torn away with a firm kick.

Because of this construction flaw, it makes sense to upgrade to a four-screw, heavy-duty, high security strike plate.  They are available in most hardware stores and home improvement centers and are definitely worth the extra expense.  Install this heavy-duty strike plate using three-inch wood screws to cut deep into the door frame stud.  Use these longer screws in the knob lock strike plate as well and use at least one long screw in each door hinge.  <u>This one step alone will deter or prevent most through-the-door forced entries.</u>

### Sliding-Glass Patio Doors

Sliding glass doors are secured by *latches* and not locks.  They are vulnerable to being forced open from the outside because of defective latch mechanisms.  This can be easily prevented by inserting a wooden dowel or stick into the track thus preventing or limiting movement.  Other precautions are metal fold-down blocking devices called "charley bars" and track-blockers that can be screwed down.

The older sliding glass doors can be lifted up and off the track which defeats the latch mechanism.  To prevent lifting, keep the door rollers properly adjusted and in good condition.  You can also install anti-lift devices such as a pin that extends through both the sliding and fixed portion of the door.  There are also locking and blocking devices available in hardware stores to prevent a sliding door from being lifted or horizontally forced.

> **A common trick used by thieves is to take only a few checks out of sequence from the checkbook instead of taking the entire checkbook.  In this way, since the victim sees the checkbook was not stolen, he doesn't realize that he is still susceptible to unauthorized charges made against his checking account. Several months after the robbery, the thief will then attempt to use the checks.  After being robbed, the victim should always check to make sure <u>all</u> checks are accounted for in the checkbook as well as any books of checks that are being stored.**

Place highly visible decals on the glass door near the latch mechanism showing an alarm system, a dog, a neighborhood watch program, and operation identification is in place. Burglars don't like alarm systems, noisy neighbors or big barking dogs.

### Windows

An open window, visible from the street or alley, may be the only reason your home is selected by a burglar.  A ground floor window is more susceptible to break-ins but upper floor windows become attractive if they can be accessed from a stairway, tree and fence or by climbing on balconies.

Since windows have latches and not locks, they should have secondary blocking devices to prevent sliding them open from the outside. Inexpensive wooden dowels work well for horizontal sliding windows and through-the-frame pins work well for vertical sliding windows. For ventilation, block the window open no more than six inches but make sure you can't reach in from the outside and remove the blocking device or reach through and unlock the door.

In sleeping rooms, these window blocking devices should be capable of being easily removed from the inside to comply with fire codes. Similar to sliding glass doors, anti-lift devices are necessary for ground level and accessible aluminum windows that slide horizontally. The least expensive and easiest method is to install screws half-way into the upper track of the movable glass panel to prevent it from being lifted out in the closed position. As a deterrent, place highly visible decals on the glass door near the latch mechanism showing an alarm system, a dog, neighborhood watch program or operation identification is in place.

### Good Neighbors

A *good* neighbor who is <u>trustworthy, honest, mature, dependable and responsible</u> is one of the best deterrents to crime in the neighborhood. Using common sense, invite the person into your home, communicate often and establish a trusting relationship. Establish a Neighborhood Watch Program and invite families throughout the neighborhood to be a part of this valuable deterrent against crime.

When choosing <u>one specific neighbor</u> to become a partner in preventing crime on your property – you must be absolutely certain this neighbor is a first-rate candidate and is *ready*, *willing* and *able* to perform necessary duties.

For example:

> While living in California, a moving truck drove into our neighborhood and parked in the driveway of one of our neighbors. Within several minutes, the movers began to load household items from the home into the truck for most of the afternoon until they finally drove away. Several days later, we all discovered that the family living in the house was away on vacation. When they returned home, the entire house had been emptied by the burglars – as the entire neighborhood watched the crime in progress. AHHHHHHHH!

- Although a disabled elderly woman down the street may certainly be trustworthy, she will not easily be able to pick up the mail and newspapers when you are out of town.

- There is absolutely no young teenager who has the maturity to take on this type of responsibility - sorry.

- The single man down the street could be considered a trustworthy candidate, but his profession takes him away on over-night business trips several times a week.

The selected neighbor will be given a significant amount of power by you to enter your home using a key to your front door and conduct daily business on your behalf. Before selecting someone for this important position, and over the course of time and casual conversations, family members should learn:

- **Past History**
    - Where they were born
    - Where they grew up
    - Where they have lived
    - Names and locations of family members
    - Professions and employment
    - Memberships in organizations
    - Religious affiliations
    - Military background
    - Criminal background

> Although good communication is important to establish between neighbors, there is specific information to *withhold* – for example, the location of any valuables, prescription drugs and emergency supplies in the house.

- **Current History**
    - Profession
    - Employment

- o Memberships in organizations
- o Religious affiliations
- o Family members (genders, ages, etc.)

When selecting the right neighbor, it is important to focus on any minor inconsistencies or glaring characteristics that point towards unacceptable character traits and lack of upstanding morals and values. There will be some who will counter "it is not for me to judge". **OH YES IT IS!** You have **EVERY** right to judge the character of a neighbor when you are handing over the key to your home.

If the neighbor has been a gang member in the past or is currently affiliated with gangs – he is definitely not an acceptable candidate. If a neighbor or a member of their family has a known drug addiction or is a member of a known terrorist organization – they are not a good choice. There are individuals who are involved in radical religious cults or who have been arrested and convicted of serious crimes. A neighbor who is a known alcoholic will not be a responsible candidate. If the neighbor's current profession is a hit man – again, probably not a good choice. You get the idea.

**DO YOUR HOME WORK AND CONDUCT A CASUAL BUT METHODICAL BACKGROUND CHECK TO GUARANTEE THE CANDIDATE IS NOT LIKELY TO BURN DOWN YOUR HOUSE, HAVE WILD PARTIES, STEAL YOUR JEWELS OR FORGET TO LOCK THE DOORS WHILE YOU ARE GONE.**

When leaving the house for an extended period of time, family members should provide the following information to the trusted neighbor:

- **<u>THE FACT YOU ARE LEAVING THE HOUSE</u>**
- An email address where a message can be sent to reach you (can be accessed anywhere in the world)
- An itinerary and schedule of where you will be each day
- Any upcoming service calls to be conducted at the home e.g. installations, repairs, maintenance
- At least two phone numbers of where you can be reached e.g. cell phone, local contact phone
- Contact numbers of standard service personnel in the event of an emergency e.g. plumber, electrician
- Requested tasks and duties to be performed e.g. pick up newspapers and mail
- Specific instructions on the care of pets and livestock
- The date you will be returning to the house
- The general location where you will be during your absence e.g. Europe - Paris - Paris Hotel
- The length of time you are scheduled to be gone
- The reason you will be gone e.g. vacation, business, sickness

This <u>trustworthy</u> neighbor will need to be given a key to the <u>front</u> door of the home. All keys to other doors, cabinets, closets or safes should not be given to anyone outside of the family. Any areas considered to be off-limits to this neighbor should be securely locked such as storage areas, safes, cabinets and closets. Requiring a service vendor to see your neighbor to retrieve and return your house key will send the message someone is watching the house. This neighborhood watch technique is called *territoriality* where all neighbors take ownership and responsibility for what occurs in the neighborhood. This concept works in both single family homes and apartment properties.

## <u>Lighting</u>

Interior lighting is necessary to show signs of life and activity <u>inside</u> the home during the evening hours because a home continually dark sends a message to burglars the occupants are not at home. Light timers are inexpensive and should be used on a daily basis. A routine is then established whereby neighbors can observe the lighting schedule and become suspicious when a normally lighted home is dark. A light-timer should be near the front and back windows with the curtains closed and the pattern of lights turning on and off should simulate actual occupancy. The same light timers can be used to turn on radios or television sets to further enhance the illusion of occupancy.

Exterior lighting becomes critical if you park in a common area parking lot or underground garage and need to walk to the front door. Exterior lighting should be bright enough to see one-hundred feet ahead and allow one to identify colors.

Another area to be well-lighted is the *perimeter* of the home or apartment and especially at the entrance. Exterior lighting on the front of a property should be on a timer to establish a routine and appearance of occupancy at all times. Common area lighting on apartment properties should be on a timer or photo-cell to turn on at dusk and turn off at dawn. The practice of leaving the garage or porch lights turned on all day on a single family home tells criminals you are out of town. Exterior lighting at the rear of a home or apartment are usually on a switch because of the proximity to the sleeping rooms and the resident can choose to leave these lights on or off. Security lights with infra-red motion sensors are relatively inexpensive and can easily replace an exterior porch light or side door light on single family homes. The heat-motion sensor can be adjusted to detect body heat and can be programmed to reset after one minute. These security lights are recommended for single family homes.

## Alarm System

A good alarm system deters burglaries by increasing the potential and fear of being caught and arrested by the police. The deterrent value comes from the alarm company lawn sign and from the alarm decals on the windows. Home and apartment burglars will generally bypass a property with visible alarm signs. Alarm systems need to be properly installed and maintained, and to be effective, all systems should have an audible horn or bell. These audible alarms should be programmed to reset automatically after one or two minutes. If using a central station to monitor the alarm, make sure your response call list is up to date.

Do not write your alarm pass code on or near the alarm keypad. Home alarms tend to be ignored but if the Neighborhood Watch Program has been established, neighbors will pay attention to these alarms and take appropriate action on your behalf. Don't forget a fire detector and carbon monoxide detector for each floor of the home!

> **If you are in a parking lot and approached by a criminal who claims to have a gun, immediately begin to wave your arms, scream and begin running away. When running, make sure you zigzag wildly back and forth. There is an eighty percent chance the criminal will run away. There is only a fifty percent chance he will try to shoot you. If he does try to shoot you, there is less than a fifty percent chance he will hit you. If he does hit you, there is less than fifty percent chance he will kill you. On the other hand, if you get in the car with him, there is a very good chance he will kill or seriously harm you. Good arithmetic to remember!**

## Home Safe

The price of a good quality home safe is a wise investment. A home safe is similar to insurance – the more protection– the higher the price. A home safe can be designed to protect against fire and water as well as stop burglars, nosey children, teenagers and dishonest babysitters or housekeepers from gaining access to important documents and personal property. Before purchasing a home safe, protection should include both fire *and* water damage. To guard against fires, buy a safe with ½-hour, 1-hour or 4-hour ratings and with an Underwriters Laboratory (UL) label or equivalent. Fire-resistant safes are available in two categories: (1) record or document safe and (2) media safe.

Safes that protect *paper* from fire are constructed of fire-resistant insulating material between two metal walls that keep the interior below the burning point of paper (350 degrees Fahrenheit). As part of the rating system, the first number (350 or 125) refers to the maximum internal temperature of the safe. The second number refers to how long the safe was tested: 350-2-hour means the safe was tested for two hours at 1700 to 2000 degrees and maintained a temperature of 350 or less internally. There are three classes of safes that protect paper documents:

- Class A Safe protects paper documents for up to 4 hours at temperatures up to 2000° Fahrenheit
- Class B Safe protects paper documents for up to 2 hours at temperatures up to 1850° Fahrenheit
- Class C Safe protects paper documents for up to 1 hour at temperatures up to 1700° Fahrenheit

A *media* safe protects anything made of plastic with magnetic or digital information or photographs. These safes are more heavily insulated since internal temperature must stay below 125 degrees Fahrenheit. If the home is located in a region prone to wildfires, the safe should have a UL 2-Hour seal of approval indicating the safe can endure intense fires for up to two hours. For home fires, a UL 1-Hour may be sufficient.

For water damage, the safe should state how long it can withstand being fully submerged in or sprayed by water. There are also safes that can withstand attempted break-ins by locksmiths armed with crow bars, torches and other tools.

These safes are heavy because of more steel in the structure of the safe.  When purchasing any home safe, *it must to be anchored into the floor or permanent shelving*.  <u>Do not purchase any safe that does not have the bolt-down feature</u>.

A burglar-resistant safe is constructed of solid metal walls and a heavy door resistant to being opened by drilling, cutting or prying.  There are two types of ratings: the class rating (1 to 5) and the UL rating.  The UL rating includes a letter designation for resistance to various types of attacks:

- **DR (drill resistant)**
- **TR (torch resistant)**
- **TRTL (torch and tool resistant)**
- **X6 (for bankers and jewelers)**

A home safe with dial combinations comes with a set code that can be reset by a locksmith.  You can also set your own code - usually three to six digits – with an electronic push button safe.  If you forget the combination for either type, the safe manufacturer can be contacted with the serial number of the safe to get the code or a reset code.  The company may require a notarized request.  When installing a safe, protect the safe code, change it on a regular basis, and always install it *away* from the master bedroom or closet.

Another practical method to secure a home safe is to literally install it <u>inside</u> a wall or floor and then cover it entirely with wood, plaster, sheetrock, carpeting, paint or wallpaper so it is no longer visible to the naked eye nor can it command detection.  This method is especially good when hiding cash, precious metals, high-priced jewelry and gems, copies of important documents and **GUNS** and **AMMUNIATION** not needed for daily activities but is being stored for emergency situations.  In this manner, during "normal" times, a robber or burglar will not find the safe and during a disaster - again - a robber or burglar will not find the safe nor will any military, government or law enforcement personnel be able to locate the safe and take your weapons.

## <u>Operation Identification</u>

The Operation Identification Program recommends owners engrave their drivers' license number (<u>not</u> social security number) on television sets, stereos, computers and small electronic appliances.  In the event of a burglary and hopeful recovery of the items, they can be identified by police and returned to the rightful owner.  In addition to engraving, photograph all valuables in their locations around the home and make a list of the *make, model,* and *serial numbers.*  Keep receipts of larger items to prove the value for insurance purposes.  Keep the list and receipts in a safety deposit box or with the out-of-state contact.

## <u>Intruder Entering The House</u>

If an intruder is inside the home when you are about to enter the house - **DO NOT ENTER.  GET AWAY AND CALL 9-1-1.**

If family members are in the home and hear what sounds like a forced entry (broken glass, a crash) or the home alarm system is activated, you are faced with a difficult situation.  The family has only a matter of *seconds* to make a decision that could save lives.  Based on the *advanced planning*, family members will be better able to determine the appropriate reaction: (1) immediately escape from the house and call 9-1-1, (2) prepare to defend yourself, (3) hide somewhere in the house to avoid detection or (4) prepare to submit to the intruder's demands.

## SHOPPING CENTERS

Shopping centers all have a parking lot.  We are all strangers in a large parking lot and violent criminals can blend in and get in close proximity to any family member.  Criminal predators can walk right by us and we allow it because of the public setting.  Because of the nature of a parking lot – we become vulnerable as possible victims of crime.

To prove my point, the next time you go to a large shopping center, observe how easy it would be for a predator to approach and attack anyone in the lot.  Shoppers walk to and from their cars consumed by their own thoughts and approach the car

> Instead of using pepper spray - purchase a can of wasp spray.  The wasp spray can shoot up to twenty feet away and is more accurate.  With pepper spray, you have to get close to the criminal who could overpower you.  Both wasp and pepper spray temporarily blinds an attacker until they get to the hospital for an antidote.

fumbling for keys and turning their backs and attention away from those nearby to load shopping bags and get children loaded inside the vehicle. Most shopping center violent crimes occur precisely at this point overwhelmingly committed by males with the most common crimes being purse-snatching and robbery. The best defense is <u>awareness</u> that allows you to anticipate the potential danger and plan ahead for the next time you go to a shopping center. Planning includes selecting a safer time to shop (daylight) and arranging (if possible) not to shop alone.

You can plan where to park (close to the shopping complex and away from any large vans or vehicles). Scan the area before parking and exiting the vehicle and plan not to park or exit the vehicle if suspicious individuals are in the area. Family members should agree *in advance* to exit and enter the vehicle quickly and lock the doors. Everyone should be trained to look around the vehicle before approaching and retreat if anyone suspicious is loitering in the area.

## BANK ATM MACHINES

Most ATM robberies occur at night between 8:00 PM and midnight. While a majority of bank ATM *robbers* are lone males under twenty-five years of age, most ATM robbery *victims* are women - alone when robbed and claim they never saw the robber approaching them. ATM robbers usually position themselves nearby waiting for a victim to approach and withdraw cash. An ATM robber will use a gun or claim to have a concealed weapon when confronting the victim and demanding cash.

If family members use ATM cash machines, here are some tips to make the process more secure:

- Use only ATM machines in well-lighted and high-traffic areas
- Avoid machines that are remote or hidden (behind buildings, pillars or away from public view)
- Beware of obvious hiding places such as shrubbery or overgrown trees
- Request a list of ATM locations from your bank and keep it in your car
- Try and limit use to daylight hours
- Scan the area for any suspicious persons and do not hesitate to walk away
- When approaching an ATM on foot, be prepared and have your access card ready
- After inserting the card and PIN number - keep an eye out behind you
- After receiving cash from the machine, immediately put it away, extract the card and walk away

If using a car at a drive-thru ATM machine, make sure there are no obvious hiding places or suspicious persons loitering in the area. Keep the car in gear and doors locked with foot firmly on the brake while using the ATM machine. Watch your rear and side view mirrors during the transaction because robbers generally approach from the rear on the drivers' side. If you see *anyone* approaching, drive off even if it means leaving your ATM card because the card can later be retrieved or cancelled. If you are confronted by an armed robber, give up the money without argument because the cash is not worth serious injury or death. Do not fight with or attempt to follow the robber; instead, drive to a safe place and immediately call police.

## HOTELS AND MOTELS

When staying in a hotel or motel, it is important to carefully select a good facility and room. The cost of the accommodation is not always a good predictor of the overall safety of the room or property. Although an upper floor is wise when attempting to avoid a robbery - the ground floor is a better choice if considering the possibility of a fire and ease of escape. I generally request a room on the third floor to reduce the risk of an intruder but at the same time, during a fire, it would be easier to escape the building.

For best protection, hotel or motel rooms should be equipped with a solid wood or metal door. Room doors should have a deadbolt lock with a one-inch throw bolt. If the lock looks worn or there are pry marks around the lock area, request another room or move to another hotel. The knob lock should be hotel-style where you can push a button on the inside knob and block out all keys. This feature is designed to prevent a former guest or housekeeper from entering once you are inside the room.

**While on the French Rivera, the manager at the hotel warned us to keep our balcony door closed due to possible cat burglars. I was on the tenth floor so naturally this warning did not apply to me. In the middle of the night I was awake (thankfully) and staring out the balcony door when much to my surprise – a burglar dressed in black came bounding over the balcony rail and directly into my room. I immediately set up in my bed and screamed "NO!" I have never seen anyone move so quickly to get out of a room and over that balcony rail. Morale of the story: These guys can climb high – and very quietly too!**

26

The room door should have a wide-angle peephole so you can view who is at the door. Hotels with electronic card access have the advantage of being able to disable key-cards issued to former guests. Do <u>not</u> rely on door chains or swing bars to secure doors. Children should be taught <u>not</u> to open the door of any hotel room. Children should not be allowed to wander the hotel grounds. Everyone at a hotel is a stranger and it is difficult to know who is a registered guest or who has criminal intentions. Do **not** leave a child unsupervised at the pool or gym since these areas are prime targets for predators.

Make sure all windows and sliding doors are secured if accessible from the ground and beware of balconies where someone can climb from one to another and enter through an open window or sliding door. Do *not* accept a room if the windows or sliding doors are not securable. Women traveling alone or with small children should take advantage of car valet service to avoid the parking lot. After checking in at the desk, ask the bellman or desk clerk to escort you to the room. After unlocking the room, quickly inspect closets, under the bed, and bathroom including behind the shower curtain.

## AUTO THEFT

There are several types of auto theft. The first type of auto theft is called *carjacking,* a violent form of motor vehicle theft where a thief approaches an occupied car and uses force and fear to steal the vehicle. The second type is called *unattended auto theft* where the thief steals the car while it is unoccupied, usually when the vehicle is sitting in the driveway of the home, on a curb, in the street, or in a parking lot.

> **My friends and I were staying in a nice hotel. While leaving the room to see the sites, a maid entered the room and stole over $500 cash we had "hidden" in a suitcase. Fortunately, a camera in the hallway caught the thief on video. Anyone with a master key can enter your hotel room and rummage through your suitcases. Lock the suitcases and use the hotel safe!**

## <u>Carjacking</u>

Carjacking occurs most often in busy commercial areas where cars are parked and when the owner is entering or exiting the parked vehicle. Most carjacking attempts occur within five miles of the victim's home. The carjacker wants the keys readily available and the car door unlocked for a quick getaway.

Carjackers tend to rob lone victims and single men are victimized more often since younger single males tend to take more chances and go to higher risk locations. Thieves look for cars at roadway intersections with a stop light and areas adjacent to retail stores with close proximity to a freeway ramp for ease of escape.

It is possible the car owner or occupants will be kidnapped during a carjacking and dropped off nearby unharmed. The worst case scenario occurs when the victim is transported to a secondary crime scene and raped, assaulted or even killed. Other drivers have been violently pulled out of their seats and left lying on the road.

> **If the car stalls in an isolated area, lock the doors, roll up the windows, get out of the car and hide in a nearby area. In this way, you can observe the car and scrutinize anyone who stops to offer assistance.**

Another scheme used by carjackers is to crash into the back of your vehicle at low speed and "bump" you with enough force to make you believe a traffic accident has just occurred. Typically, drivers get out of both vehicles to exchange insurance information. At this point, the carjacker robs you of your vehicle and drives away. The accomplice drives away in the carjacker's car. The carjacking of parked vehicles ultimately depends on the attentiveness of the car owner to the surroundings. Most victims claim they never saw the carjacker until he/she appeared at the car door.

To reduce the risk of being carjacked, follow the steps below:

- Always park in a well-lighted area if you plan to arrive or leave after dark
- As you <u>approach</u> your car - look under, around, and inside the car
- As you <u>walk</u> to your car, be alert of suspicious persons sitting in cars
- Be aware of young males loitering in the area (handing out flyers or smoking)
- If area and vehicle are safe, open the door, enter quickly, lock the doors, start the car and drive away
- Be suspicious of anyone who offers to repair your car or a flat tire
- Do not argue, fight or chase the robber
- Do not park in isolated or visually obstructed areas near walls or heavy foliage

- Do not pick up hitchhikers or offer any stranger a ride
- Do not turn your back while loading packages into the car
- If forced to drive, consider crashing the car near a busy intersection
- If bumped in traffic by young males, be suspicious of the accident
- If confronted by an <u>armed</u> carjacker  - **DO NOT RESIST** - give up car, keys and/or money
- <u>Never</u> agree to be kidnapped - and if possible, drop the keys, run and scream for help
- Request a security escort if alone at a shopping center
- Use valet parking or an attended garage when driving alone
- **WHEN DRIVING – ALWAYS KEEP THE DOORS LOCKED AND WINDOWS ROLLED UP!**
- When stopped in traffic, always leave room ahead to maneuver and escape
- Call police to report the crime and provide detailed information

## <u>Unattended Auto Theft</u>

Auto theft is a profitable business in this country and there are organized groups of car thieves who fill orders for contract buyers.  Some cars are stolen for shipment out of the country or young car thieves steal cars as a prank or for a joy ride.  Some intend to personally drive or sell the stolen car after disguising the vehicle with new paint, plates and wheels.  Most cars are stolen for the value of their parts.  An experienced car thief can steal a car in less than a minute. According to insurance companies, a $20,000 stolen vehicle can be stripped and sold for $30,000 in parts inventory to unscrupulous scrap and auto-body shops.

Motor vehicles are stolen from shopping malls, streets, driveways, parking lots, garages, and car dealerships but in greater frequency where large groups of cars are parked together for extended periods of time such as airports, shopping centers, colleges, sporting events, fairgrounds, movie complexes and large apartment complexes. High-rise and subterranean parking structures and fee parking lots experience a lower auto theft rate due to a reduced number of escape routes and the possibility of video cameras.

To reduce the risk of unattended auto theft, follow the steps below:

- <u>Always</u> lock the car and roll up your windows
- Carry drivers license, registration and insurance card with you - don't leave it in the car
- Copy license plate and vehicle identification (VIN) numbers on a card and keep them with you
- Do not leave credit cards in your vehicle
- In a fee garage, take the pay-ticket with you (it's also the thief's ticket out of the garage)
- Install a highly-visible steering wheel or brake pedal locking device
- <u>Never</u> leave the car running and unattended - even for a few minutes
- <u>Never</u> leave the keys in the car or ignition - even inside a locked garage
- <u>Never</u> leave valuables in the car – even if the car is locked
- Park in a high-traffic and well-lighted area
- Purchase an auto alarm system and display an alarm decal near the door handle
- When using valet parking, leave <u>only</u> the ignition key with the attendant

---

**If stopped by law enforcement in an <u>isolated location</u>, immediately lock the car doors and roll up all windows with the exception of the driver side – roll it up so there is only a two inch opening at the top of the window. Do NOT <u>ever</u> get out of the car or agree to a search of your vehicle – <u>even if directed to do so</u>. If the police insist you get out of the car, calmly but firmly state because of security reasons and concern for your own safety, before you will leave the vehicle, you insist on driving to the nearest police station or public location. Inform the officers you intend to call 9-1-1 if further coercion is initiated by them. If they are legitimate police, they will understand your action. If they are imposters or unscrupulous officers, you could save yourself from being raped, robbed or killed.**

---

## IDENTITY THEFT

Identity theft is one of the fastest growing crimes in the world. Credit and debit card numbers, savings and checking accounts, driver's license numbers, passports, social security numbers, date of birth, and other personal identification can net criminals thousands of dollars in a very short period of time.

In many cases, identity thieves get the victims personal identification numbers by having the victims credit cards, goods and services delivered to <u>their</u> address. Since the bills for charges incurred are sent to the thief's address, the victim will be unaware of the mounting debt until the account reaches the collections department and by that time, the victim's credit report will have excessive late payment histories and many accounts in collections.

Identity theft can take many forms. The illegal immigrants in this country use a "legitimate" social security number and date of birth belonging to a <u>citizen</u> for employment purposes or to obtain a birth certificate. Go online to the Social Security Administration if someone is using your social security number to obtain a birth certificate, gain unlawful employment or establish credit or new accounts. If fraud is suspected, contact the SSA Hotline: (800) 772-1213.

There are several guidelines that can be used by family members to avoid being a victim of identity theft.

- Every six months, request a credit report to discover unknown credit inquiries or unauthorized accounts. All three major credit reporting agencies in the United States have toll free telephone numbers. Equifax (888) 532-0179; Experian (800) 311-4769; Trans Union (800) 680-7289. Report suspected fraud to the credit reporting agencies and request your account be red flagged with a fraud statement posted at the top of your report at all three credit reporting agencies. This will stop future credit from being issued until you are contacted and will remain in place for seven years or until you cancel the request. These agencies will also help clear up negative information on the reports due to fraud.

- Reconcile statements in a timely fashion and immediately challenge any suspicious purchases.

- Limit the number of credit and debit cards used and cancel any inactive accounts.

- Immediately <u>destroy</u> and <u>shred</u> all unused pre-approved credit card and loan applications.

- <u>Never</u> provide strangers who call on the phone and claim to be from the government, utility companies, department store or any other business with date of birth or personal driver's license, credit card, bank account and social security numbers.

- Minimize exposure of your drivers' license number for check cashing purposes, ask if the business has alternative options such as using a check-cashing card or go elsewhere to conduct business.

- <u>Never</u> give out your date of birth or social security number in order to cash a check at a business.

- <u>Shred</u> all pay stubs, utility bills, tax returns, bank statements, checks, credit and debit cards and transaction receipts prior to disposal.

- Scrutinize all <u>utility and subscription bills</u> to guarantee proper charges.

- Immediately <u>destroy and shred all checks</u> when closing a checking account.

- <u>Memorize</u> your passwords and personal identification (PIN) numbers.

- Maintain and carry a list of pertinent information (including the issuer and contact number) on all personal bank and identification cards in the event of missing or stolen cards. Immediately report all stolen cards to the issuers and request that new card numbers be issued. Always respond to written credit card receipt notifications received in the mail.

- Do not publicize personal information on the Internet.  Full names, dates and places of birth, and current address will provide an identity thief with information he needs to get your duplicate birth certificate.

- Instead of using a mail box in front of your home  to receive mail, strongly consider renting a mail box at the post office or install a lockable mail box that can only be opened by the postal worker and you.  Thieves routinely search outside mail boxes to retrieve tax refunds, social security, retirement, pension and paychecks as well as steal important account numbers from the monthly bills.

- Do not use your mother's maiden name as a password.  Maiden names are often used as passwords to access accounts over the telephone.

- Never leave a purse or wallet unattended – anywhere – any time – or for any reason.

## SCAM ARTISTS

Scam artists are more prevalent because of the Internet where it is easy to anonymously reach out and trick someone into relinquishing private information or access to bank accounts.  Since our society has evolved into a credit-based culture, with just a few strokes on a computer keyboard, a person can unwittingly provide all the personal information necessary for a scam artist to steal their identity.

Frankly, in many cases, both the greed and laziness of the scam artist <u>and</u> the victim are to blame for the desire of wanting to get something for nothing.  Something free.  Something easy.  Well – allow me to let you in on a little secret - **<u>there is no free lunch – and one way or the other – SOMEBODY has to pay for the meal</u>**.

Family members should be <u>vigilant</u>, <u>responsible</u> and <u>accountable</u> for the methods used in making transactions with their hard-earned money **AND** be intelligent enough to recognize that **WHAT SOUNDS TOO GOOD TO BE TRUE – OFTEN IS TOO GOOD TO BE TRUE.  SO WISE UP!**

There is a buffet of scams just waiting for the next victim.  For example:

- There is an e-mail in your inbox verifying a credit card charge of $500.00 for online purchases at a porno website and if you have questions about the charge, you are instructed to call a toll-free telephone number.  The number is in the Caribbean and is not toll-free but instead is charged at an inflated international rate.  The victim will be placed on hold or forced to listen to a long recorded message while long distance charges are being charged at an exorbitant rate.  Most credit card companies will not send you an e-mail message.  Be very suspicious of dialing unfamiliar area codes.

- The victim appears to be investing in gems or precious metals with low risk and a great return on investment!  The buyer relies on counterfeit "grading certificates" or "appraisals" with information about the worth of these investments.  They are generally not worth the money paid by the victim and they have little resale value.

- A victim is being asked to make payments for shipping, taxes or handling fees before receiving the $25,000 prize.  A legitimate company or sweepstakes will <u>never</u> require any payment or purchase in order for the prize to be awarded to the winner.  The scam artists may also request private information such as a social security number and birth date in order to use this information for further identity theft purposes.

- There are many scams involving bargain vacations or an exotic trip that includes airfare for only $150.  What the scam neglects to disclose is the fact that you will be tied to the wheels of the airplane and as the plane flies over Fiji, they will untie the ropes and allow you to fall to the island.  The luxury hotel turns out to be a mud hut in the middle of a mosquito invested swamp.  The victim will also be required to pay undisclosed taxes and other fees *in advance* of the trip.  The admission is free – you pay to get out.  Investigate these travel offers with a reputable travel agency.

- The "Been Ripped Off - We'll Get Your Money Back!" scams get the names of people who have been defrauded in other scams and then call, claiming to be federal attorneys or agents who can get your lost money back in return for a fee.  When the federal government sues scam artists, there is never a charge to consumers to return any recovered money.

- There are phone solicitors representing charitable organizations.  In many cases, the victim believes they are donating to a good cause but the telephone calls are from scam artists who claim to be collecting on behalf of the police, firefighters or highway patrol officers.  It is important to donate money to legitimate charities, but refrain from making <u>any</u> donations over the phone or to solicitors who come to your home.  Do not provide any solicitor with personal information such as credit or debit card numbers or checking account numbers in order to make the donation.  Many charitable organizations – although legitimate - command a huge percentage of donations as administrative costs with very little money actually going towards the intended cause.  Always investigate any charity before making a donation.

- The victim is promised they can get a loan even with bad credit.  These scams require an advanced fee but then the paperwork stall begins and a loan is never approved.  A person who knows nothing about you but promises to get you a loan and demands money up front is running a scam.

- The scam artists promise to remove damaging information from your credit report and claim they can get truthful information removed from your credit report for a fee.  Accurate information can be reported for five to ten years.  If your report has errors, you can get it corrected at no cost through the credit reporting agency.

- An unsolicited letter from Nigeria arrives from a high government official or officer of an oil company asking your assistance in moving millions of dollars from a contract "overpayment" out of Nigeria.  In return for the assistance, they offer to let you retain millions of dollars.  The victim simply needs to provide personal financial information and an advanced fee to pay for transfer costs.

- The victim is offered a chance to invest in a promising company with a guaranteed high return.  The idea is you invest and recruit others to do the same and you get a percentage share from each investor you enlist in the program.  When the pyramid collapses (either the pool of new investors dries up or the swindler is caught), everyone loses - except the person at the top.

- Scam artists will advertise fake charities using similar names of legitimate charities such as the National Cancer Society to cause confusion with the legitimate American Cancer Society or the National Heart Institute to cause confusion with the American Heart Institute.  There are times when legitimate volunteers will canvas the neighborhood requesting donations for legitimate charities.  In these cases, accept the flyers and brochures from the individual and advise them you will personally mail in the donation.

- During an emergency situation, scam artists pretend to be employed by Federal Emergency Management Administration (FEMA), the Small Business Administration (SBA) or other agencies.  To safeguard against disaster-related fraud, officials recommend the following precautions:

  - Ask for proper identification.  A shirt or jacket with FEMA or SBA on the back or front is not absolute proof of someone's affiliation with an agency.  Always ask to see the laminated official photo identification card carried by all federal employees. If they don't have it, they are not official representatives.  Applicants should also be aware they may receive visits from more than one official inspector or representative.

  - Under no circumstances are FEMA representatives or other agency representatives allowed to accept money.  FEMA does not charge for any programs or services.  While FEMA inspectors assess damage, the agency does not hire or endorse specific contractors.

  - Safeguard personal information.  If someone requests personal information outside of an official registration process, do not provide it.  FEMA inspectors never require this information.  Applicants who register for FEMA assistance receive a registration number, and official FEMA and/or SBA representatives will have that number with them.

The Federal Trade Commission has published free consumer brochures on scams providing details on how the scams work and how to avoid them. Copies of the brochures are available from the FTC's Public Reference Branch, Room 130, 6th Street and Pennsylvania Avenue, N.W., Washington, D.C. 20580; or call (202) 326-2222.

## NEIGHBORHOOD WATCH PROGRAM

A Neighborhood Watch Program may be the most effective and least costly means to prevent crime and reduce the fear of crime in your neighborhood. A *Neighborhood Watch Program* teaches residents how to observe and report suspicious persons, vehicles and activity in their neighborhoods. Law enforcement officers want and need assistance of residents to report suspicious persons, vandalism, abandoned cars, or other behavior that causes a resident to feel uncomfortable.

During peaceful or "normal" times – this program can significantly reduce crime in the area. During a disaster situation – the Neighborhood Watch Program becomes even more important in protecting the families in the neighborhood. During a dangerous event - whether the disaster is a manmade or natural occurrence and whether the length of the crisis is one hour or one year - law enforcement, fire and first responders will be occupied in maintaining critical electrical, water and sewer systems, directing traffic and securing public domains.

**Every family must recognize their role in protecting themselves and their property from those who would take advantage of a chaotic environment**. As an organized and united group – neighbors will serve as a legitimate deterrent to gangs, thieves, muggers, kidnappers and other thugs who may threaten the neighborhood.

Talk to several of your neighbors to learn the level of interest in the neighborhood and select a coordinator to oversee the project. Once a coordinator is chosen, he/she needs to find interested people to serve as block captains. The coordinator would serve as a liaison between law enforcement and the block captains. Block captains gather information from the neighborhood residents. The block captains then bring the neighbors comments to the coordinator who then relays it to law enforcement.

Continue to establish interest and attention in the program and gather the facts about crime in your neighborhood. Check police reports, conduct victimization surveys and learn residents' perceptions about crime. Create a neighborhood bulletin or newsletter and distribute by hand or through email. Include information particular to your neighborhood such as highlights of achievements by residents or upcoming neighborhood events.

Arrange a time and place to meet with residents in the neighborhood. Residents may need persuasion to attend these meetings. Make sure to aggressively advertise the event by distributing flyers and making phone calls *well in advance* of the first meeting. Hold it at a convenient location and time (Tuesday, Wednesday or Thursday evenings are usually well attended). Consider providing simple refreshments. At this meeting, choose block captains and compile a list of concerns and fears to present to law enforcement for suggestions and recommendations.

At a second meeting, arrange for a police officer to attend to train the group in crime prevention methods and to provide ideas for the program. Hold a potluck block party and speak on crime in your area or hold a neighborhood clean up contest and provide treats for the family who cleans up the most trash. Physical conditions like abandoned cars or overgrown vacant lots contribute to crime so encourage residents to beautify the area and ask them to turn on outdoor lights during the evening hours.

Consider linking with an existing organization, such as a citizens' association, community development office, tenants' association or housing authority. They may be able to provide an existing infrastructure that can be utilized by your program. You can approach neighbors who are disabled or seldom leave their homes and ask them to be "window watchers" looking out for children and reporting any unusual activities in the neighborhood. Some neighborhoods expand efforts to reduce crime by organizing a system where trained citizen volunteers drive or walk within their immediate neighborhood to be a visible deterrent to crime after participating in training sponsored by the local law enforcement office.

Families can ban together to provide a higher level of support and protection. By *planning in advance*, households can determine the best approach to take in supporting each other during dangerous events. Emphasize neighborhood watch programs should <u>not</u> have a vigilante attitude nor should they assume the role of the local police. **Their duty is to ask neighbors to be alert, observant, caring and to report suspicious activity or crimes immediately to law enforcement officials.**

# NATURAL DISASTERS

A *natural disaster* is the result of a <u>natural</u> hazard occurring in nature e.g. flood, tornado, hurricane, thunderstorm, volcanic eruption, earthquake, heat wave or landslide. A natural disaster is generally considered to be created by a higher force of nature or through the Power of God. Natural disasters are common and are increasing at an alarming rate throughout the world. There are some regions in the country and around the world prone to <u>specific</u> types of disasters.

**LOOK AROUND YOU!** It is wise to identify each type of disaster and analyze the possibility of such disasters occurring in <u>your region</u>. For example, if you live in Kansas and are told to run to high ground because a tsunami is coming – you have more to worry about than taking a swim and getting wet, but if you are told to take cover because of an impending tornado – take heed of the warning.

The eastern, western and gulf coastlines in the United States are not only targets for a tsunami but have a higher probability of experiencing a hurricane than some other parts of the country. States located on fault lines or have dormant or active volcanoes such as California, Oregon and Washington are more likely to experience an earthquake or volcanic eruption. Communities residing along major dams, rivers or lakes are more likely to experience flooding than cities located in desert regions.

<u>**As part of *planning in advance*, family members should determine what type of *natural* disasters are probable in their region and as part of their overall strategic emergency preparedness plan, prepare a *mini* plan to accommodate each *type* of disaster possible or probable in their area**</u>.

For example, if family members reside along the coast, there should definitely be a tsunami mini plan integrated into the overall emergency preparedness plan. Those individuals living in Kansas – I wouldn't worry about a tsunami mini plan but I would be vigilant about making sure a mini plan is in place to survive that pesky tornado.

In the United States, natural disasters can be classified as Level 1 (1 hour to 7 days), Level 2 (7 days to 1 month) and in some cases, Level 3 (1 month to 1 year) disasters. The damage or destruction to utilities, communication systems, transportation modes, medical facilities and commercial markets have at times been severe, but the length of time it would take to replace or repair the damage has been limited to a few hours up to several months. Citizens were able to return to normal after a relative short period of time. However, things are changing. The United States has <u>still</u> not fully recovered from Hurricane Katrina, Hurricane Sandy or the BP Oil Spill. Due to the severity of these disasters, it is taking <u>much longer</u> for the country to fully recover from the affects.

Each family should prepare for and be ready for all possible levels and types of natural disasters:

- <u>**Determine the types of natural disasters *probable* and *possible* in your region. Attempt to analyze the probable severity, damage and destruction that may occur as a result of these disasters and how long it may realistically take to fully recover from the affects.**</u>

- Always consider the *worst case scenario* and plan accordingly. If it happens, you are prepared. If is doesn't happen, you are still prepared. Win/Win.

- Prepare an overall family emergency plan. Your family may not be together when disaster strikes, so it is important to know how you will contact one another, how you will get back together and what you would do in case of a specific type of disaster.

- Prepare emergency pantries and supply kits stocked to support all probable natural disasters, including the home, place of refuge (cabin, motor home or camper), auto, work and evacuation kits. These kits should include basic essentials such as food and water, and specialty items for <u>specific</u> disasters e.g. face masks during a volcanic eruption. The specialty items in these kits would be contingent on the region where family members reside and possible disasters that could occur in the area.

- Consider the health and safety of pets and livestock into the overall plan and determine appropriate actions based on each type of disaster that could occur in your area.

- Depending on the severity of the disaster, government agencies and first responders may not be equipped to support the entirety of the devastation. Families should <u>not plan on support from outside sources</u> during the first phase of a natural disaster and should be prepared to support the survival of the family members for the <u>entire duration</u>.

- Consider a designated public shelter or alternative evacuation site if the home or place of refuge has been damaged or destroyed and is no longer safe.

- Attempt to listen to Emergency Broadcast messages, the NOAA Weather Radio, television, radio or check the Internet for official news and instructions as information become available.

After a natural disaster, the safety and security of family members should be the major priority during clean up and recovery. As a first priority, all family members should check for injuries and get first aid for themselves, as well as pets and livestock as needed and then immediately locate and assemble emergency supplies. If someone needs to be rescued, work with first responders. Many people have been killed or injured trying to rescue others on their own. Family members should wear long pants, long-sleeved shirt, sturdy shoes, safety glasses and work gloves during recovery and cleanup exercises. A face mask should be used in areas with dust, chemicals and other hazardous materials in the atmosphere.

## VOLCANIC ERUPTION

A volcano is a mountain that opens downward into a reservoir of molten rock below the surface of the earth. A vent is created at the surface of the earth down into the molten rock and these vents are where molten rock escapes back up to the earth's surface. Eruptions have lava flows, flattened landscapes, poisonous gases or flying rock and ash that travel hundreds of miles. Fresh volcanic ash is abrasive, acidic, gritty, gassy and odorous and causes lung damage in small infants, older adults and those suffering from severe respiratory illnesses.

Volcanic ash also damages machinery and equipment and ash mixed with water can collapse a roof. Volcanic eruptions can be accompanied by other natural disasters including earthquakes, mudflows, flash floods, rock falls, landslides, acid rain, fire, and under special conditions - even tsunamis.

According to the National Geological Survey, the United States is ranked third behind Indonesia and Japan in the number of historically active volcanoes with over ten percent of the 1,500 volcanoes that have erupted in the past 10,000 years located in the United States. Most of these volcanoes are found in the Aleutian Islands, the Alaska Peninsula, the Hawaiian Islands, and the Cascade Range of the Pacific Northwest; the remainder is widely distributed in the western part of the country. There are several volcanoes in the United States that have produced some of the largest and most dangerous types of eruptions in this century.

The map below shows volcanoes (active and inactive) spread across the United States. It appears families living on the west coast of the country (and especially in Alaska and Hawaii) should prepare emergency pantries to support the possibility of a volcanic eruption.

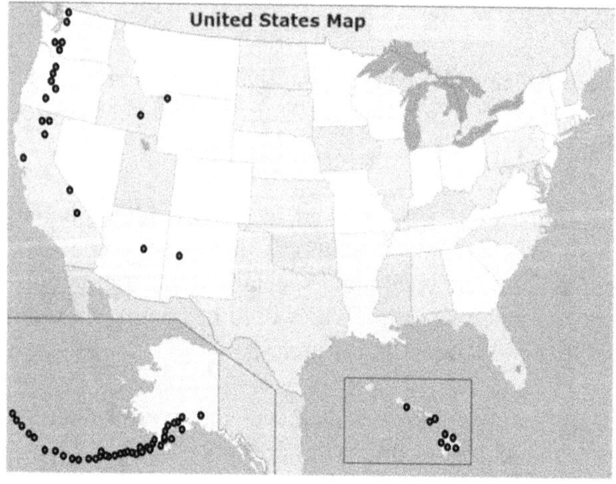

<u>**Before a Volcanic Eruption**</u>

Prior to a volcanic eruption, evacuation of the area may be necessary or depending on the circumstances, family members may be able to remain at the home *before, during* and *after* the eruption. If there is reasonable knowledge the home may be in imminent danger, immediately gather emergency supplies and evacuate family members, pets and livestock from the volcano area. As part of *planning in advance,* family members should have a place of refuge including a public shelter or another property site selected that is *outside* the danger zone of a volcanic eruption. This place could be the home of a friend or relative, or even an outside location.

If the family is able to remain at the home, protection from falling ash is important so close all windows, doors, fireplace or woodstove dampers and turn off all fans, heating and air conditioning systems in the home. If realistic, pets and livestock should be brought into enclosed shelters or livestock should be released from enclosures in order to give them the opportunity to move from the danger area. All cars, vehicles and equipment should be moved into an inside enclosure. Locate and gather emergency supplies to be ready for use. Use a radio or television for the latest emergency information.

<u>**During a Volcanic Eruption**</u>

During a volcanic eruption, driving can stir up volcanic ash that clogs engines, damages moving parts and stalls vehicles. Try to avoid driving in heavy ash fall because moving parts can be damaged from abrasion including bearings, brakes and transmissions. If you have to drive, keep the speed to 35 miles per hour, keep car windows rolled up and do not operate the air conditioning system.

Family members should beware of mudflow that increases near stream channels and with prolonged heavy rains. Mudflows can move faster than a person and most animals can walk or run so always look upstream before crossing a bridge and do not cross a bridge if a mudflow is approaching. Avoid river valleys and low-lying areas.

<u>**After a Volcanic Eruption**</u>

After the eruption, continue to avoid driving in heavy ash and stay away from volcanic ash fall areas. Stay <u>indoors if possible</u>. Wear long-sleeved shirts and long pants. Use goggles and wear eyeglasses instead of contact lenses. Wear a face mask designed to protect against lung damage from small particles. If a family member has a respiratory ailment, avoid contact with any amount of ash. If outside, cover the mouth and nose. Clear the roofs of ash to avoid collapsing a roof.

## EARTHQUAKE

An earthquake is the sudden and rapid shaking of the earth caused by shifting rock as it releases a buildup of stress in the earth that has accumulated over a long period of time. There are forty-five (45) states and territories in the United States that have moderate to high risk for earthquakes including the New Madrid fault line in the central region of the United States. Many family members may have experienced a small earthquake in the past and have a false sense of safety; you didn't do anything or perhaps you got under a desk or ran outside and still survived with no injuries.

Most family members have never experienced the kind of strong earthquake shaking possible in much larger earthquakes - the sudden and intense back and forth motions of several feet per second will cause the floor or the ground to jerk sideways right out from under you, and every unsecured object will topple, fall, or become airborne in a matter of seconds. That is why you must learn to immediately protect yourself after the first jolt - don't wait to see if the earthquake shaking will be strong! Everyone must learn to be proactive!

Throughout the world, there are high level earthquake zones that generally follow the tectonic plates.

In the United States, although California is known for the famed San Andreas Fault, there are several lesser-known fault zones in the country that are dangerous and unpredictable. Some of these faults are capable of producing an earthquake larger and more threatening than the San Francisco earthquake in 1906. One of the main reasons why these particular fault lines are unknown is because of the time period between major jolts.

## PACIFIC NORTHWEST

A much greater hazard in terms of sheer magnitude known as the Cascadian Subduction Zone exists to the north of the San Andreas Fault where the ocean crust is being forced beneath the North American continent. This zone stretches 680 miles and is a colliding land mass fifty miles offshore of Oregon, Washington and southern British Columbia. The most active volcanoes in the chain include Mt. St. Helens, Mt. Baker, Lassen Peak, and Mt. Hood. This fault is capable of generating a magnitude 9 earthquake on the Richter Scale. There could be unprecedented damage and thousands of deaths.

## NEW MADRID

A majority of major earthquakes in the world occur at tectonic plate boundaries where land masses are colliding or pushing past one another but one exception is in the middle of the United States near New Madrid, Missouri. In 1811 and 1812, three massive earthquakes struck near New Madrid - the largest of which exceeded a magnitude 8 and was felt over two million square miles or nearly two-thirds of the country.

During these earthquakes, the ground rose and fell, trees were uprooted, deep cracks opened in the ground, landslides rolled down hills, huge waves washed boats out of the Mississippi River and river banks, islands and sand bars were destroyed. An earthquake near this junction of Missouri, Illinois, Kentucky, Tennessee and Arkansas today would produce serious property damage and loss of life.

## ALASKA

One of the largest earthquakes ever recorded was in Alaska's Prince William Sound in 1964. This magnitude 9.2 earthquake was the result of the oceanic plate being forced beneath the continental plate and killed 128 people due to the resulting tsunami. In some places, the ground was uplifted almost thirty-eight feet and in other areas it dropped more than seven feet.

The major concern for Alaska is the <u>Denali Fault</u> which had a thirty-mile-long rupture in a magnitude 7.9 earthquake in 2004. Alaska's biggest vulnerability is its transportation infrastructure where virtually all traffic going anywhere in the state passes through Anchorage. The airport sits on ground that could easily suffer liquefaction — where sediments act like a liquid when shaken in an earthquake. This could seriously damage runways and isolate the rest of the state.

## UTAH

Running along the base of the western edge of the Rocky Mountains, the <u>Wasatch Fault</u> lies underneath Salt Lake City and the state's urban corridor which is home to two million people. The fault is 240 miles in length and is one of the world's longest standard faults where the land on one side of the fault drops down relative to the other side during an earthquake.

The Wasatch Fault has distinct segments that act independently of one another, each with its own history of earthquakes. On average, every 300 to 350 years, one of the central segments near Salt Lake City and Provo has had a major earthquake. The last one occurred three hundred years ago. The possibility of a major earthquake in the region is increased because of a segment under Salt Lake City and a segment to the north of the area averages a large earthquake every 1,300 years. The Salt Lake City segment last ruptured approximately 1,300 years ago and the area to the north ruptured approximately 2,100 years ago.

## HAWAII

The <u>Hawaiian Islands</u> were formed by a massive plume of magma rising through the molten mantle between the crust and core of the earth creating a volcano. As the Pacific plate slowly moved over the stationary plume, new volcanic islands were formed as older ones became dormant. The island of Hawaii is where the magma is currently active. Even more dangerous are the earthquakes caused by the expansion of the volcano as new magma pushes out from below the surface of the earth. These jolts can cause destructive tsunamis resulting in a high death toll.

One of the major problems with the Hawaiian Islands is if there is an earthquake, volcanic eruption or even a tsunami, there aren't many places for the people to run to safety. The Hawaiian Islands are after all - islands. At some point as you are running away from the danger - you are going to run into the ocean.

## CONNECTICUT

<u>Cameron's Line</u> begins near Ridgefield, Connecticut, descends from New England and runs beneath the Bronx and East Rivers, touching the western edge of Queens, looping into the lower third of Manhattan, and then heads south beneath New York Bay and Staten Island. The line separates the prehistoric North American continent from the oceanic plate that smashed against it 450 million years ago.

The rocks of the Manhattan Formation located on the western side of Cameron's line are sedimentary rocks that have been tectonically stable over a large period of time but the other side of the line has different rocks which have experienced great tectonic movement in a westward direction on top of the underlying bedrock near New York City. This fault line is in close proximity to three major airports in the country (Newark, LaGuardia and Kennedy) - can't get any better than that - right?

## MID-ATLANTIC

The <u>Ramapo Fault</u> System spans more than 185 miles in the states of *New York*, *New Jersey*, and *Pennsylvania*. The faults include Ramapo, Hopewell, Chalfont and the Flemington-Furlong fault. It is a system of faults between the northern Appalachian Mountains and Piedmont areas. These faults are perhaps the best known fault zone in the Mid-Atlantic region, especially with the proximity to the Indian Point Nuclear Plant in New York.

Shown below is a map of some of the major fault systems throughout the United States:

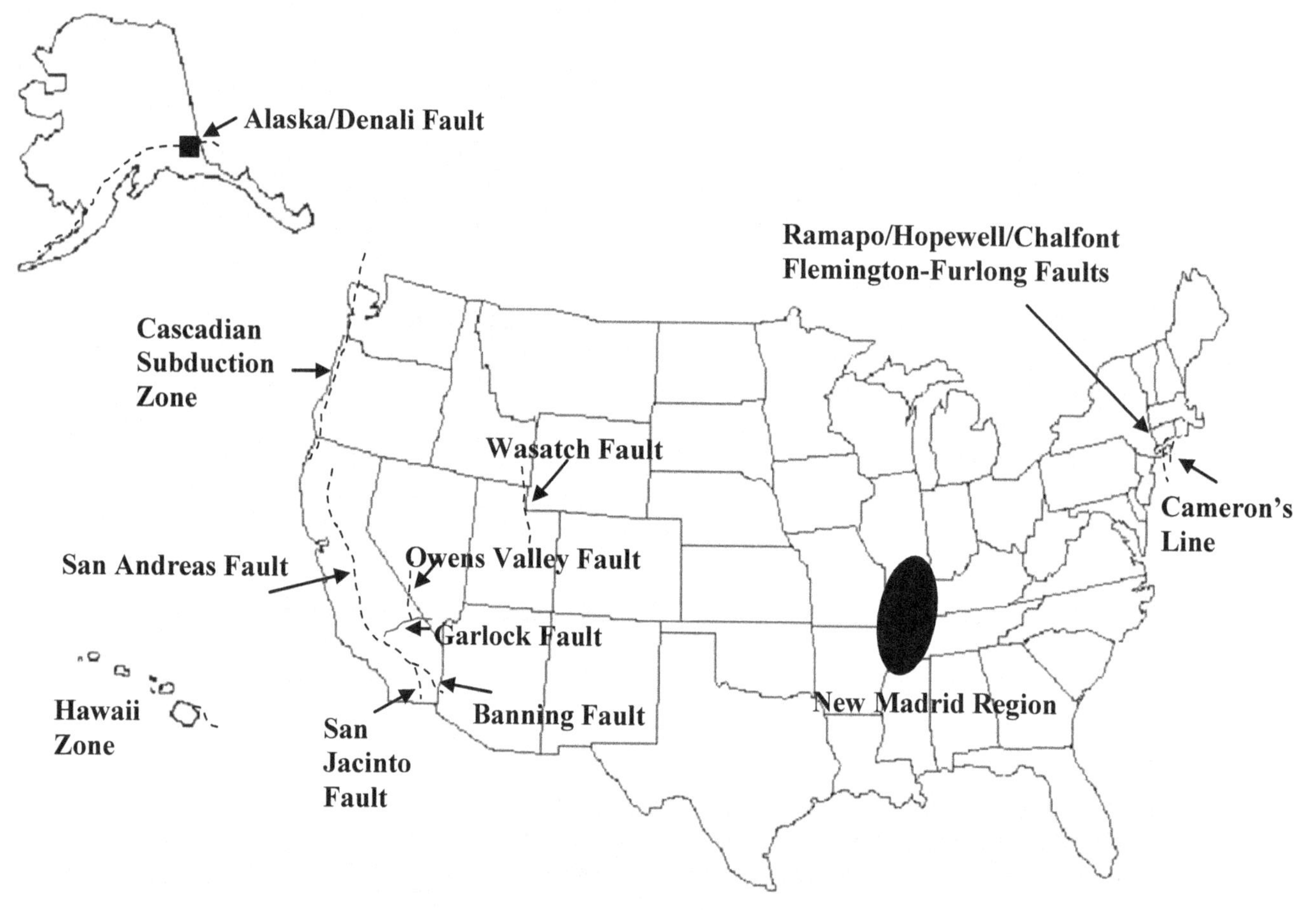



Based on locations of major faults in the country, the United States Geological Survey determined the highest hazard for serious earthquake is obviously in the western region of the country (including Alaska and Hawaii) along the west coast as well as in the New Madrid region.

**IF FAMILY MEMBERS ARE LOCATED IN THE VICINITY OF KNOWN EARTHQUAKE FAULT LINES, *PLAN IN ADVANCE* TO PREPARE FOR THE POSSIBILITY OF AN EARTHQUAKE AND THE CONSEQUENCES THAT CAN OCCUR AS A RESULT INCLUDING EXTENDED ELECTRICAL OUTAGES, GAS AND SEWER DISRUPTION, DAMAGE TO TRANSPORTATION INFRASTRUCTURE, VEHICLES AND SYSTEMS, DESTRUCTION OF MEDICAL FACILITIES AND INCREASED INJURIES.**

We now know in the United States, the western region has the most earthquakes. The State of Alaska leads the country in the highest number of earthquakes with 57.2% or 12,053 earthquakes between 1974 and 2003 out of a total of 21,080. All family members living in the western part of the country or in states identified as prone to earthquakes should ensure all emergency pantries support earthquake preparation.

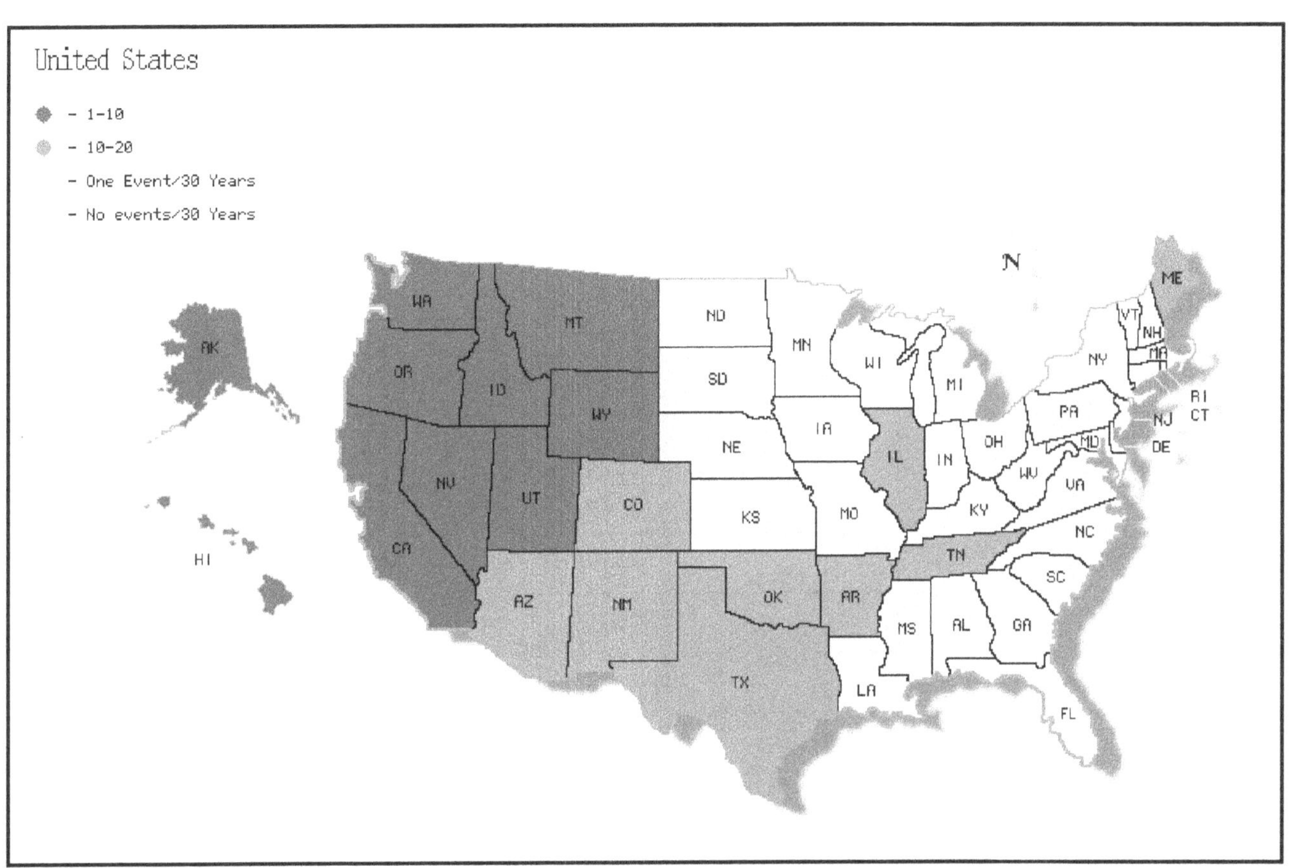



| RANK | STATE | AMOUNT 1974-2003 | PERCENT OF TOTAL | RANK | STATE | AMOUNT 1974-2003 | PERCENT OF TOTAL |
|---|---|---|---|---|---|---|---|
| **1** | **Alaska** | **12,053** | **57.2 %** | 26 | Virginia | 10 | - |
| 2 | California | 4,895 | 23.2 % | 27 | Nebraska | 8 | - |
| 3 | Hawaii | 1,533 | 7.3 % | 28 | Ohio | 8 | - |
| 4 | Nevada | 778 | 3.7 % | 29 | Georgia | 7 | - |
| 5 | Washington | 424 | 2.0 % | 30 | Indiana | 6 | - |
| 6 | Idaho | 404 | 1.9 % | 31 | New Hampshire | 6 | - |
| 7 | Wyoming | 217 | 1.0 % | 32 | Pennsylvania | 6 | - |
| 8 | Montana | 186 | 0.9 % | 33 | Kansas | 4 | - |
| 9 | Utah | 139 | 0.7 % | 34 | North Carolina | 3 | - |
| 10 | Oregon | 73 | 0.3 % | 35 | Massachusetts | 2 | - |
| 11 | New Mexico | 38 | 0.2 % | 36 | Michigan | 2 | - |
| 12 | Arkansas | 34 | 0.2 % | 37 | Minnesota | 2 | - |
| 13 | Arizona | 32 | 0.2 % | 38 | Mississippi | 2 | - |

| RANK | STATE | AMOUNT 1974-2003 | PERCENT OF TOTAL | RANK | STATE | AMOUNT 1974-2003 | PERCENT OF TOTAL |
|---|---|---|---|---|---|---|---|
| 14 | Colorado | 24 | 0.1 % | 39 | New Jersey | 2 | - |
| 15 | Tennessee | 22 | 0.1 % | 40 | Louisiana | 1 | - |
| 16 | Missouri | 21 | - | 41 | Rhode Island | 1 | - |
| 17 | Texas | 20 | - | 42 | West Virginia | 1 | - |
| 18 | Illinois | 17 | - | 43 | Connecticut | 0 | - |
| 19 | Oklahoma | 17 | - | 44 | Delaware | 0 | - |
| 20 | Maine | 16 | - | 45 | Florida | 0 | - |
| 21 | New York | 16 | - | 46 | Iowa | 0 | - |
| 22 | Alabama | 15 | - | 47 | Maryland | 0 | - |
| 23 | Kentucky | 15 | - | 48 | North Dakota | 0 | - |
| 24 | South Carolina | 10 | - | 49 | Vermont | 0 | - |
| 25 | South Dakota | 10 | - | 50 | Wisconsin | 0 | - |

**SOURCE:  United States Geological Survey**

<u>**Before an Earthquake**</u>

Contact your insurance representative about the possibility of getting earthquake insurance - and especially if you are located in an earthquake zone.  In general, the insurance will cost around $200 to $500 per year with a deductible of around $10,000.  Although the deductible is high, remember if your home is damaged or destroyed due to an earthquake, regular home owner's insurance will not cover the damage due to "by Acts of God" clause prevalent in most home owner's insurance policies.  If the home was to be shaken from the foundation, if the roof collapses or if there is serious damage to personal belongings - the cost can easily reach and surpass the $10,000 deductible.  If the house catches fire and is damaged or destroyed as a result of the earthquake - the fire insurance portion of your home owner's policy will generally cover the damage.  Talk to your insurance agent and make sure you understand the coverage to be included in the earthquake policy.

As a precautionary measure, fasten shelves securely to walls and place large or heavy objects on lower shelves.  Breakable items such as bottled foods, glass and dishes should be stored in low and closed cabinets with latches.  Weed killers, pesticides and flammable products should be stored securely in closed cabinets with latches and on bottom shelves.  Fasten heavy items such as pictures and mirrors securely to walls and away from beds and couches.

Brace overhead light fixtures and top heavy objects.  Repair defective electrical wiring and leaky gas connections.  Install flexible pipe fittings that are more resistant to breakage to avoid gas or water leaks.  Secure the water heater, refrigerator, furnace and gas appliances by strapping them to wall studs and bolting them to the floor.  If recommended by the gas company, have an automatic gas shut-off valve installed that is triggered by strong vibrations.  Repair any deep cracks in ceilings or foundations.  Get expert advice if there are signs of structural defects.  Be sure the home is firmly anchored to its foundation.  Locate safe spots in each room under a sturdy table or against an inside wall.  Hold earthquake drills and remember -

# DROP, COVER AND HOLD ON

<u>**During an Earthquake**</u>

<u>**Indoors**</u>

When indoors during an earthquake: **DROP** to the ground, take **COVER** by getting under a sturdy table or other a piece of furniture and **HOLD ON** until the shaking stops. **DO NOT** run outside or to other rooms during the shaking. Research has shown most injuries occur when people inside buildings attempt to move to a different location inside the building or try to leave the building. The areas near the exterior walls of a building are the most dangerous place to be during an earthquake. Windows, facades and architectural details are often the first parts of the building to collapse. DO NOT use the elevators. The shaking can be so strong you will not be able to move far without falling down and objects may fall or be thrown at you. Injuries can be avoided if you drop to the ground before the earthquake drops you.

**DO NOT** stand in a doorway. Many believe a doorway is the safest place to be during an earthquake. It is true if you live in an old, unreinforced adobe house or some older wood frame house. In modern houses, however, doorways are no stronger than any other part of the house, and the doorway does not protect you from the most likely source of injury - falling or flying objects. You also may not be able to brace yourself in the door during strong shaking. You are safer under a table or desk and if there is no table or desk, cover your face and head with your arms and crouch in an inside corner of the building.

<u>**Outdoors**</u>

If outside during an earthquake - <u>stay outside</u>. Move away from buildings, streetlights and utility wires and head towards an open area until the shaking stops. The greatest danger exists directly outside buildings, at exits and alongside exterior walls. If in a moving vehicle during an earthquake, stop as quickly as possible and stay in the vehicle. Avoid stopping near or under buildings, trees, overpasses and utility wires. Proceed cautiously once the earthquake has stopped. <u>Avoid roads, bridges, overpasses or ramps that may have been damaged by the earthquake</u>.

If a family member becomes trapped under debris, do <u>not</u> light a match, move around or kick up dust. Cover your mouth with a handkerchief or clothing. Tap on a pipe or wall so rescuers can locate you. Use a whistle if one is available. Shout only as a last resort as shouting can cause you to inhale dangerous amounts of dust.

<u>**After an Earthquake**</u>

When in a commercial building during an earthquake, and when the shaking stops, look around to make sure it is safe to move and then exit the building. At the home, search for and extinguish small fires and then listen to a radio or television for the latest emergency information. Locate and assist pets and livestock. Open cabinets cautiously and beware of objects that can fall off shelves. Immediately clean up any spilled medicines, bleaches, gasoline or other flammable liquids. Leave the area if you smell gas or fumes from other chemicals. Inspect the entire length of chimneys for damage. Use the telephone only for emergency calls.

Inspect all utilities as follows:

- <u>**Check for gas leaks**</u>. If you smell gas or hear a blowing or hissing noise, open a window and quickly leave the premises. If possible, turn off propane at the valve located on top of the tank or the natural gas at the outside main valve. Call the gas company using a cell phone a long distance away from the house. <u>If you turn off the natural gas for any reason, it must be turned back on by a professional.</u>

- <u>**Look for electrical system damage**</u>. If you see sparks, broken or frayed wires, or if you smell hot insulation, turn off the power at the main fuse box or circuit breaker. DO NOT step in water to get to the fuse box or circuit breaker - call an electrician for instructions.

- <u>**Check for sewage and water line damage**</u>. If sewage lines or septic tanks are damaged, avoid using the toilets and contact a plumber. If water lines and pipes are damaged, turn off the water coming into the house, avoid using water from the tap and contact the water company.

After an earthquake, you should expect aftershocks. These secondary shockwaves are usually less violent than the main quake but can be strong enough to do additional damage to weakened structures and can occur in the first hours, days, weeks or even months after the quake.  If family members live in coastal areas, be aware of possible tsunamis.  When local authorities issue a tsunami warning, assume a series of dangerous waves are on the way and stay away from the beach.

## TSUNAMI

A tsunami is a series of giant, long ocean waves created by an underwater disturbance such as an earthquake, landslide, volcanic eruption or meteorite.  From the area where the tsunami originates, waves travel outward in all directions.  A tsunami can move hundreds of miles per hour in the open ocean, and once the wave approaches the shore, it builds in height and smashes into land with high waves.  There may be more than one wave and each one may be larger than the one before it.

In the United States, the most destructive tsunamis have occurred along the coasts of *California, Oregon, Washington, Alaska* and *Hawaii*.  According to the National Geophysical Data Center, more than fifty percent of the population in the United States now live in coastal communities and may be at risk for impacts from a tsunami and as more people continue to move to the coast, the risk of death and damage will continue to increase.  Drowning is the most common cause of death associated with a tsunami and other hazards include flooding, contamination of drinking water and fires from gas lines or ruptured tanks.

Areas with the greatest risk are less than twenty-five feet above sea level and within a mile of the shoreline.  However, all structures made of wood, mud, thatch and sheetrock, and structures without proper anchorage to foundations within ten to twenty miles of low lying coastal areas are vulnerable to direct impacts of tsunami waves and the debris brought by these waves.

Settlements in adjacent areas could also be vulnerable to floods.  Infrastructure facilities such as ports and harbors, telephone and electrical poles, cables, ships and fishing boats, roads, electrical and nuclear power plants and banking services can be destroyed or damaged and could bring a community to their knees within an hour.

| REGION | HAZARD BASED ON RUNUPS | HAZARD BASED ON FREQUENCY | HAZARD BASED ON LOCAL EARTHQUAKES |
|---|---|---|---|
| **Atlantic Coast** | Very Low - Low | Very Low | Very Low - Low |
| **Gulf Coast** | Very Low | Very Low | Very Low |
| **Puerto Rico/Virgin Islands** | *High* | *High* | *High* |
| **West Coast** | *High* | *High* | *High* |
| **Alaska** | *Very High* | *Very High* | *High* |
| **Hawaii** | *Very High* | *Very High* | *High* |
| **Pacific Island Territories** | Moderate | *High* | *High* |

**SOURCE:  National Science Foundation**

Based on the above table, and over the course of several hundred years, by far the largest number of tsunamis has occurred in Hawaii (1,592) and Alaska (352).  In the Atlantic Coast region, the states of New Jersey (8) and New York (7) have experienced the highest number of tsunami events in the continental states.  Along the Gulf Coast region, the state of Texas has experienced one tsunami.  Puerto Rico has experienced over 142 and the Virgin Islands have experienced 30 tsunami events.  On the West Coast, tsunami events have occurred in California (19), Oregon (5) and Washington (1).  The Pacific Island territories of American Samoa (60), Guam (23) and Northern Mariana (1) have also experienced tsunami events.

Unfortunately, this natural disaster can completely wipe out an entire city, town or village including every structure in its path.  A family could spend years and expend thousands of dollars on emergency supplies, and a tsunami could demolish everything in seconds.  As a precaution, if the home and the homes of other family members are within a tsunami zone, individual backpacks should be equipped and ready for immediate evacuation.  If evacuation is possible by car, the auto kit should be fully stocked and have adequate supplies that could be used at a pre-determined place of refuge or a public shelter.  Another suggestion is to store emergency supplies in a nearby area not likely to be impacted by a tsunami but still close enough for family members to reach – perhaps the home of a friend or relative.  It is also a good idea to have some money in a bank not located in the tsunami zone.

Since everything you own could be destroyed, make sure the emergency backpack and the auto kit have copies of identification for all family members, other important documents and some type of debit or credit card that can be used to purchase additional supplies.  The out-of-state contact should have copies of all important documentation.

### Before a Tsunami

At the location of the home, know the height of the street above sea level and the distance of the street from the coast or other high-risk waters.  Evacuation orders may be based on these numbers.  If family members live near a coastal area, create and practice an evacuation plan.  Be able to follow the escape route at night and during inclement weather.  All family members should be able to reach the designated safe location <u>on foot</u> within fifteen minutes.

The family should make necessary arrangements to transport children, the elderly, disabled family members, and of course, pets and livestock.  Practicing the plan *in advance* makes the appropriate response more of a reaction and should require less thinking during an actual emergency.  Know community warning systems and disaster plans, including evacuation routes.

If the school evacuation plan requires a family member to pick up children from school or from another location, be aware telephone lines during a tsunami may be overloaded and routes to and from schools may be jammed.  If you are a tourist, familiarize yourself with local tsunami evacuation protocols.  You may be able to safely evacuate to the third floor and higher in reinforced concrete hotel structures.

### Prior to a Tsunami

Evacuate family members and pets immediately and follow the instructions given by authorities.  If necessary, livestock should be released from enclosures to give them a chance to reach higher ground.  Pick areas one-hundred feet above sea level and attempt to go <u>at least</u> two miles inland and away from the coastline.  If you cannot get this high or far, go as high or far as you can because every foot inland or upward may make a difference between life and death.  <u>Never</u> go to the beach to watch an approaching tsunami.  If there is noticeable recession in water away from the shoreline, this is nature's tsunami warning and it should be heeded.  If you can see the wave - you are too close to escape it.  You should move away immediately.  Save yourself - not your possessions.

### After a Tsunami

If the home was in the path of the tsunami, the home will no longer exist.  Gone.  No More.  The End.  Remember a tsunami is a series of waves that may continue for hours.  Stay away from debris in the water that may pose a safety hazard to people and pets.  Stay out of any building with water around it.  Tsunami water can cause floors to crack or walls to collapse.  Use caution when re-entering buildings or homes.

## FLOODS

In the United States, floods are one of the most common natural disasters.  Flooding can be local, impacting a single family, neighborhood or community, or very large affecting entire river basins and multiple states.  There are several types of floods that can occur around the country.  A *flash* flood can develop in just a few minutes from excessive rainfall, a dam or levee failure or a sudden release of water held by an ice jam.  Flash floods often have a dangerous wall of roaring water carrying rocks, mud and other debris.

*Overland* flooding typically occurs if rivers or streams overflow their banks as a result of excessive rain caused by thunderstorms, hurricanes or tornadoes, a tsunami, or even a possible levee breach can cause flooding in surrounding areas.  Overland flooding also occurs when rainfall or snowmelt exceeds the capacity of underground pipes or the capacity of streets and drains designed to carry flood water away from urban areas.  Flood hazards are more likely in low-lying areas, near waterways, behind a levee or downstream from a dam.  Even very small streams, gullies, creeks, culverts, dry streambeds or low-lying ground that appear harmless in dry weather can flood during severe rain storms.  Do not camp or park your vehicle along streams, rivers or creeks, particularly during threatening conditions.

## Before a Flood

The prudent decision would be to avoid building in a floodplain - period!  However, if the family insists on doing so, the home should be elevated and reinforced.  Elevate the furnace, water heater and electric panel in the home if you live in an area with a high flood risk.  Consider installing "check valves" to prevent flood water from backing up into drains of the home and homes of other family members.  If feasible, construct barriers to stop floodwater from entering the building and seal walls in basements with waterproofing compounds.

The Federal Emergency Management Administration (FEMA) has compiled statistical data on river flows, storm tides, hydrologic/hydraulic analyses, and rainfall and topographic surveys to create flood hazard maps that outline your community's different flood risk areas.  The agency manages the National Flood Insurance Program (NFIP), providing federally-backed flood insurance in communities who agree to adopt and enforce floodplain management ordinances to reduce future flood damage.

Flood losses are not typically covered under renter and home owner's insurance policies, however, flood insurance is available in most communities through insurance agents but there is a thirty-day waiting period before flood insurance becomes active.  Find out if the home or business is at risk for flooding and become educated on the impact a flood could have on the family.  To find out more about the NFIP, visit www.FloodSmart.gov.

If experiencing high levels of rainfall, listen to the radio or television for information on possible flood areas.  If there is a possibility of flash floods, do not wait for instructions to move to higher ground.  Be aware of streams, drainage channels, canyons and other areas known to flood.  Flash floods can occur in these areas with or without typical warnings such as rain clouds or heavy rain.  If you must prepare to evacuate, secure the home and the homes of family members.  If there is time, bring in outdoor furniture and move essential items to an upper floor.  Disconnect electrical appliances and turn off utilities at the main switches or valves if instructed to do so.  Do not touch electrical equipment if you are wet or standing in water.  Make arrangements for pets and livestock.

## During a Flood

Stay on high ground or on the upper level or floor of a solid structure or building.  Do not walk through moving water - six inches of moving water can cause you to fall!  If you *must* walk in flood areas, use a stick to check the firmness of the ground in front of you.  Try not to drive into flooded areas.  If flood waters rise around the car, the vehicle can be swept away, so abandon the car and move to higher ground.

## After a Flood

Be aware of roads where flood waters have receded - they may have weakened and could collapse under the weight of a car.  Emergency workers would be assisting people in flooded areas - you can help them by staying off the roads and out of the way.  Roads may still be closed because they have been damaged or are covered by water.  Barricades will be placed for your protection; if you come upon a barricade or a flooded road, go another way.  Stay away from damaged areas unless assistance has been specifically requested by police, fire, or relief organizations.

Try not to walk in standing water - the water may be electrically charged from underground or downed power lines.  In the home, turn off the electricity at the main breaker or fuse box, even if the power is off in the surrounding community.  When the home is dry, the power can be turned back on.

Flooding may have caused familiar places to change because flood waters often erode roads and walkways.  Flood debris may hide animals and broken bottles, and it may also be slippery.  Water may be contaminated by oil, gasoline or raw sewage and mud left from flood waters can contain sewage and chemicals.  Clean and disinfect all wet property and supplies.  Assist pets and livestock.

Stay out of buildings if they are surrounded by flood waters.  Use caution when entering buildings; there may be hidden damage in foundations.  Contact your insurance agent to discuss claims.  Service damaged septic tanks, cesspools, pits and leaching systems as soon as possible.  Damaged sewer systems are serious health hazards.  If you hire cleanup or repair contractors, check references and be sure they are qualified to do the job.  Be suspicious of individuals who drive through the neighborhood offering assistance in cleaning up or repairing your home.

## TORNADOES

Tornadoes appear as a rotating, funnel-shaped cloud starting in a thunderstorm and going all the way to the ground with winds reaching up to 300 miles per hour. Damage paths can be one mile wide and fifty miles long. Because a tornado is part of a convective storm and these storms occur all over the earth, tornadoes are not limited to any specific geographic location. In fact, tornadoes have been documented on every continent on earth with the exception of Antarctica.

In terms of absolute tornado counts, the United States leads the world with an average of over one thousand tornadoes recorded each year. In a very distant second place is Canada with around one-hundred per year. Other locations experiencing tornadoes include northern Europe, western Asia, Bangladesh, Japan, Australia, New Zealand, China, South Africa and Argentina. The United Kingdom has more tornadoes relative to its land area than any other country but these tornadoes are relatively weak.

In the United States, there are four regions with a disproportionately high frequency of tornadoes. Although the names and boundaries are <u>extremely debatable among experts</u>, I have identified these regions as follows:

| NAME | STATES |
|---|---|
| **TORNADO ALLEY** | *Iowa, Kansas, Minnesota, Nebraska, North Dakota, Oklahoma, South Dakota, Texas, Wisconsin* |
| **DIXIE ALLEY** | *Alabama, Arkansas, Florida, Georgia, Louisiana, Mississippi, Missouri, Tennessee* |
| **CAROLINA ALLEY** | *North Carolina, South Carolina* |
| **HOOSIER ALLEY** | *Illinois, Indiana, Kentucky, Michigan, Ohio* |

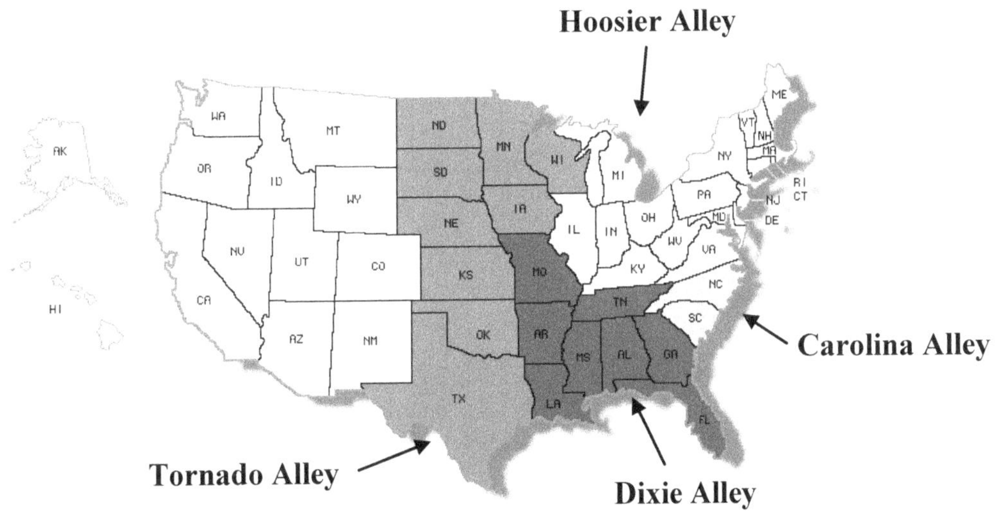


According to the National Weather Service, strong to violent tornadoes are relatively rare and do not typically occur outside the United States. In the United States, seventy-seven percent of tornadoes are considered weak and the remaining twenty-five percent are categorized as violent tornadoes. The results from one analysis indicated that Dixie Alley has the highest frequency of long-track violent tornadoes, making it the most active region in the United States followed by Tornado Alley, Hoosier Alley and Carolina Alley. Family members who reside in regions more susceptible to tornados should include provisions in emergency pantries to support tornado disasters.

### <u>Before a Tornado</u>

All family members should be alert to changing weather conditions and watch for approaching storms. Listen to NOAA Weather Radio or to commercial radio or television newscasts for the latest information and instructions. If you see approaching storms or any other danger signs, secure pets and livestock (release livestock in order to allow them to move out of the danger zone) and be prepared to take shelter immediately.

Look for the following danger signs:

- Dark, often greenish sky
- Large hail
- A large, dark, low-lying cloud (particularly if rotating)
- Loud roar similar to a freight train

## During a Tornado

If family members are under a tornado warning, seek shelter immediately!

| IF YOU ARE IN | ACTION |
|---|---|
| **Outside** | Lie flat in a nearby ditch or depression and cover head with hands (you are safer in a low, flat location).  Be aware of the potential for flooding.  Do not get under an overpass or bridge.  Never try to outrun a tornado in a car or truck in urban or congested areas.  Leave the vehicle immediately for safe shelter and watch for flying debris. |
| **Structure** <br> *Residence* <br> *Small building* <br> *School* <br> *Nursing home* <br> *Hospital* <br> *Factory* <br> *Shopping center* <br> *High-rise building* | Family members and pets should go directly to a pre-designated shelter area such as a safe room, basement, storm cellar or the lowest building level.  If there is no basement, go to the center of an interior room on the lowest level (closet, interior hallway) away from corners, windows, doors and outside walls.  Put as many walls as possible between you and the outside.  Get under a sturdy table and use your arms to protect your head and neck.  In a high-rise building, go to a small interior room or hallway on the lowest floor possible. <br><br> <u>Do not open the windows.</u> |
| **Vehicle** <br> **Trailer** <br> **Mobile Home** | Family members and pets should get out immediately and go to the lowest floor of a sturdy, nearby building or storm shelter.  Mobile homes, even if tied down, offer little protection from tornadoes. |

## Safe Room

The home for family members may be built "to code" but does not mean it can withstand winds from tornadoes and major hurricanes.  The purpose of a safe room or a wind shelter is to provide an area that offers a high level of protection where family members and pets can seek refuge.  A safe room can be built in one of several places in or around the home as follows:

- Basement at home
- Atop a concrete slab-on-grade foundation or garage floor
- An interior room on the first floor
- Separate underground shelter adjacent to home (best choice)

Safe rooms built below ground level provide the greatest protection, but a safe room built in a first-floor interior room can also provide good protection.  Below-ground safe rooms must be designed to avoid accumulating water during heavy rains that often accompany severe windstorms.  To protect its occupants, a safe room must be built to withstand high winds and flying debris, even if the rest of the residence is severely damaged or destroyed.

## After a Tornado

Injury may result from the direct impact by a tornado or it may occur when people walk among debris and enter damaged buildings.  In Illinois, a study of injuries after a tornado showed that fifty percent of tornado-related injuries occurred during rescue attempts, cleanup and other post-tornado activities.  <u>Nearly a third of the injuries resulted from stepping on nails</u>, so wear sturdy shoes or boots, long pants, long sleeved shirt and gloves when handling or walking on or near debris.

Be aware of downed power lines, broken gas lines and electrical systems.  There could also be possible structural, electrical or gas-leak hazards in the home.  Use a flashlight to avoid risk of fire or explosion.  In general, if you suspect any damage to the home, shut off electrical power, natural gas and propane tanks to avoid fire, electrocution or explosions until safety is confirmed.

Secure and assist pets and livestock.  Never use generators, pressure washers, grills, camp stoves or other gasoline, propane, natural gas or charcoal-burning devices inside the home, basement, garage or camper - or even outside near an open window, door or vent.  Clean up spilled medicines, drugs, flammable liquids and other potentially hazardous materials.  Hang up displaced telephone receivers that may have been knocked off by the tornado.  Recognize cell phone towers and telephone lines may also be damaged or destroyed.

## HURRICANES

A hurricane is a tropical cyclone or severe tropical storm accompanied by thunderstorms, and in the Northern Hemisphere, a counterclockwise circulation of winds near the surface of the earth.

*Hurricane Alley* is an area of warm water in the Atlantic Ocean stretching from the west coast of northern Africa to the east coast of Central America and the Gulf Coast of the southern United States.  Areas of the Southwest and the Pacific Coast also experience heavy rains and floods from hurricanes spawned off Mexico.  The Atlantic hurricane season lasts from June to November with the peak season from the middle of August to late October.  The Eastern Pacific hurricane season begins the middle May and ends in November each year.

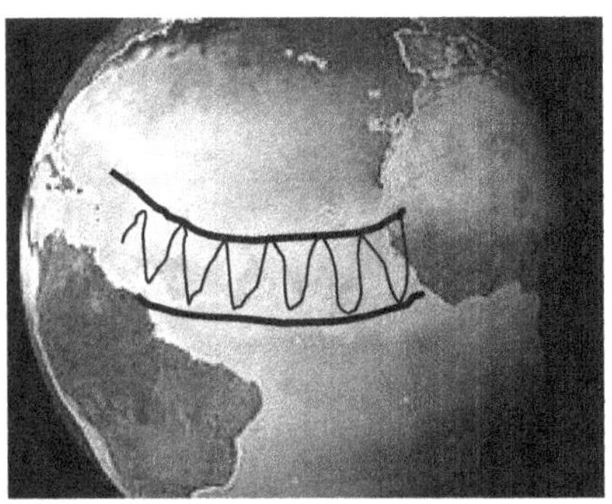

**Warm waters of Hurricane Alley depicted between dark black lines**

According to the National Hurricane Center, a hurricane can produce winds exceeding 155 miles per hour, and microbursts and storm surges along the coast can cause extensive damage from heavy rainfall.  Floods and flying debris from excessive winds can often be the deadly and destructive results of these weather events.

Slow moving hurricanes traveling into mountainous regions tend to produce especially heavy rain triggering landslides, flash floods or mud slides.  The greatest potential for loss of life is from the storm surge (water pushed toward the shore by the force of the winds swirling around the storm).  This advancing surge combines with normal tides to create the hurricane storm tide that can increase the water level to impact roads, homes and other critical infrastructure.

Hurricanes are classified into five categories based on wind speed, central pressure and the potential of damage:

| SAFFIR-SIMPSON HURRICANE WIND SCALE SUMMARY | | |
|---|---|---|
| **CATEGORY** | **MILES PER HOUR** | **DAMAGE** |
| 1 | *74-95* | ***Very dangerous winds will produce some damage***<br>• Minor damage to exterior of homes<br>• Toppled tree branches, uprooting of smaller trees<br>• Extensive damage to power lines, power outages |
| 2 | *96-110* | ***Extremely dangerous winds will cause extensive damage***<br>• Major damage to exterior of homes<br>• Uprooting of small trees and many roads blocked<br>• Guaranteed power outages for long periods of time |

| SAFFIR-SIMPSON HURRICANE WIND SCALE SUMMARY | | |
|---|---|---|
| **CATEGORY** | **MILES PER HOUR** | **DAMAGE** |
| 3 | *111-130* | ***Devastating damage will occur***<br>• Extensive damage to exterior of homes<br>• Many trees uprooted and many roads blocked<br>• Extremely limited availability of water and electricity |
| 4 | *131-155* | ***Catastrophic damage will occur***<br>• Loss of roof structure and/or some exterior walls<br>• Most trees uprooted and most power lines down<br>• Isolated residential due to debris pile up<br>• Power outages lasting for weeks to months |
| 5 | *Over 155* | ***Catastrophic damage will occur***<br>• A high percentage of homes will be destroyed<br>• Fallen trees and power lines isolate residential areas<br>• Power outages lasting for weeks to months<br>• Most areas will be uninhabitable |

**SOURCE:  National Hurricane Center**

The map and table below shows the states most susceptible to hurricanes although many other states experience hurricanes as well.  Based on statistics from the National Hurricane Center, the State of **Florida** is the proud owner of the Number One position for having the most hurricanes.  Based on all hurricanes and the corresponding damage estimates, **Florida** again secures the Number One position.

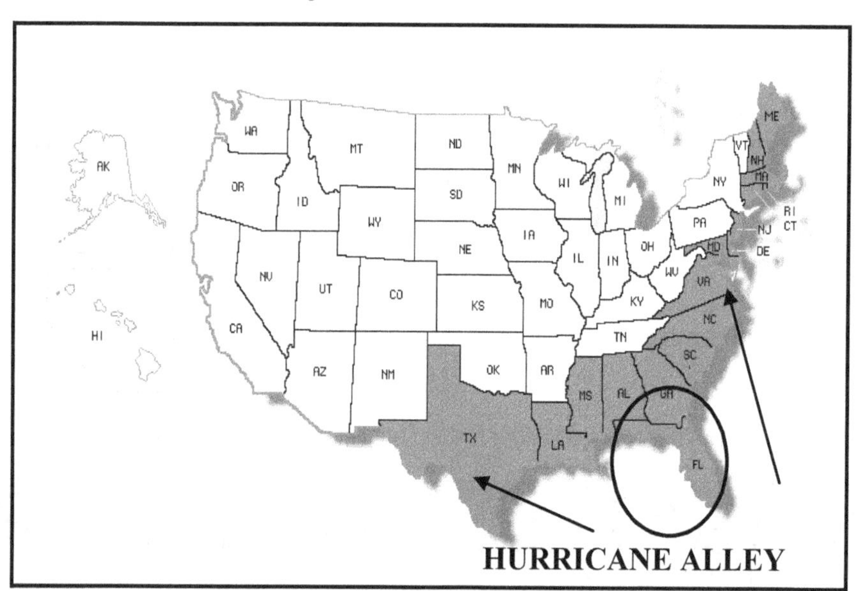



| RANK | HURRICANE | YEAR | STATES | CATEGORY | DAMAGE (Billion $) |
|---|---|---|---|---|---|
| 1 | Great Miami | 1926 | **Florida**, Alabama | 3-4 | 157.0 |
| 2 | Katrina | 2005 | Louisiana, Mississippi | 3 | 81.0 |
| 3 | Galveston | 1900 | Texas | 4 | 78.0 |
| 4 | Sandy | 2012 | New York, New Jersey, Connecticut, Rhode Island | 3-4 | 70.0 |
| 5 | Galveston | 1915 | Texas | 4 | 61.7 |
| 6 | Andrew | 1992 | **Florida**, Louisiana | 3-5 | 57.7 |
| 7 | New England | 1938 | Connecticut, Maryland, New York, Rhode Island | 3 | 39.2 |

| RANK | HURRICANE | YEAR | STATES | CATEGORY | DAMAGE (Billion $) |
|---|---|---|---|---|---|
| 8 | 11 | 1944 | **Florida** | 3 | 38.7 |
| 9 | Lake Okeechobee | 1928 | **Florida** | 4 | 33.6 |
| 10 | Donna | 1960 | **Florida**, North Carolina, New York | 3-4 | 29.6 |
| 11 | Camille | 1969 | Louisiana, Mississippi | 5 | 21.2 |
| 12 | Betsy | 1965 | **Florida**, Louisiana | 3 | 20.7 |
| 13 | Wilma | 2005 | **Florida** | 3 | 20.6 |
| 14 | Agnes | 1972 | **Florida**, Connecticut, New York | 1 | 17.5 |
| 15 | Diane | 1955 | North Carolina | 1 | 17.2 |
| 16 | 4 | 1947 | **Florida**, Louisiana, Mississippi | 3-4 | 16.8 |
| 17 | Hazel | 1954 | North Carolina, South Carolina | 4 | 16.5 |
| 18 | Charley | 2004 | **Florida** | 4 | 16.3 |
| 19 | Carol | 1954 | Connecticut, New York, Rhode Island | 3 | 16.1 |
| 20 | Ivan | 2004 | **Florida** | 3 | 15.5 |
| 21 | Hugo | 1989 | South Carolina | 4 | 15.3 |
| 22 | 2 | 1949 | **Florida** | 3 | 14.7 |
| 23 | Carla | 1961 | Texas | 4 | 14.2 |
| 24 | 7 | 1944 | Connecticut, New York, North Carolina, Rhode Island, Virginia | 3 | 13.2 |
| 25 | 2 | 1919 | **Florida**, Texas | 4 | 12.9 |
| 26 | 9 | 1945 | **Florida** | 3 | 12.3 |
| 27 | Frederic | 1979 | Alabama, Mississippi | 3 | 10.3 |
| 28 | Rita | 2005 | Texas | 3 | 10.0 |
| 29 | Frances | 2004 | **Florida** | 2 | 9.7 |
| 30 | 8 | 1933 | Virginia | 2 | 8.2 |
| 31 | Dora | 1964 | **Florida** | 2 | 7.7 |
| 32 | Jeanne | 2004 | **Florida** | 3 | 7.5 |
| 33 | Alicia | 1983 | Texas | 3 | 7.5 |
| 34 | Floyd | 1999 | North Carolina | 2 | 6.7 |
| 35 | Allison | 2001 | Texas | 2 | 6.6 |
| 36 | 6 | 1935 | **Florida** | 2 | 6.4 |
| 37 | Opal | 1995 | **Florida** | 3 | 6.1 |
| 38 | Freeport | 1932 | Texas | 4 | 5.9 |
| 39 | Fran | 1996 | North Carolina | 3 | 5.8 |
| 40 | Celia | 1970 | Texas | 3 | 5.6 |
| 41 | 1 | 1916 | Alabama, Mississippi | 3 | 5.3 |

**SOURCE: National Weather Service**

## Before a Hurricane

Prior to a hurricane, adults should learn the elevation level of the property, whether the land is flood-prone, where the home is located and the locations of homes where all family members reside during normal times. This information will assist family members in evaluating how the property will be affected when a storm surge or tidal flooding is forecast in the area. In addition, identify levees and dams in the area and learn whether they pose a hazard to the family, learn community hurricane evacuation routes and how to find higher ground and decide where family members would go and how you would get there if an evacuation is warranted.

Make plans to secure the home and surrounding property including the procedure for covering all windows. Permanent storm shutters offer the best protection for windows. A second option is to board windows with 5/8" marine plywood, cut to fit and ready to install. Remember - tape does <u>not</u> prevent windows from breaking. Install straps or additional clips to securely fasten the roof to the frame structure.

Make sure trees and shrubs around the home are well trimmed and clear loose and clogged rain gutters and downspouts. Reinforce garage doors; if wind enters a garage it can cause dangerous and expensive structural damage. Make arrangements to protect pets and livestock.

Turn off all utilities including propane tanks. Turn the refrigerator thermostat to its coldest setting and keep the door closed. Have a supply of water ready for drinking and sanitary purposes such as cleaning and flushing toilets. Fill the bathtub and other larger containers with water. Plan to bring in all outdoor furniture, decorations, garbage cans and anything else not tied down and establish how and where to secure a boat. Finally, if family members reside in a location that is hurricane prone, consider building a safe room.

## <u>During a Hurricane</u>

During a hurricane, everyone should evacuate if directed to do so by local authorities. If family members live in a mobile home or temporary structure – such shelters are particularly hazardous during a hurricane no matter how well fastened to the ground. If the home or the home of all/some family members is in a high-rise building – hurricane winds are stronger at higher elevations so as part of the evacuation plan, make sure the alternate site is lower than the tenth floor of the building. If family members live on the coast, on a flood plain, near a river, or on an island waterway, plan to evacuate the home and/or homes and go to an alternate site.

If unable to evacuate the home, take refuge in a small interior room, closet or hallway on the <u>lowest</u> level. Stay indoors and away from windows and glass doors, keep curtains and blinds closed, close all interior doors and secure and brace external doors. Lie on the floor under a table or another sturdy object. Do *not* be fooled if there is a lull; it could be the eye of the storm – winds will pick up again.

## <u>After a Hurricane</u>

After a hurricane, stay alert for extended rainfall and flooding even after the hurricane or tropical storm has ended. Inspect the home for damage - there could be structural, electrical or gas-leak hazards. Use a flashlight to avoid the risk of fire or explosion. In general, if you suspect any damage to the home, shut off electrical power, natural gas and propane tanks to avoid fire, electrocution or explosions.

Clean up spilled medicines, drugs, flammable liquids and other potentially hazardous materials. Avoid drinking or preparing food with tap water until verified it is not contaminated. Check refrigerated food for spoilage. Hang up displaced telephone receivers that may have been knocked off by the hurricane. Take pictures of the damage for insurance purposes - both of the building and its contents.

Cell phone towers and telephone lines may also be damaged and not working. When going outside, family members should be aware of downed power lines, broken gas lines and electrical systems. Locate and secure pets and livestock. Watch pets and livestock closely and keep them under your direct control. Watch out for wild animals, especially poisonous snakes. When walking in the area, use a stick to poke through debris.

> **FEMA has established the <u>National Emergency Family Registry and Locator System (NEFRLS)</u> developed to help reunite families who are separated during a disaster. The NEFRLS system gives displaced individuals the ability to enter personal information into a website database so they can be located by others during a disaster. The <u>American Red Cross</u> also maintains a database to help find family members. Contact the local American Red Cross Chapter where you are staying for information. Do <u>not</u> contact the chapter in the disaster area.**

## LIGHTNING AND THUNDERSTORMS

According to the National Weather Service (NWS), every thunderstorm produces lightning and in the United States lightning continues to be a storm-related killer. Thunderstorms may occur singly, in clusters or in lines and typically produce heavy rain from thirty minutes to an hour. About ten percent of thunderstorms produce hail at least three-quarters of an inch in diameter, has winds sixty miles per hour and higher or produces a tornado.

A warm and humid condition is highly favorable for thunderstorm development. Lightning often strikes outside of heavy rain and may occur as far as ten miles away from any rainfall. "Heat lightning" is actually lightning from a thunderstorm too far away from thunder to be heard. Most lightning deaths and injuries occur when people are caught outdoors in the summer months during the afternoon and evening hours.

<u>**Before a Thunderstorm and Lightning**</u>

Remove dead or rotting trees and branches, secure outdoor objects that could blow away or cause damage from around the home and postpone outdoor activities. Close windows, shut window blinds, shades or curtains and secure outside doors. Unplug any electronic equipment well before the storm arrives. Monitor pets and livestock closely and keep them under your direct control.

Family members should move inside the home, building, or hard top automobile. Although you may be injured if lightning strikes a car, you are much safer inside than outside a vehicle. <u>Rubber-soled shoes and rubber tires provide NO protection from lightning</u>. The steel frame of a hard-topped vehicle gives increased protection providing you are not touching metal.

| **30-30 RULE** |
| --- |
| **The 30/30 Lightning Safety Rule says: Go indoors if after seeing lightning, you cannot count to thirty before hearing thunder. Stay indoors for thirty minutes after hearing the last clap of thunder.** |

<u>**During a Thunderstorm and Lightning**</u>

Family members should avoid contact with corded phones - use a corded telephone only for emergencies. Cordless and cellular telephones are safe to use. Power surges from lightning can cause serious damage to electrical and electronic devices and equipment so unplug appliances, computers and televisions and turn off furnaces and air conditioners. Avoid contact with electrical equipment or cords. Plumbing and bathroom fixtures can conduct electricity so do not wash your hands, take a shower, wash dishes or do laundry during the storm. Stay away from windows and doors, stay off porches, do not lie on concrete floors and do not lean against concrete walls.

Immediately seek shelter when outside during a lightning storm. For example, in a forest, seek shelter in a low area under a thick growth of *small* trees. If on water, immediately get to land. Avoid natural lightning rods such as tall and isolated trees in an open area and avoid hilltops, open fields, the beach or a boat on the water. Avoid contact with anything metal (tractors, farm equipment, motorcycles, golf carts, golf clubs and bicycles) and avoid isolated sheds or small structures in open areas.

| **Lightning strike victims carry no electrical charge and should be attended to immediately.** |
| --- |

If your hair stands on end – *squat* low to the ground on the balls of the feet. Place hands over the ears and put head between your knees. Make yourself the smallest target possible and minimize contact with the ground. <u>**DO NOT** lay flat on the ground</u>. If driving, attempt to safely exit the roadway and park the vehicle. Stay in the vehicle and turn on the emergency flashers until the heavy rain subsides. Avoid touching metal that conducts electricity.

<u>**After a Thunderstorm or Lightning**</u>

If lightning strikes a person, call 9-1-1 for medical assistance as soon as possible. The following should be checked when attempting to give aid to a victim of lightning:

- **Breathing** - if breathing has stopped, begin mouth-to-mouth resuscitation
- **Heartbeat** - if the heart has stopped, administer CPR
- **Pulse** - if the victim has a pulse and is breathing, look for other possible injuries

## WINTER STORMS AND EXTREME COLD

A winter storm and/or extreme cold outside temperatures can become <u>lethal</u> to citizens in entire communities. The severity of a winter storm and extreme cold can disrupt electrical power for hours – and even days. There have been countless instances where people have frozen to death in their homes because electricity was out and the furnace would not work.  In these cases, there had been no *advanced planning* to prepare for alternative heat sources during winter storms and cold temperatures.

**If living in a region with cold temperatures, the home and homes of all family members <u>must</u> be equipped to survive extreme cold temperatures <u>inside the home</u> resulting from electrical outages and lack of fuel supplies during the winter months.  This includes extra bedding, blankets and sleeping bags which may be the only method to keep family members warm until power and fuel supplies are restored.**

A storm dropping just eight inches of snow can make unplowed roads impassable and automobiles stuck in the snow – even in Utah!  Road conditions could become so severe family members would not even be able drive to locations offering food and other necessities.  Snowstorms exceeding twelve inches can cave in the roofs of homes and bring down trees and cause power outages.

Even a few inches of dry snow can form high drifts under windy conditions.  Mountain snowstorms can produce cornices and avalanches.  Deaths can occur from hypothermia, infections due to frostbite, fires and carbon monoxide poisoning or car accidents due to slippery roads.  Large amounts of snow known as a *whiteout* can significantly reduce visibility in an area causing major accidents on the road.  Heart attacks increase from overexertion while shoveling heavy wet snow.

Heavy showers of freezing rain are one of the most dangerous types of winter storm.  They typically occur when a layer of warm air hovers over a region, but the ambient temperature a few feet above the ground is near or below 32 °F and the ground temperature is sub-freezing.

A snowstorm dropping four inches of snow is manageable but a comparable ice storm dropping four inches of ice can paralyze even the northern region of the country.  Driving becomes extremely hazardous, telephone and power lines are damaged and crops can be ruined.  Because ice storms do not require extreme cold, they often occur in warm temperature climates (such as the southern United States).  Ice storms in Florida can destroy entire citrus crops.

<u>**Before a Winter Storm and Extreme Cold**</u>

Prior to winter months that bring storms and cold temperatures, family members should winterize the home by insulating walls and attics, caulking and weather-stripping doors and windows, and installing storm windows or covering windows with plastic.  **The home should be stocked with *alternatives* or *layers* for heating the house in the event power is out, including a wood-burning stove and adequate fuel, sleeping bags, <u>blankets</u> and <u>winter clothing</u> for all family members.**

Winterize barns, sheds or other structures that could provide shelter for people, pets, livestock or equipment.  Clear rain gutters, repair roof leaks and cut away tree branches by the house or other structures.  Review steps necessary to drain water pipes to avoid freezing.

Maintain heating equipment and chimneys by having them cleaned and inspected every year.  Insulate pipes with insulation and allow faucets to drip during cold weather.  Maintain fire extinguishers and make sure adult and young adult family members know how to use them.

**Make sure a shovel, windshield scraper, small broom, chains or rope, road salt and sand, emergency flares, distress flag, booster cables, warm blankets, sleeping bag and warm clothes and boots are included in automobile kits.**

Bring pets/companion animals inside during winter weather and move other animals or livestock to sheltered areas with non-frozen drinking water.

Before winter approaches, family members should add the following supplies to the respective emergency kits at the home, place of refuge (motor home, camper, trailer or cabin) and automobiles:

- Rock salt to melt ice on walkways
- Sand to improve traction
- Snow shovels and other snow removal equipment
- Sufficient heating fuel for fireplace or stove
- Adequate clothing and blankets to keep warm

Attempt to minimize travel prior to a winter storm warning.  If travel <u>is</u> necessary, make sure the emergency kit in the vehicle is fully stocked to support the storm and cold temperatures.

Inspect or have a mechanic check the following items on the vehicles <u>prior</u> to the winter months:

- **Antifreeze Levels** - sufficient to avoid freezing
- **Battery and Ignition System** - should be in top condition and battery terminals should be clean
- **Brakes** - check for wear and fluid levels
- **Exhaust System** - check for leaks and crimped pipes and repair or replace as necessary
- **Fuel/Air Filters** - replace and keep water out of the system by using additives and maintaining a full tank
- **Heater and Defroster** - works properly
- **Lights and Flashing Hazard Lights** - check for serviceability
- **Oil** - check level and weight (heavier oils congeal and do not lubricate as well at low temperatures)
- **Thermostat** - works properly
- **Windshield Wiper Equipment** - repair any problems and maintain proper washer fluid level
- **Winter Tires** - tires have adequate tread

Although many regions are susceptible to winter storms, the map below illustrates areas in the continental United States that are <u>prone</u> to heavy winter storms and/or extreme cold temperatures.

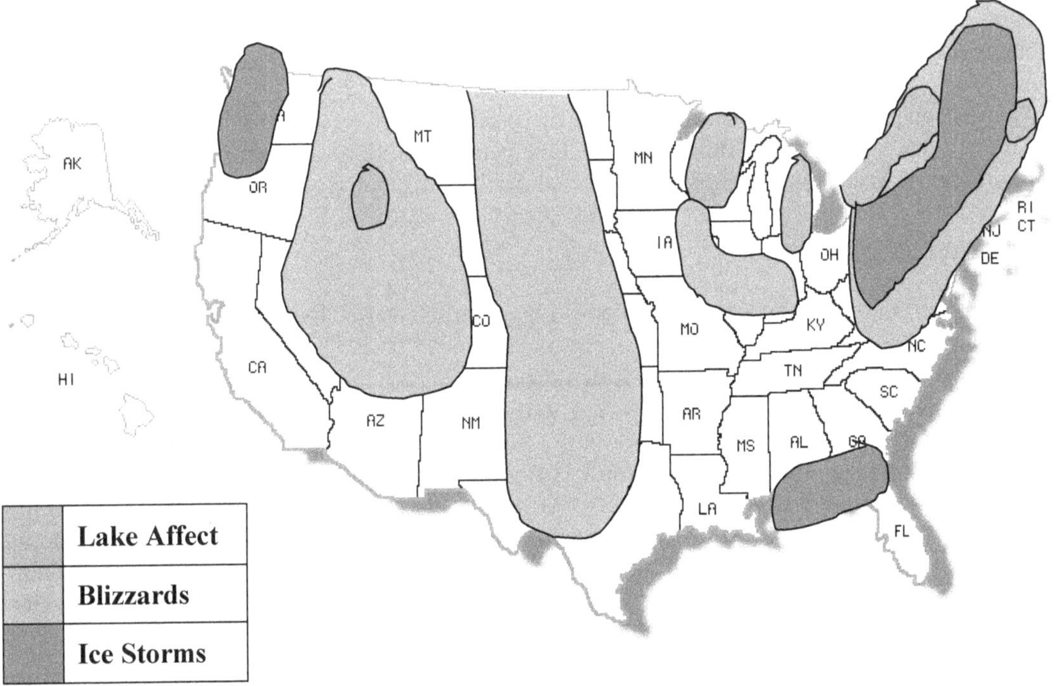


### During a Winter Storm and Extreme Cold

Stay indoors during a storm and walk carefully on walkways.  Remember to avoid overexertion when shoveling snow because overexertion can bring on a heart attack.  When shoveling snow, stretch before going outside.

If you must go outside, wear several layers of loose-fitting, lightweight, warm clothing rather than one layer of heavy clothing.  The outer garments should be tightly woven and water repellent.  Wear mittens, (they are warmer than gloves), a hat to prevent loss of body heat, and cover your mouth with a scarf to protect the lungs.

> **On 14 April 1921, the world record for the most snowfall in 24-hours was set in Silver Lake, Colorado, where 76 inches of snow fell. Eighty-seven inches of snow was recorded for the entire storm which lasted less than 28 hours. OUCH!**

Wet clothing loses insulating value and rapidly looses heat so change wet clothing frequently to prevent loss of body heat.  Watch for signs of frostbite (loss of feeling and white or pale appearance in extremities such as fingers, toes, ear lobes and the tip of the nose), and signs of hypothermia (uncontrollable shivering, memory loss, disorientation, incoherence, slurred speech, drowsiness and exhaustion).  If symptoms of hypothermia are detected, get victim to a warm location, remove wet clothing, warm the center of the body first and give warm, *non-alcoholic* beverages if victim is conscious.  Get medical help as soon as possible.

If you <u>must</u> drive during a storm, travel during the day, do not travel alone, keep others informed of the destination, the route, and expected arrival time, stay on main roads and avoid back road shortcuts.  If trapped in a vehicle during a blizzard, pull off the highway, turn on hazard lights and hang a distress flag from the radio antenna or window.  Remain in the vehicle where rescuers are most likely to find you.  Do <u>not</u> set out on foot unless you can see a building close by where you <u>know</u> you can take shelter.  Be careful; distances are distorted by blowing snow.  A building may seem close, but be too far to reach on foot in deep snow.

While in the vehicle, and if you have *planned in advance* and have an auto kit in the car, you could use a solar garden light for light, a blanket for heat and a hand crank radio for communication.  If for some ridiculous reason you do not have an emergency auto kit, run the engine and heater about ten minutes each hour to keep warm.  When the engine is running, open a downwind window slightly for ventilation and <u>periodically clear snow from the exhaust pipe</u> to protect from possible carbon monoxide poisoning.

It is also a good idea to "exercise" while in the vehicle to maintain body heat, but avoid overexertion.  The exercise could include the extension of arms and legs and turning the waist from one side to the other side.

> **If there is no heat in the house during cold temperatures, place heavy blankets and quilts over a card table or dining room table.  Ensure blankets touch the floor on all sides.  Now - get inside the "tent" with sleeping bags.  Body heat will help maintain an overall heat in the tent.  The kids will love the adventure and will not view the incident as a bad experience.**

In extreme cold, use road maps, seat covers and floor mats for insulation.  If more than one person is in the vehicle, take turns sleeping.  One person should be awake at all times to look for rescue crews or dangerous situations.  Use emergency supplies, eat and drink fluids, but <u>avoid caffeine and alcohol</u>.

### <u>After a Winter Storm and Extreme Cold</u>

Continue to protect yourself from frostbite and hypothermia by wearing warm, loose-fitting, lightweight clothing in several layers.  Stay indoors.

> **As an experiment, I wanted to learn what it would be like without heat during cold temperatures.  During one of the coldest winters on record, I turned off my furnace in the *middle of March* while it was still fairly cold outside, but was not cold enough to freeze pipes inside the house.  I figured all I would have to do is put on a heavy coat, hat and socks.  Even though I wore warm clothing, - my NOSE WAS COLD!  The heavy clothing was so bulky it was hard to move and complete simple tasks.  I also noticed the chilly temperatures inside the house made me feel sluggish and I didn't have any energy.  Within a short time, I became irritable, ornery and very bad-tempered.  Even my cats noticed my sour disposition.  Keep in mind I still had electricity - but even with the convenience of power, I was miserable.  Can you imagine what it would have been like without heat <u>and</u> electricity?????**

## HEAT WAVES

A heat wave is an extended period of extreme heat and is often accompanied by high humidity.  During extended and extreme heat waves, an entire region can be crippled with over-extended power demands and plants and crops die from exposure and/or lack of water.  Without proper shelter, humans and animals would succumb to death in a very short time.

Older adults, young children and those who are unhealthy or overweight are more likely to be affected by extreme heat.  People living in urban areas may be at greater risk from the affects of a prolonged heat wave than those living in rural areas because asphalt and concrete store heat longer and gradually release heat at night, which can produce higher nighttime temperatures known as the "urban heat island affect."

<u>**Before a Heat Wave**</u>

Prior to summer months and with the possibility of extreme heat temperatures, the home should be well insulated both in the ceiling and walls. Install window air conditioners and/or check central air-conditioning ducts for proper insulation. Electric fans placed throughout the house will re-circulate the air and in some cases, replace the need for central air conditioning. A heat wave places a severe strain on power resources so expect power outages during extended hot periods.

Some heat-reducing tips is to install temporary window reflectors (for use between windows and drapes), such as aluminum foil-covered cardboard that reflects the heat outside. Keep windows closed and cover windows receiving morning or afternoon sun with drapes or shades. Outdoor awnings or louvers can reduce the heat entering a home by up to eighty percent.

> **One of my best investments was to re-insulate the ceiling and install new windows in my home. Over the years, the insulation had deteriorated and was no longer effective. After installing insulation and windows, there was an immediate drop in my heat and electric bill and I noticed the house maintained heat during the winter and stayed cool in the summer - even without air conditioning.**

It is also a good idea to keep storm windows up all year. Make sure all doors and sills have weather stripping to keep cool air inside the home. To reduce sun rays from hitting the home, plant fast-growing shade trees around the residence. Another good emergency supply during a heat wave and when the power is out is an old fashioned fan used by ladies many years ago. These simple fans re-circulate the air and would be a good addition to the home, place of refuge, auto and evacuation kits.

<u>**During a Heat Wave**</u>

Stay indoors as much as possible, stay on the lowest floor out of the sunshine if air conditioning is not available and limit exposure to the sun. Avoid strenuous work during the warmest part of the day, postpone outdoor games and activities and consider spending the warmest part of the day in public buildings such as libraries, schools, movie theaters, shopping malls and other community facilities.

In the house, keep doors and windows **SHUT** and drapes **CLOSED** during the hot times of the day. This method helps keep the heat outside and the cool air inside. I use electric fans to circulate the air inside the house. Circulating air can cool the body by increasing the perspiration rate of evaporation. Consider the purchase of a hand-held fan - it works!

Drink plenty of water even if you do not feel thirsty but avoid drinks with caffeine and limit the intake of alcoholic beverages. Persons who have epilepsy, heart, kidney or liver disease, on fluid-restricted diets or have a problem with fluid retention should consult a doctor before increasing the intake of liquids. Eat well-balanced, light, and regular meals. Avoid using salt tablets unless directed to do so by a physician.

Dress in loose-fitting, lightweight, and light-colored clothes that cover as much skin as possible but avoid dark colors because they absorb the sun's rays. Protect face and head by wearing a wide-brimmed hat. Make sure pets and livestock have adequate shelter and a continuous supply of water and check on animals frequently to ensure they are not suffering from the heat. <u>Never leave children or pets alone in closed vehicles.</u>

The following table lists heat induced illnesses, their symptoms and the first aid treatment:

| CONDITION | SYMPTOMS | FIRST AID |
|---|---|---|
| **Sunburn** | Skin redness and pain, possible swelling, blisters, fever, headaches | Shower using soap to remove oils from pores that prevent the body from cooling. Apply dry and sterile dressings to any blisters. |
| **Heat Cramps** | Painful spasms, usually in leg and abdominal muscles; heavy sweating | Get victim to a cooler location. Lightly stretch and gently massage affected muscles to relieve spasms. Give sips of up to a half glass of cool water every 15 minutes. Do not give liquids with caffeine or alcohol. Discontinue liquids if victim is nauseated. |

| CONDITION | SYMPTOMS | FIRST AID |
|---|---|---|
| **Heat Exhaustion** | Heavy sweating but skin may be cool, pale or flushed.  Weak pulse.  Normal body temperature is possible, but temperature will likely rise.<br><br>Fainting, dizziness, nausea, vomiting, exhaustion, or headaches. | Get victim to lie down in a cool place.  Loosen or remove clothing.  Apply cool, wet clothes.  Fan or move victim to air-conditioned location.  Give sips of water if victim is conscious.  Give a half glass of cool water every 15 minutes. Discontinue water if victim is nauseated. Seek immediate medical attention if vomiting occurs. |
| **Heat Stroke** | High body temperature (105+); hot, red and dry skin; rapid and weak pulse; rapid and shallow breathing.   Victim will probably not sweat unless victim was sweating from recent strenuous activity. Possible unconsciousness. | Immediately move a victim to a cooler environment and remove clothing. Try a cool bath, sponging, or wet sheet to reduce body temperature. Use fans and air conditioners. Watch for breathing problems.  Call 9-1-1 or get the victim to a hospital. |

## DROUGHT

A drought is an extended period of months or years when a region experiences a lack of precipitation.  Drought can have significant environmental, agricultural, health, economic and social consequences and the affect varies according to vulnerability.

The United States Department of Agriculture, the National Drought Mitigation Center and NOAA's National Climatic Data Center issues a weekly drought assessment called the *United States Drought Monitor*.  The monitor provides a depiction of national drought conditions based on a combination of drought indicators and field reports.

In 2011, the United States seasonal drought outlook depicted a persistent and intense drought condition in many of the southern states, the Hawaiian Islands and along the east coast including the following states:

*Alabama (eastern part of the state)

*Arizona (most of the state)

*Arkansas (western part of the state)

*Florida (northern part of the state)

*Georgia (most of the state)

*Hawaii (most of main island and up to ½ of other islands)

*Iowa (large part of state)

*Kansas (southern part of the state)

*Louisiana (western part of the state)

*Minnesota (southern part of state)

*New Mexico (most of the state)

*North Carolina (mid section of state)

*Oklahoma (all of the state)

*South Carolina (all of the state)

*Texas (all of the state)

*Wyoming (southeast part of the state)

This map is updated on a regular basis:

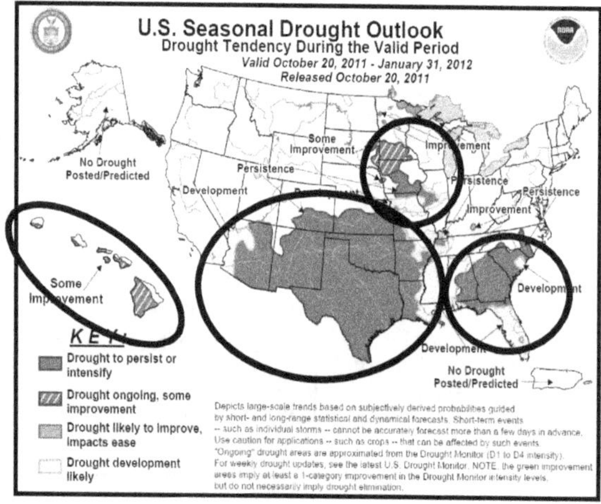

In 2005, parts of the Amazon basin experienced the worst drought in over one-hundred years.  The Woods Hole Research Center conducted a study and concluded that the forest in its present form could survive only three years of drought.  The Brazilian National Institute of Amazonian Research concluded this drought response, coupled with the affects of deforestation on regional climate is pushing the rainforest towards a "tipping point" where it would irreversibly begin to die. It concludes the rainforest is on the brink of being turned into a savanna or desert with catastrophic consequences for the world's climate.  The United Nations estimates an area of fertile soil the size of Ukraine is lost every year because of drought, deforestation and climate instability.

The lack of precipitation causing a drought does not happen immediately but is spread across months or even years and by the time most people actually recognize a problem, it may be too late.  For example, if you put a frog in a pot of boiling water, it will immediately jump out of the pot.  But, if you put the frog in a pot of cool water and gradually heat the water to boiling, the frog will remain in the pot and will cook to death.  So it is with us - simply phrased - "we never miss the water until the well runs dry".

The best method to *prepare in advance* for a drought is to have adequate food and water supplies stored in emergency pantries.  Storing cash to buy food and water could present a problem - would you really have enough cash to buy these very expensive and limited items?

## LANDSLIDES

Landslides occur in all states throughout the country and are caused by earthquakes, storms, volcanic eruptions, fire or by human modification to the land.  They develop when water rapidly accumulates in the ground or during heavy rainfall or rapid snowmelt, which in turn changes the earth into a flowing river of mud, rock, earth or debris saturated with water that moves down a slope.

A landslide can strike with no warning at avalanche speeds and can travel several miles from the source, growing in size as it picks up trees, boulders, cars and other materials.  In the United States, the greatest danger from landslides is in the Rocky and Appalachian Mountain regions and the west coast along the California coastline.  Family members living in regions with hills or mountains should be aware of landslides.

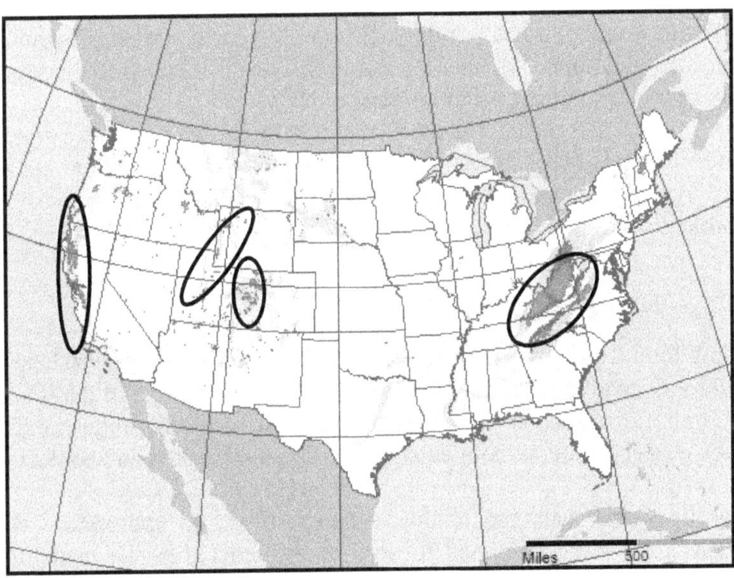

**SOURCE:  United States Geological Survey**

### Before a Landslide

Follow proper land-use procedures - avoid building near steep slopes, close to mountain edges, near drainage ways or along natural erosion valleys.  As part of *planning in advance* and before building, get a ground assessment of the property and learn whether debris flows have previously occurred in the area.  Slopes where debris flows have occurred in the past are likely to happen again in the future.

Protect property by planting ground cover on slopes and building retaining walls. In mudflow areas, build channels or deflection walls to direct flow around buildings. If you are at risk from a landslide, talk to an insurance agent - debris flow may be covered by flood insurance offered by the National Flood Insurance Program.

The best way to prepare for a landslide is to stay informed about changes in and around the home that can signal a landslide is likely to occur in the area. Family members should recognize landslide warning signs:

- Changes in landscape patterns (drainage on slopes, land movement, small slides, leaning trees)
- Doors or windows stick or jam for the first time
- New cracks appear in plaster, tile, brick or foundations
- Outside walls, walks or stairs begin pulling away from the building
- Slowly developing and widening cracks appear on ground or paved areas (streets or driveways)
- Underground utility lines break
- Bulging ground appears at the base of a slope
- Water breaks through the ground surface in new locations
- Fences, retaining walls, utility poles or trees tilt or move

As a landslide approaches, there is usually a faint rumbling sound that increases in volume. The ground slopes downward in one direction and may begin shifting in that direction under your feet. Unusual sounds, such as trees cracking or boulders knocking together may indicate moving debris. Collapsed pavement, mud, fallen rocks, and other indications of possible debris flow can be seen when driving (embankments along roadsides are particularly susceptible to landslides).

## During a Landslide

During a severe storm, stay alert and awake since many deaths from landslides occur when people are sleeping. Family members should listen to local news stations for warnings of heavy rainfall. All members should listen for unusual sounds that might indicate moving debris such as trees cracking or boulders knocking together.

If you see a landslide in progress, move away from the debris flow as quickly as possible. The danger from a mudflow increases near stream channels and with prolonged heavy rains. If you are near a stream or channel, be alert for any sudden increase or decrease in water flow and notice whether the water changes from clear to muddy; these changes may indicate there is debris flow activity upstream so be prepared to move quickly.

Mudflows can move faster than a person can walk or run so look upstream before crossing a bridge and do not cross the bridge if a mudflow is approaching. Avoid river valleys and low-lying areas. If caught in a landslide and escape is not possible, curl into a tight ball and protect your head.

## After a Landslide

After the landslide, check the building foundation, chimney and surrounding land for damage to help assess the safety of the area. All family members should stay away from the slide area - there may be danger of additional slides. Flooding sometimes follows landslides and debris flows because they may both be started by the same event. Check for injured and trapped persons, pets or livestock near the slide without entering the direct slide area and contact authorities.

Look for and report broken utility lines and damaged roadways and railways to appropriate authorities. Replant damaged ground as soon as possible since erosion caused by loss of ground cover can lead to flash flooding and additional landslides in the future.

# MANMADE DISASTERS

The human population can claim a significant number of disasters generally caused by negligence, error or failure of a manmade system. In fact, there are so many disasters caused by humans – it is difficult to estimate the number of deaths, the environmental impact and the financial cost of our irresponsible actions.

There are countless *social* hazards happening throughout the world. Modern societies generally regard crime as an offense against the state and many of these crimes create serious disasters, both to individual citizens as well as the general population in the form of death to humans and animals and environmental and property damage. For example, *arson* fires cause death and destroy buildings, bridges, vehicles and private property. A *terrorist* act creates fear in order to achieve political, religious or ideological goals and target civilians, government officials, military personnel or individuals serving the interests of government. *Warfare* has destroyed entire cultures, countries, economies and inflicted great suffering on humanity and the environment.

There are also *technological* hazards created by humans including industrial disasters such as the Bhopal disaster in 1984 where a gas and chemical leak at a pesticide plant in India resulted in exposure to thousands of people. The official immediate death toll was 2,259 and 3,787 deaths related to the gas release. Others estimate 3,000 died within weeks and another 8,000 have since died from gas-related diseases.

The Chernobyl disaster may be regarded as the worst *nuclear* accident where in 1986, at the Chernobyl Nuclear Power Plant in Ukraine, an explosion and fire released large quantities of radioactive contamination into the atmosphere spreading over most of Western Russia and Europe. The battle to contain the contamination ultimately crippled the economy. The estimated human death toll ranged from 4,000 to as many as 25,000 direct casualties and over 200,000 related deaths. We are still waiting on statistics involving the earthquake and tsunami and the resulting nuclear meltdown that occurred in Japan on 11 March 2011.

## FIRE

It is important to understand the basic characteristics of fire. Fire can spread very quickly, leaving no time to gather valuables or make a phone call. In just two minutes, a fire can become life-threatening and in five minutes, the home could be engulfed in flames. Heat and smoke from fire can be more dangerous than flames and inhaling the super-hot air can sear lungs. Fire produces poisonous gases that make a person drowsy and disoriented so instead of being awakened by a fire, you may fall into a deeper sleep. Asphyxiation is the leading cause of fire deaths, exceeding burns by a three-to-one ratio.

### <u>Preventive Measures</u>

As a proactive measure, family members should take steps to <u>prevent</u> a fire from occurring in the first place. Most home fires occur in the kitchen while cooking and are the leading cause of injuries from fire. Common causes of fires at night are carelessly discarded cigarettes, sparks from fireplaces without screens or glass doors, and heating appliances left too close to furniture or other combustibles. These fires are particularly dangerous because they may smolder for a long period of time before igniting into a fire.

### <u>Cooking</u>

Stay in the kitchen when frying, grilling or broiling food. If leaving the kitchen for even a short period of time, turn off the stove. When cooking, wear short, close-fitting or tightly rolled sleeves. Do not cook when tired, drinking alcohol, or taking medication that causes drowsiness. Keep children and pets away from cooking areas by enforcing a "restricted zone" of three feet around the stove. Position barbecue grills at least eight to ten feet away from siding and deck railings and out from under eaves and overhanging branches.

### <u>Smoking</u>

The majority of home fires caused by smoking start inside the home, so if you smoke, <u>smoke outside</u>. Place cigarettes in a can filled with sand and make sure cigarettes and ashes are out. Soak cigarette butts and ashes in water before throwing them away and never toss hot cigarette butts or ashes in the trash can. If people have been smoking in the home, check for cigarettes under cushions.  Never smoke in a home where oxygen is used, even if it is turned off.  And for heavens sake - don't smoke in bed!  And even better - **STOP SMOKING!**  Wise up!

## Electrical and Appliance Safety

Replace all worn, old or damaged appliance cords and do not run cords under rugs or furniture.  Always purchase electrical products evaluated and approved by Underwriters Laboratories (UL).  If an appliance has a three-prong plug, use it only in a three-slot outlet and never force it to fit into a two-slot outlet or extension cord.  Never overload extension cords or wall sockets.  Immediately shut off and replace lights that flicker and light switches that spark when turned on/off or are hot to the touch.

## Portable Space Heaters

Keep combustible objects at least three feet away from portable heating devices.  Buy only heaters evaluated and approved by Underwriters Laboratories (UL).  The portable heater should have a thermostat control mechanism that switches off automatically if the heater falls over or becomes overheated.

## Fireplaces and Woodstoves

Inspect and clean woodstove pipes and chimneys annually and check monthly for damage or obstructions.  Use a fireplace screen heavy enough to stop rolling logs and big enough to cover the entire opening of the fireplace to catch flying sparks.  Make sure the fire is completely out before leaving the house or going to bed.  Store cooled ashes in a tightly sealed metal container outside of the home.

## Children

Take the mystery out of fire by teaching children fire is a tool and not a toy.  Store matches and lighters in a locked cabinet out of children's reach.  Teach children *not* to pick up matches or lighters and tell an adult immediately of the discovery.  Never leave children unattended near operating stoves or burning candles.  Check under beds and in closets for evidence children may be playing with fire.  Teach children <u>not</u> to hide from firefighters.

## Before a Fire

At least two times each year, all family members should practice the fire escape plan that includes feeling your way out of the house in the dark or with your eyes closed.  As part of the strategy, include the safety and security of pets in the overall plan.  Purchase escape ladders if the residence has more than one level and make sure burglar bars and other antitheft mechanisms blocking outside window entries are easily opened from the *inside* of the house.  On a regular basis, clean out storage areas and avoid the accumulation of trash, newspapers and magazines.

As part of *planning in advance* and common sense, home owners should carry home owners insurance.  Make sure you have fire coverage in the event the fire destroys all or part of the house.  Make copies of all important documents and place them in a safety deposit box or scan the documents and email them to yourself.  For older adults and persons with special needs, attempt to live near an exit of the building.  If you live in a multi-story home, arrange to sleep on the ground floor and near an exit.  Keep a phone near the bed and be ready to call 9-1-1 or your local emergency number in the event of a fire.  You will be safest on the ground floor if living in an apartment building.

If using a walker or wheelchair, check all exits to be sure you can get through the doorways and make arrangements to provide exit ramps and wide doorways to facilitate an emergency escape.  As part of *planning in advance*, speak to other family members, the building manager or neighbors about your fire safety plan and practice it with them.  Contact the non-emergency line of the fire department and explain special needs issues.

## During a Fire

When the smoke alarm sounds - get out of the house!  You may only have seconds to safely escape.  Smoke is toxic and first collects along the ceiling so when escaping through smoke, crawl low under any smoke to your exit.  If there is smoke blocking or coming around the door, leave the door closed and use an alternative route out of the building.  **<u>If unable to remove pets trapped inside the house, inform firefighters right away</u>.**

Before opening a door, feel the doorknob and door and if either is hot, leave the door closed and use an alternative escape route. When opening a door, open it slowly and be ready to shut it quickly if heavy smoke or fire is present. If you cannot vacate the building, try to reach a room with an outside window. If trapped inside a building, close all doors in the room and cover vents and cracks around doors with cloth or tape. Stay where you are and signal for help by yelling out the window or use some type of distress signal such as a light-colored cloth or a flashlight.

If your clothes catch fire, **STOP, DROP, COVER AND ROLL** – *stop* immediately, *drop* to the ground, *cover* your face with your hands and *roll* over and over or back and forth until the fire is out. If you or someone else cannot stop, drop, cover and roll, smother the flames with a blanket or towel. Use cool water to treat any burns for three to five minutes, cover with a clean, dry cloth and get medical assistance.

## After a Fire

Firefighters will advise family members when the residence is safe to enter and whether utilities are safe to use. If utilities have been disconnected (especially natural gas), the gas company must reconnect the gas to the home. As a general rule, don't attempt to reconnect utilities but contact qualified representatives to assist in this task.

Contact the insurance company for detailed instructions on conducting an inventory, filing claims and contacting fire damage restoration companies. As part of the recovery process, it will be necessary to locate and gather items that can be salvaged and conduct an inventory of damaged property and items. Do not throw away any damaged goods until after an inventory. Access documents and records and be prepared to provide information to various government agencies and the insurance company. Begin saving receipts on money expended as a result of the fire. Receipts may be required by the insurance company and for verifying losses claimed on income tax returns. If there is a mortgage on the home, notify the mortgage company of the fire.

## WILDFIRES

As people continue to construct homes in woodland settings, near forests, rural areas or remote mountain sites, the possibility of a wildfire becomes an increased danger to life and property. Wildfires often begin unnoticed and are usually triggered by lightning or humans who are careless or have set fires purposely to cause destruction.

According to the National Oceanic and Atmospheric Administration (NOAA), although a wildfire may occur in almost any region of the country, there are certain states that may be more prone to wildfire, due to warm and dry conditions, density of population, fuel sources and wind currents. Depending on the current climatic conditions, the probably of wildfires in a specific state can dramatically change each season. The National Interagency Fire Center (NIFC) reports that during January through March of 2012, there were 10,351 wildfires of various sizes that burned 182,417 acres in the United States.

There are several states that seem to continually experience wildfires each season, including **California, Colorado** and **Texas**. However, there are other states that also claim a high number or serious wildfires each season, including *Arizona, Oklahoma, Kansas, Nebraska, South Dakota, Minnesota, Missouri* and *Arkansas* with even hot spots occurring in *Florida*. Many of these states provide a large percentage of grains, fruits and vegetables for the country.

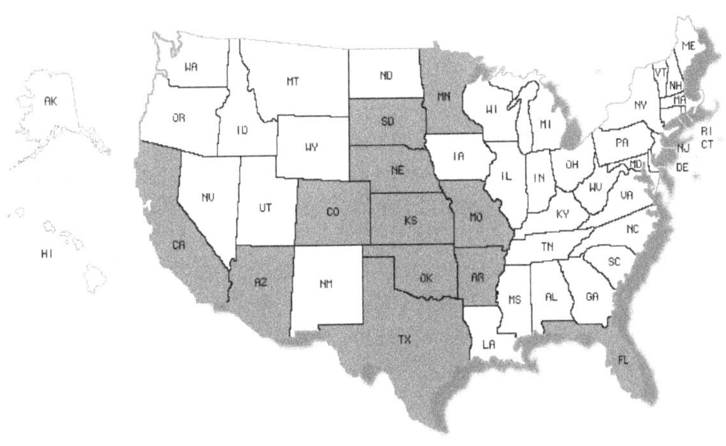

<u>**Before a Wildfire**</u>

Every year across the country, some homes actually survive a major wildfire, due to *advanced planning* in preparing for the eventuality of fire. If building in a woodland area, design and landscape the home with wildfire safety as a *top priority* and select materials and plants that help contain fire rather than fuel it. For example, use fire-resistant or noncombustible materials on the roof and exterior structure of the dwelling, or treat wood or combustible material used in roofs, siding, decking or trim with fire-retardant chemicals. Plant fire-resistant shrubs and trees. For example, a hardwood tree is less flammable than pine, evergreen, eucalyptus or fir trees.

On a regular basis, mow grass, rake leaves, remove dead limbs and twigs extending over roofs, clear flammable vegetation, clean roof and gutters, remove leaves and rubbish from under structures around the home, remove vines from the walls of the home and prune tree branches and shrubs within fifteen feet of a stovepipe or chimney outlet. If necessary, request the power company clear any branches from and around power lines.

**Teams should create a 30 to 100 foot safety zone around the home and homes of other family members living in a woodland environment. Homes built in pine forests should have a minimum safety zone of 100 feet. If your home sits on a steep slope, standard protective measures may not suffice. Contact your local fire department or forestry office for additional information.**

Thin a fifteen-foot space between tree crowns, remove limbs within fifteen feet of the ground and clear a ten-foot area around propane tanks and the barbecue grill. Place a screen over the grill and use nonflammable material with mesh no coarser than one-quarter inch. Place stove, fireplace and grill ashes in a metal bucket, soak in water for two days and bury the cold ashes in mineral soil.

Inspect chimneys at least twice a year and clean them at least once a year. Equip chimneys and stovepipes with a spark arrester that meets the requirements of National Fire Protection Association Standard 211 and keep the dampers in good working order. Stack firewood at least one-hundred feet away and uphill from the home! Use only wood-burning devices evaluated by Underwriters Laboratories (UL).

Regularly dispose of newspapers and rubbish at an approved site. Store gasoline, oily rags and other flammable materials in approved safety cans and place in a safe location *away* from the base of buildings. Make sure the home is equipped with fire tools: a rake, axe, handsaw or chain saw, bucket and shovel and keep a ladder by the home that will reach the roof.

Identify and maintain an adequate outside water source such as a small pond, cistern, underground well, spring, swimming pool or hydrant. Install freeze-proof exterior water outlets on at least two sides of the home and near other structures on the property and install additional outlets at least fifty feet from the home. Store a garden hose that is long enough to reach any area of the home and other structures on the property.

Install dual-sensor smoke alarms on each level of the home, especially near bedrooms; test monthly and change the batteries at least once each year. Teach adult family members how to use a fire extinguisher (ABC type) and make sure everyone knows where it is stored. And finally, review the home owner's insurance policy for the home and prepare and continually update a list of home contents.

<u>**During a Wildfire**</u>

When observing <u>any</u> wildfire, including one near the home, immediately call 9-1-1 and do <u>not</u> assume someone else has already made the call. Describe the location of the fire, speak slowly and clearly and answer any questions asked by the dispatcher.

Family members should immediately change into protective clothing – sturdy shoes, cotton or woolen clothes, long pants, a long-sleeved shirt, gloves and a handkerchief to protect the face. Attend to pets and livestock. Begin to gather fire tools such as a rake, axe, handsaw or chainsaw, bucket and shovel into one location.

**I know you may not want to - but if evacuating the home due to a wildfire, leave doors and windows closed and unlocked. It may be necessary for firefighters to gain quick entry into the home to fight fire.**

If equipped with gas-powered pumps for water, make sure they are fueled and ready to operate. Connect garden hoses and fill any pools, hot tubs, garbage cans, tubs or other large containers with water. Place lawn sprinklers on the roof and near above-ground fuel tanks and wet the roof. Place a ladder in clear view against the house.

Close outside attic, eaves and basement vents, windows, doors (inside and outside) and pet doors. Remove flammable drapes and curtains and close all shutters, blinds or heavy non-combustible window coverings to reduce radiant heat. Open the damper on the fireplace but close the fireplace screen. Shut off any natural gas, propane or fuel oil supplies at the source. Close all garage doors and then disconnect any automatic garage door openers so the doors can still be opened by hand if the power goes out. Back cars into the driveway but leave the keys in the ignition, shut and unlock the doors and roll up the windows. <u>Turn on outside lights and leave a light on in every room to make the house more visible in heavy smoke.</u>

Place valuables that will not be damaged by water in a pool or pond and place valuable papers, mementos and important valuables inside the car ready for quick departure. Move flammable furniture into the center of the residence away from the windows and sliding-glass doors. Any pets still with you should also be put in the car. Release livestock to give them a chance to retreat from the fire.

**If trapped at the home,** stay inside and away from outside walls. Keep the entire family and pets together and try to remain calm.

**If in a vehicle,** survival *is* possible in the firestorm <u>if you stay in the car</u>. It is much less dangerous to stay in the vehicle than trying to outrun the fire. Roll up the windows, close the air vents and drive slowly with headlights on. Be aware the engine may stall and not restart and air currents may rock the car. Watch for other vehicles and pedestrians but do <u>not</u> drive through heavy smoke.

If you have to stop, park away from the heaviest trees and brush. Again, turn the headlights on and the ignition off, roll up the windows and close air vents. Get on the floor and cover up with a blanket or coat. There may be some smoke and sparks that enter the vehicle and the temperature inside the vehicle will increase but metal gas tanks and containers rarely explode. **STAY IN THE VEHICLE UNTIL THE MAIN FIRE PASSES. DO NOT RUN!**

**If caught outside in an open area,** the best *temporary* shelter is in a sparse fuel area. For example, on a steep mountainside, move to the back side of the mountain and avoid canyons, natural "chimneys" and saddles. If a road is nearby, lie face down along the road or in a ditch on the uphill side. Cover yourself with anything that will shield you from the heat. If hiking in the back country, seek a depression with sparse fuel. Clear fuel away from the area while the fire is approaching and then lie face down in the depression and cover yourself. Stay down until *after* the fire passes!

In the event of an evacuation order, arrange temporary housing for family members, pets and livestock outside the threatened area. If advised or ordered to evacuate by officials, do so immediately. Make sure all family members have their respective evacuation kits, and depending on the situation, either drive or walk using a route away from the fire hazard. Watch for changes in speed and direction of the fire and smoke. Attempt to inform someone of the date and time of the evacuation, the names of family members and the location of the temporary shelter.

## After a Wildfire

In the event the family remained at the home during the wildfire, check the roof immediately after the fire danger has passed. Put out any roof fires, sparks or embers and check the attic for hidden burning sparks. For several hours after the fire, maintain vigilance by continually re-checking for smoke and sparks throughout the house. In order to minimize breathing dust particles, wet debris down.

When going outside, all family members should wear leather gloves and heavy soled shoes to protect hands and feet. Watch animals closely and take steps to keep them under your direct control. Hidden embers and hot spots could burn pets' paws or hooves. Avoid damaged or fallen power lines, poles and downed wires. Use caution when entering burned areas as hazards may still exist, including hot spots, which can flare up without warning. Watch for and identify ash pits and warn family members and neighbors to keep clear of the pits.

When a family is forced to evacuate, and upon returning to the home, if a building inspector has placed a color-coded sign on the home, do not enter until you get more information, advice and instructions about what the sign means and whether it is safe to enter the building. Once it is safe to enter the home, dispose of any cleaning products, paint, batteries and damaged fuel containers to avoid risk.

Do NOT use water that may be contaminated to drink, wash dishes, brush teeth, prepare food, wash hands, make ice or prepare baby formula. If you have a safe or strong box, it can hold intense heat for several hours. If the door is opened before the box has cooled, the contents could burst into flames.

## PESTILENCE

A pandemic (pestilence) is an epidemic of an infectious disease that spreads through human and animal populations across states, countries, multiple continents or even throughout the world. A disease or condition is not a pandemic simply because it is widespread or kills many people or animals; it must also be infectious. For instance, cancer and heart disease are responsible for many deaths but is not considered pandemic because the diseases are not infectious or contagious.

In most cases, a flu pandemic excludes the recurrence of seasonal flu. Throughout history there have been many pandemics including smallpox, malaria, tuberculosis, influenza, HIV and the H1N1 pandemic. Family members can take proactive steps in preparing for a pandemic by ensuring all family members are immunized. Knowledge of the magnitude of what can happen during a pandemic outbreak and what actions to take to lessen the impact is essential for survival. During a pandemic, it may not be possible to get to a store, or stores may be out of supplies, so as part of *planning in advance*, store at least a two week supply of water and food. Check prescription drugs periodically for a continuous supply in the home and store nonprescription drugs and other health supplies, including pain relievers, stomach remedies, cough and cold medicines, fluids with electrolytes and vitamins.

When you are sick, keep your distance from others to protect them from getting sick. If possible, stay home from work, school and running errands. Cover mouth and nose with a tissue when coughing or sneezing. Germs are often spread when a person touches something contaminated with germs and then touches the eyes, nose or mouth. Washing hands often will help protect from germs. Discuss with family members about the possibility of becoming ill and what would be realistic to care for them. Practice other good health habits; get plenty of sleep, be physically active, manage stress, drink plenty of fluids and eat nutritious food.

## FAMINE

A famine is a widespread scarcity of food caused by natural and manmade disasters including drought, heat waves, cold weather, flooding, fire, tornadoes, winds and war as well as overpopulation and government policies. The consequence of these disasters is crop (grain, fruits, vegetables) failure and the loss of cattle, sheep, hogs, chickens and other animals that provide meat (protein) sources to the human and animal population.

This phenomenon is usually accompanied or followed by regional malnutrition, starvation, epidemic and increased mortality rates. The mortality rates are concentrated among children and the elderly and male mortality exceeds female, due to perhaps the obvious superiority of females (!) and greater female resilience under the pressure of malnutrition. Every continent in the world has experienced a period of famine. Many countries continue to have extreme cases of famine.

It is interesting to note in the Bible, in Revelations 6:5-6, the third horseman rides a black horse and is generally understood to be famine. The horseman carries a pair of weighing scales suggesting bread would be weighed during a famine. Perhaps the price of grain is so high it takes an entire day's wages to buy enough wheat for one person or enough barley for three persons so poor and middle class workers would struggle to feed their families.

> **When the Lamb opened the third seal, I heard the third living creature say, "Come and see!" I looked, and there before me was a black horse! Its rider was holding a pair of scales in his hand. Then I heard what sounded like a voice among the four living creatures saying, "A quart of wheat for a day's wages, and three quarts of barley for a day's wages, and do not damage the oil and the wine!"**

Of the four horsemen, the black horse and its rider are the only ones whose appearance includes a vocal pronunciation. John hears a voice that speaks of the prices of <u>wheat</u> and <u>barley</u>.  Some suggest the black horse's famine is to drive up the price of grain but leave oil and wine supplies unaffected (though out of reach of the ordinary worker).   One explanation is that grain crops would be more naturally susceptible to famine years or locust plagues than olive trees and grapevines.

Food shortages in a population are generally caused either by a lack of food or by difficulties in food distribution.  It may also be worsened by natural climate fluctuations and by extreme political or economic conditions related to oppressive government or warfare.  Throughout the world, the number of people who are hungry is staggering.  There are over seven billion people in the world and over thirteen percent or 925 million are hungry – or almost one in seven people.

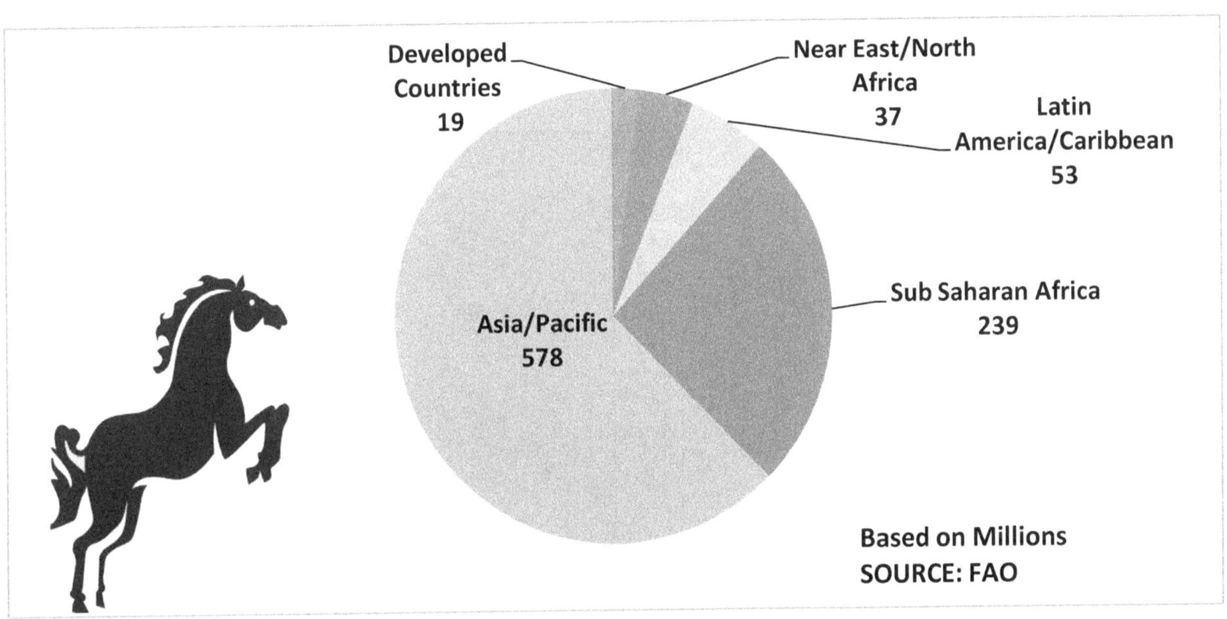


The world produces enough food to feed everyone.  According to the Food and Agriculture Organization of the United Nations (FAO), the world agriculture produces seventeen percent more calories per person today than it did thirty years ago, despite a seventy percent increase in population.  This is enough to provide everyone in the world with at least 2,720 kilocalories per person per day.  The principal problem is many people in the world do not have sufficient land to grow or income to purchase enough food.

In the United States, we have been so truly blessed that many of us cannot process the possibility of this great nation being assaulted by a famine disaster.  Over the past several years, there has been an increase in the number of people in <u>this</u> country who are facing starvation and countless millions are malnourished.  The price of most food has been increasing so dramatically it is becoming not only hard – but impossible – for families to put food on the table.  The regions that grow our food are experiencing severe climate changes affecting the amount of food being produced in this country.

<u>As family members, we must recognize the urgent need to fill our emergency pantries – **INCLUDING OUR FOOD PANTRIES** as quickly as possible to make certain we have enough food to eat during serious disasters and other dangerous events that can disrupt our food supply</u>.  It appears John (in Revelations) may be onto something – the climate conditions are affecting the amount of food being produced, the "oil" may not be cooking oil at all but the price of gasoline (oil) needed to transport and distribute the food, and the price of food continues to rise with no end in sight - the affects being felt by those in the poor and middle class families.  If you believe the availability of food is difficult to obtain and the price of food is high now – wait until you see the availability and prices during a long-term famine.

## HAZARDOUS MATERIALS

There are chemicals used to purify drinking water, increase crop production and simplify household chores.  And yet hazardous materials in various forms can cause death, serious injury, long-lasting health affects and damage to buildings, homes, environment and other property. Hazards can occur during production, storage, transportation, use or disposal. These products are shipped on the highways, railroads, waterways and pipelines every day.

There are many sources of hazardous materials, including chemical manufacturers, service stations, hospitals and waste sites. According to the Environmental Protection Agency, varying quantities of hazardous materials are manufactured, used or stored at an estimated 4.5 million facilities in the United States from major industrial plants to local dry cleaning establishments or garden supply stores. Hazardous materials come in the form of explosives, flammable and combustible substances, poisons and radioactive materials. All family members and the community are at risk if a chemical is used unsafely or released in harmful amounts into the environment.

In the United States, the *eastern* and *central* regions of the country are where most toxic chemicals are manufactured, processed and used in significant amounts. Another region that claims a high use of toxic chemicals is the *western* coast line of **California**, **Oregon** and **Washington**. Family members who reside in areas susceptible to chemical spills should have a "shelter-in-place" location available at the home. In addition, make sure adequate emergency supplies supporting a chemical spill are included in the various pantries. Include pets and livestock in the overall plan.

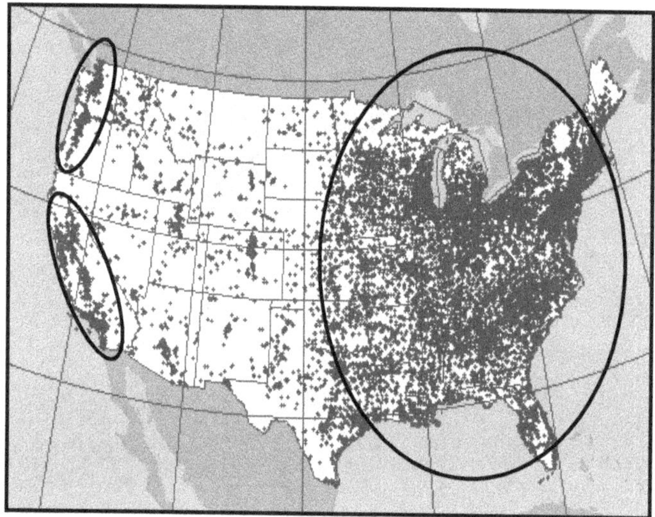

**SOURCE:  Environmental Protection Agency**

## Before a Hazardous Materials Incident

Many communities have a Local Emergency Planning Committee (LEPC) whose responsibilities include collecting information about hazardous materials in the community and distributing this information to the public upon request. These committees are tasked with developing an emergency plan to prepare for and respond to chemical emergencies in the community. The method of notifying the public and actions the public must take in the event of a release are part of the plan. Contact the LEPC in your area to find out more about chemical hazards and what needs to be done to minimize the risk to individuals and the community from these materials.

## During a Hazardous Materials Incident

Listen to local radio or television stations for detailed information and follow the instructions. Stay away from the area to minimize risk of contamination. Remember that some toxic chemicals are odorless.

| IF YOU ARE | THEN |
|---|---|
| **Asked To Evacuate** | Gather evacuation kits and evacuate immediately. Stay tuned to radio or television for information on evacuation routes, temporary shelters and procedures. Follow the routes recommended by the authorities. If you have time, minimize contamination in the house by closing all windows, shutting all vents and turning off attic fans. Make arrangements for pets and livestock. |

| IF YOU ARE | THEN |
| --- | --- |
| **Caught Outside** | Move away from the accident scene and do not walk into or touch any spilled liquids, airborne mists or condensed solid chemical deposits. Stay upstream, uphill, and upwind! Attempt to go at least one-half mile (usually eight to ten city blocks) from the danger area. Cover mouth with a cloth while leaving the area so as not to inhale gases, fumes and smoke. Stay away from accident victims until the hazardous material has been identified. |
| **In A Motor Vehicle** | Stop and seek shelter in a permanent building. If you must remain in the car, keep car windows and vents closed and shut off the air conditioner and heater. |
| **Requested To Stay Indoors** | In large buildings, set ventilation systems to 100 percent <u>recirculation</u> so no outside air is drawn into the building. Otherwise, ventilation systems should be turned off.<br><br>At the home, bring pets inside and release livestock from enclosures to allow them to get away from the danger zone. Close and lock all exterior doors and windows, vents, fireplace dampers and interior doors and turn off air conditioners and ventilation systems. Family members and pets should then immediately go to the shelter-in-place room. Seal gaps under doorways and windows, air conditioning units, bathroom and kitchen exhaust fans, and stove and dryer vents with wet towels or plastic sheeting using duct tape. If gas or vapors could have entered the building, take shallow breaths through a cloth or a towel.<br><br>Avoid eating or drinking any food or water that may be contaminated. |

**SOURCE: Environmental Protection Agency**

<u>**After a Hazardous Materials Incident**</u>

Do not leave the safe room in the home until instructed to do so by authorities. Listen to local radio or television stations for the latest emergency information and follow decontamination instructions. You may be advised to take a shower or stay away from outside water. Find out from local authorities how to clean up your land and property. Seek medical treatment of any unusual symptoms for family members, pets and livestock as soon as possible.

## HOUSEHOLD CHEMICALS

Chemicals are found in kitchens, medicine cabinets, basements, garages and gardens. Nearly every household uses products containing hazardous materials or chemicals. Although there is minimum risk of a chemical accident, knowing how to handle these products and how to react during an emergency can reduce the risk of injury. According to the Environmental Protection Agency, chemicals causing chemical poisoning include *toxins* and *toxicants*. Chemicals that are produced by living organisms are called *toxins*. There are a wide variety of toxins, including biotoxins that cause biotoxin poisoning. Examples of biotoxins include snake venom, honey bee venom and cyanotoxin (produced by blue-green algae).

A *toxicant* is a synthetic chemical that are natural substances not produced by a living organism. There are a wide variety of toxicants such as pesticides, chlorine, ammonia, pepper spray and acetone. Toxins and toxicants that cause chemical poisoning come in different forms, including gas, liquids or solids, and are taken into the body by inhaling and ingesting the substance. Symptoms and complications vary depending on the specific chemical, its form, and the amount of exposure to the chemical.

As a <u>proactive</u> measure, family members should inspect the home and the homes of other family members to see where chemicals are located. Once a product has been located, check the label and take the appropriate steps to use, store and dispose of the material.

<u>**Avoiding a Chemical Accident**</u>

Read the instructions and labels <u>before</u> using a new chemical product and store household chemicals according to the instructions on the label.

Warning labels on commercial chemicals are as follows:

- **DANGER** - chemical harmful or fatal if swallowed.  Ingestion of a small taste to a teaspoon could kill an average sized adult

- **WARNING** - chemical harmful if swallowed.  Ingestion of a teaspoon to an ounce could kill an average sized adult

- **CAUTION** - chemical harmful if swallowed.  Ingestion of an ounce to a pint could kill an average sized adult

Avoid mixing household chemical products since deadly toxic fumes result from the mixture of chemicals, such as chlorine bleach and ammonia.  Never smoke while using household chemicals or use hair spray, cleaning solutions, paint products, or pesticides near an open flame, pilot light, lighted candle, fireplace or wood-burning stove.  Although you may not be able to see or smell them, vapor particles in the air could ignite or explode.

Clean up spilled chemicals with rags and protect eyes and skin by wearing gloves and goggles or safety glasses.  Allow fumes in the rags to evaporate outdoors and then dispose of the rags by wrapping them in newspaper, placing them in a sealed plastic bag and putting them outside in the trash can.  Disposing of chemicals properly ensures they will not adversely affect the environment, the health and well being of the public, family, pets and livestock.

Be aware animals are more likely to explore substances within their reach, particularly those with an attractive odor (<u>including substances such as antifreeze and chocolate which is toxic to most pets</u>).  Animals will often lick their paws, fur or skin and swallow a substance.  Wash your animals' paws and coat if necessary and prevent licking as much as possible until you have taken the animal to the veterinarian.

Family members should also take extra precautions when *using, storing* and *disposing* of these agents:

- **Air Freshener** - interferes with ability to smell by disabling nasal passages with an oil film or a nerve-deadening agent.  Common chemicals in air fresheners include formaldehyde (carcinogen) and phenol (causes hives, convulsions, circulatory collapse, coma, and even death).  Who knew?????

- **Ammonia** - volatile chemical that damages eyes, respiratory tract and skin.

- **Antibacterial Cleaner** - contains triclosan that is absorbed through the skin and linked to liver damage.  Antibacterial soaps may also contribute to the development of drug-resistant bacteria.

- **Bleach** - strong corrosive that damages skin, eyes and respiratory tract.

- **Carpet and Upholstery Shampoo** - contains highly toxic substances such as perchlorethylene (carcinogen that damages liver, kidneys and nervous system) and ammonium hydroxide (corrosive that irritates eyes, skin and respiratory passages).

- **Dishwasher Detergent** - contains concentrated chlorine which is the leading cause of child poisonings.

- **Drain Cleaner** - contains lye (burns skin and eyes and esophagus and stomach if ingested), hydrochloric acid (corrosive eye and skin irritant that damages kidneys, liver and digestive tract), or tricholoroethane (eye and skin irritant and nervous system depressant).

- **Furniture Polish** - contains phenol and nitrobenzene that is a highly flammable and toxic chemical easily absorbed through the skin, causing skin and lung cancer.

- **Laundry Room Products** - contains sodium or calcium hypocrite (corrosive agent that irritates skin and eyes) and hypochlorite bleach (corrosive that burns eyes, skin and respiratory tract).  If exposed to other chemicals, hypochlorite bleach may form chlorine fumes that can be fatal.

- **Mold and Mildew Cleaner** - contains sodium hypochlorite (corrosive causing fluid in the lungs) and formaldehyde (carcinogen).

- **Oven Cleaner** - contains lye (sodium hydroxide) that burns the skin and eyes and the esophagus and stomach if ingested.

- **Toilet Bowl Cleaner** - contains hydrochloric acid or hypochlorite bleach (corrosive eye and skin irritant that damages kidneys, liver and digestive tract).

Additional dangerous chemicals used around the house include the following:

| **Lawn and Garden Products** | | |
| --- | --- | --- |
| <br>• *Fungicides*<br>• *Herbicides*<br>• *Insecticides* | **IT IS IMPORTANT TO STORE HOUSEHOLD CHEMICALS IN PLACES WHERE CHILDREN AND PETS CANNOT ACCESS THEM.** | |
| **Cleaning Products**<br><br>• *Car wash and shampoo*<br>• *Pool chemicals*<br>• *Tub, tile, shower cleaners*<br>• *Wood/metal cleaners*<br>• *Polishes* | **Indoor Pesticides**<br><br>• *Ant sprays and baits*<br>• *Bug sprays*<br>• *Cockroach sprays and baits*<br>• *Flea repellents/shampoo*<br>• *Houseplant insecticides*<br>• *Moth repellents*<br>• *Mouse/rat poisons and baits* | **Miscellaneous**<br><br>• *Batteries*<br>• *Driveway sealer*<br>• *Fluorescent light bulbs*<br>• *Hair Spray*<br>• *Lice shampoo*<br>• *Mercury thermostats*<br>• *Nail Polish/Remover* |
| **Automotive Products**<br><br>• *Air conditioning refrigerants*<br>• *Antifreeze (pets)*<br>• *Automotive batteries*<br>• *Brake fluid*<br>• *Carburetor cleaners*<br>• *Fuel additives*<br>• *Fuel injection cleaners*<br>• *Motor oil*<br>• *Starter fluids*<br>• *Transmission fluid* | **Workshop/Painting Supplies**<br><br>• *Adhesives and glues*<br>• *Fixatives and other solvents*<br>• *Furniture strippers*<br>• *Oil or enamel-based paint*<br>• *Paint strippers/removers*<br>• *Paint thinners*<br>• *Photographic chemicals*<br>• *Stains and finishes*<br>• *Turpentine*<br>• *Wood preservatives* | **Fuel Products**<br><br>• *Diesel*<br>• *Gas cylinders*<br>• *Gas/oil mix*<br>• *Home  heating oil*<br>• *Kerosene*<br>• *Lamp Oil*<br>• *Lighter fluid*<br>• *Propane* |

## After a Chemical Accident

When burned by chemicals - call 9-1-1 and administer first aid.  Remove clothing and jewelry from around the injury and pour clean, cool water over the burn for fifteen to thirty minutes.  Loosely cover the burn with a sterile or clean dressing so it will not stick to the burn.  If there is danger of a chemical fire or explosion - leave the area.  To avoid breathing toxic fumes, always stay upwind and away from the danger area.

If victim has been exposed to toxic chemicals, wash the hands, arms or other body parts that may have been exposed to the toxic chemical since chemicals continue to irritate the skin until washed off. Remove clothing being careful not to pull it over the face. Cut the clothing off if necessary and discard clothing that may have been contaminated by toxic chemicals. If you know or have reason to believe exposure to the chemical may cause poisoning, call the Poison Control Center at 1-800-222-1222. If your pet appears to have been exposed to a poison or other toxin, call your veterinarian or the Animal Poison Control Center at 1-888-426-4435. Post these numbers by all telephones.

According to the Poison Control Center, the list below provides *possible* signs and symptoms family members *may* have from being poisoned. Depending on the severity of the reaction, symptoms are *mild*, *moderate* or *severe*:

| <u>**MILD**</u> | <u>**MODERATE**</u> | <u>**SEVERE**</u> |
|---|---|---|
| *Nausea* | *Drooling* | *Breathing Difficulty* |
| *Headache* | *Severe Diarrhea* | *Fever* |
| *Fatigue* | *Severe Nausea* | *Extreme Thirst* |
| *Dizziness* | *Excessive Swearing* | *Rapid Breathing* |
| *Weakness* | *Abdominal Cramps* | *Muscle Twitching* |
| *Restlessness* | *Tremors* | *Narrowed Pupils* |
| *Perspiration* | *Lack of Coordination* | *Convulsions* |
| *Diarrhea* | *Severe Weakness* | *Unconsciousness* |
| *Loss of Appetite* | *Mental Confusion* | |
| *Weight Loss* | *Blurred Vision* | |
| *Thirst* | *Cough* | |
| *Joint Pain* | *Rapid Pulse* | |
| *Moodiness* | *Flushed Skin* | |
| *Skin/Eye Irritation* | *Yellow Skin* | |
| *Respiratory Irritation* | *Watery Eyes* | |

## RIOTS

A riot is civil disorder by groups of individuals in a sudden and intense rash of violence against authority, property or other citizens. Riots often occur in reaction to a perceived grievance or out of dissent for an existing law or policy. Riots have historically occurred due to poor working or living conditions, government oppression, food supply, taxation, forced recruitment into the military, frustration with legal channels, conflicts between ethnic groups or religions and even the outcome of a sporting event. A riot typically involves vandalism and destruction of private and public property including shops, homes, cars, restaurants, state-owned institutions and religious buildings.

Getting caught in a riot can be serious and life threatening and is not something to take lightly. If you are unfortunate enough to be caught in the middle of a riot or recognize the possibility of an impending riot, family members can take some simple precautions to manage the situation. There may be signs of public anger and violence at least one day (in some cases even 3-4 days) prior to the actual riot. Reading the newspapers and following the news may give you a warning about impending protests, rallies and marches. Being informed and avoiding troubled areas will be your best defense.

- A motorcycle helmet or a large towel wrapped around the head can protect the head if bricks or other large items are being thrown.

- Attempt to learn the reason for the riot because knowing the cause of a riot can help determine an appropriate response.

- Avoid public transportation since buses, subways, and trains will likely be out of service and stations and depots will be overwhelmed with frightened citizens.

- Be prepared for the worst - the unexpected can happen at any moment. Crowds are dangerous when angry and good-natured citizens can become frenzied just by being in a mob environment.

- Carry small amounts of cash to arrange transportation, pay off looters or bribe police at checkpoints.

- Chemicals cling to oil based moisturizer and sunscreen. Wear glasses, swimming goggles or a gas mask to protect the eyes and remove contact lenses since tear gas behind the lenses will cause severe pain. Carry toothpaste and smear it under the eyes if tear gas is released and you have nothing else available.

- Do not confront rioters or looters to prevent property damage.

- Do not drive towards police lines which can be interpreted by police as a means to use the car as a weapon against them. An activist will also fear cars that can involve irate non-participants running down protesters. Do not walk towards police lines in an attempt to cross to safety. Police are in place to confine the unrest and prevent its spread and their orders are usually not to allow anyone to pass.

- Get inside and stay inside a building. Riots typically occur in the streets and being inside a large and sturdy structure can be the best protection. Attempt to move to inside rooms where the danger of being hit by stones or bullets is minimized. Gravitate towards a basement, sub-basement or an interior doorway. Keep doors and windows locked and avoid watching the riot from windows or balconies. Locate at least two possible exits – especially in the event of fire.

- If in a car when the riot begins, remain inside the car unless the car becomes a focus for the riot – then calmly and swiftly leave the car and get to safety. If you have no alternative but to drive, lock the doors, <u>do not stop the car</u> and stay on streets *away* from the rioting. Avoid all main routes and keep alert for news of mob location. If people block the escape route; honk the horn and carefully drive through or around them at a moderate speed.

- If traveling abroad, register with the consulate and carry your passport and/or visa with you at all times. Always have proper identification and emergency contact information with you in the event of arrest, injury or death.

- Investigate possible escape routes and safe havens and look for homes that can serve as "safe houses". Obtain permission from the owner, if possible.

- Never touch a tear gas canister with bare hands - once discharged they are very hot.

- Remain calm. Adrenaline and survival instincts will surface but attempt to think rationally and pursue safety using a methodical approach. Avoid confrontation by keeping your head down and walk at all times because if you run or move too quickly, you might attract unwanted attention.

- Stay on the sidelines and do not take sides in the argument. Try to look inconspicuous and slowly and carefully move to the outside of the mob. Stay close to walls or other protective barriers and avoid bottlenecks such as tunnels, pillars, high fences and walls.

- To protect the mouth, place wet bandanas around the mouth if tear gas is released. The bandana will need constant replacement as the cloth will keep soaking up the gas. Wear vinyl or latex gloves to protect hands from pepper spray. Avoid rubbing hands or fingers into eyes, nose and mouth after a chemical attack.

- Try to avoid being hit by riot control chemicals or weapons. Police may deploy riot control agents such as tear gas, water cannons and rubber bullets to disperse a crowd. These riot control agents can kill if correctly targeted and can cause severe pain, respiratory distress and blindness. Learn to recognize the signs that a riot control agent has been used and how to manage exposure.

- Use the social media for alerts. Just as the rioters have started using social media and texting to alert one another where to go, you can use the media to learn safe and unsafe areas. Messages informing you of streets and areas currently being targeted provide instantaneous warnings of areas to avoid.

- Watch your footing in a mob situation. If you stumble and fall to the ground, you could easily be trampled. If you fall down, pull yourself up into a ball. Protect your face, ears and internal organs.

- Wear dark clothes that minimize the amount of exposed skin (long pants and long-sleeved shirts) when going out into the mob.  Do not wear clothing that could be interpreted as military or police clothing and avoid wearing anything that looks like a uniform.  If the anger of rioters is directed toward foreigners – blend in.  If rioters are divided into factions - appear neutral.  Avoid looking conspicuously wealthy.

There is a home made decontamination spray that may help reduce the affects of riot chemicals. If attacked by chemicals, spray on eyes, nose and skin:

- **Gather antacids (Tums, Pepto-Bismol, Gaviscon, Milk of Magnesia, Alka-Seltzer or baking soda)**
- **Dilute with water**
- **Place mixture in a spray bottle that can easily be carried**

## ELECTRICAL GRID

According to the United States Department of Energy, electric-power *transmission* is the bulk transfer of electrical energy from generating power plants to the electrical substations located near demand centers.  A *transmission grid* is a network of power stations, transmission circuits and substations.  Electric power *distribution* is the local wiring between the high-voltage substations and the customers.  The transmission lines when interconnected with each other become transmission networks or power grids.  These networks use components such as power lines, cables, circuit breakers, switches and transformers.

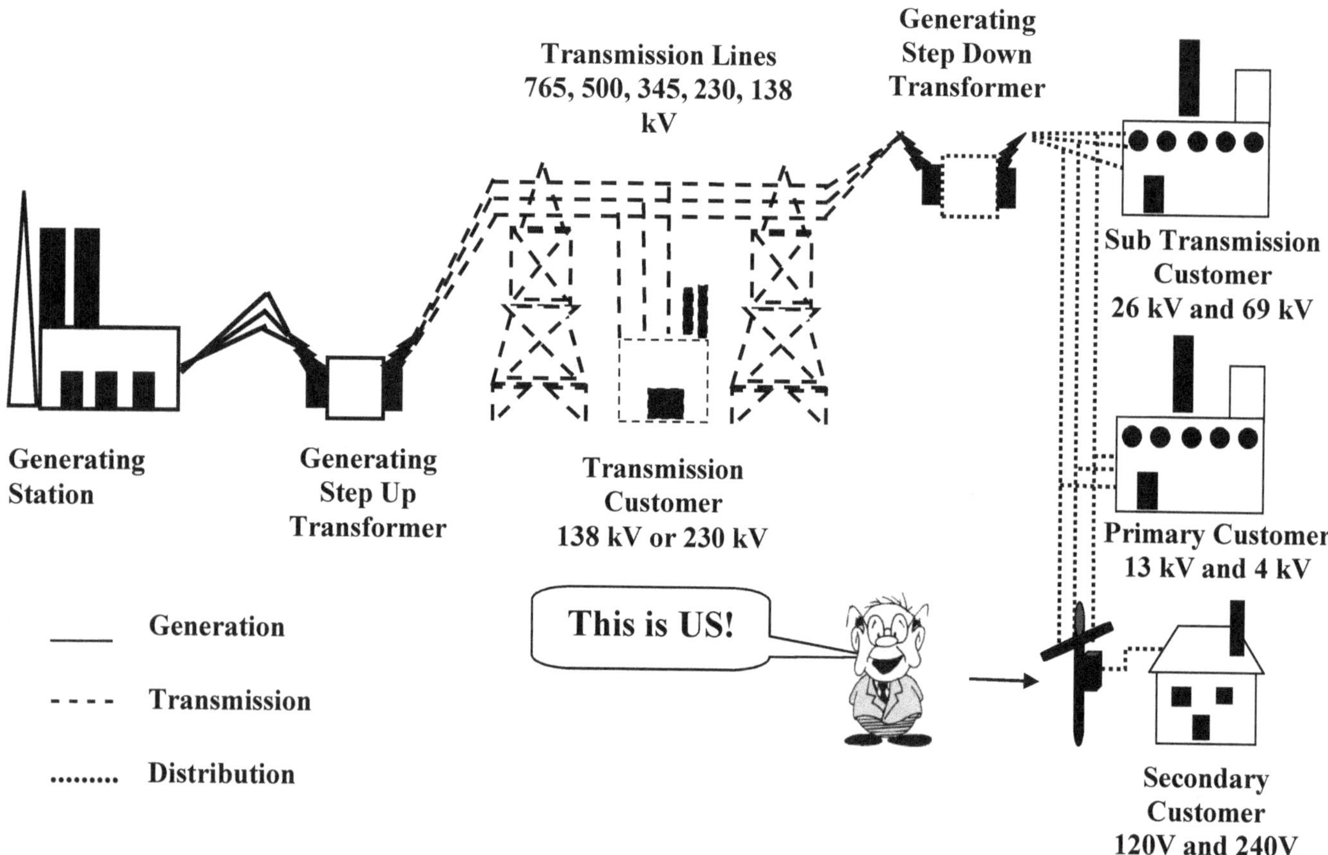


The capital cost of electric power stations is so high and electric demand is so variable it is often cost effective to import power than to generate it locally.  Because nearby loads are often correlated (hot weather in the Southwest of the United States might cause many people to use air conditioners), electricity often comes from distant sources.  Because of the economics of load balancing, wide area transmission grids now span across countries and even large portions of continents.  For example, New York City purchases a significant amount of electricity from Canada.

Electricity is transmitted at high voltages (110 kV or above) to reduce the energy lost in long-distance transmission. Electrical power is usually transmitted through overhead power lines because underground power transmission has a significantly higher cost and greater operational limitations.

With minor exceptions, the key limitation in the distribution of electricity is that <u>electrical energy cannot be stored and therefore must be generated as needed</u>. A sophisticated system of control is required to guarantee the electric generation very closely matches the demand. If supply and demand is not in balance, generation plants and transmission equipment can shut down and lead to major regional blackouts. The power generating stations require *fuel* in order to produce the electricity and the major fuel types used include *coal*, *natural gas*, *nuclear*, *hydro* (water) and *oil*, although other alternative fuel sources such as wind and solar power are used.

According to the United States Department of Energy, in the United States, when comparing fuels used to generate electricity, fossil fuel generation (mainly coal) was by far the largest source of fuel used to generate electricity.

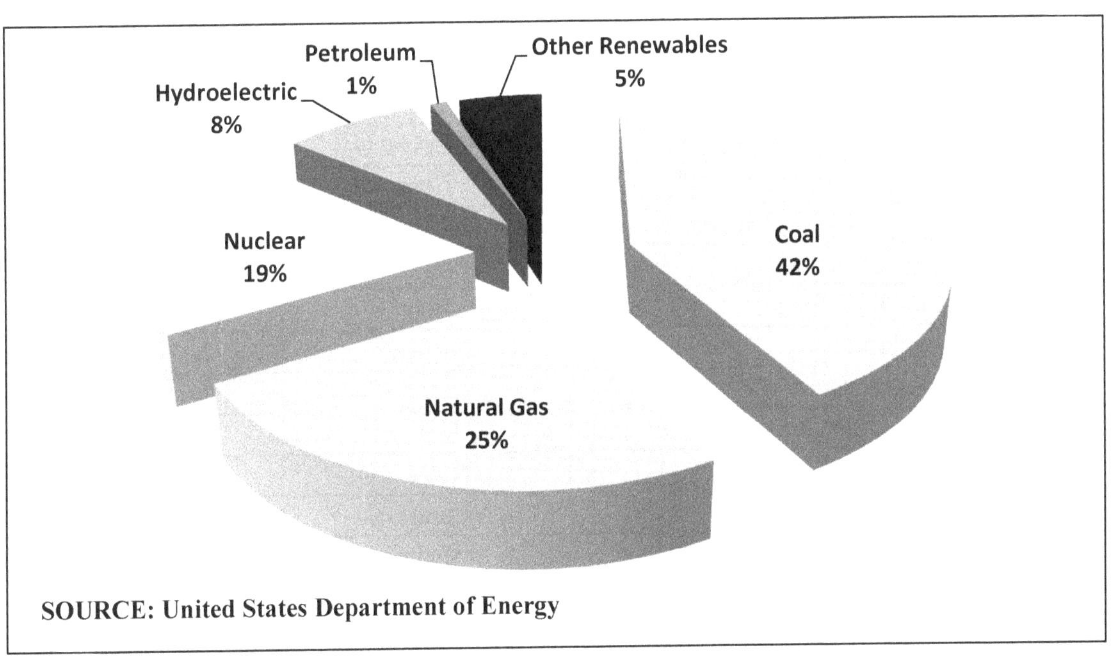


**SOURCE: United States Department of Energy**

There is hundreds of generating and power stations located throughout the United States and a large majority of these plants provide electrical output based on *kilowatts*. These particular stations generally serve a specific region adjacent to the plant. There are other generating stations providing electrical output based on *megawatts* and these stations produce a huge amount of electricity serving millions of people in the vicinity or the electricity is transported through the transmission lines to other states.

The capacity of the plant varies depending on capital improvements, environmental regulations, improved technology and other factors that have an impact on electrical output. The Grand Coulee Power Station located near Grand Coulee, Washington commands the top position, generating a staggering 7,079 megawatts of electricity with the assistance of the Grand Coulee Dam and the Columbia River. Many of the hydro (using dams and rivers) electric plants are located in the western region of the country – with many of these stations assigned to the state of Washington, including the Grand Coulee Dam Power Station.

| RANK | PLANT | FUEL | STATE | CAPACITY (MW) |
|---|---|---|---|---|
| 1 | **Grand Coulee Dam Power Station** | **Hydro** | **WA** | **7,079** |
| 2 | Martin Power Plant | Coal/Oil | FL | 4,300 |
| 3 | Palo Verde Nuclear Plant | Nuclear | AZ | 3,937 |
| 4 | West County Energy Center | Natural Gas | FL | 3,750 |
| 5 | W A Parish Generating Station | Coal/Natural Gas | TX | 3,664 |

| RANK | PLANT | FUEL | STATE | CAPACITY (MW) |
|---|---|---|---|---|
| 6 | Plant Scherer | Coal/Oil/Natural Gas | GA | 3,520 |
| 7 | Plant Bowen | Coal | GA | 3,499 |
| 8 | Wansley Power Station | Coal | GA | 3,437 |
| 9 | Gibson Power Station | Coal | IN | 3,340 |
| 10 | Turkey Point Station | Nuclear | FL | 3,322 |
| 11 | Browns Ferry Station | Nuclear | AL | 3,309 |
| 12 | Monroe Generating Station | Coal | MI | 3,293 |
| 13 | Crystal River Energy Complex | Nuclear | FL | 3,151 |
| 14 | Bath County Pumped Storage Station | Hydro | VA | 3,003 |
| 15 | John E Amos Power Station | Coal | WV | 2,933 |
| 16 | James H Miller Power Station | Coal | AL | 2,822 |
| 17 | Manatee Power Station | Oil/Natural Gas | FL | 2,735 |
| 18 | James M. Barry Generating Plant | Coal/Natural Gas | AL | 2,671 |
| 19 | General James M Gavin Power Plant | Coal | OH | 2,640 |
| 20 | Chief Joseph Dam Power Station | Hydro | WA | 2,620 |
| 21 | Rockport Power Station | Coal | IN | 2,610 |
| 22 | Cumberland Power Station | Coal | TN | 2,600 |
| 23 | South Texas Project | Nuclear | TX | 2,560 |
| 24 | Roxboro Power Station | Coal | NC | 2,558 |
| 25 | Paradise Power Station | Coal | KY | 2,558 |
| 26 | Oconee Station | Nuclear | SC | 2,538 |
| 27 | Moss Landing Power Plant | Natural Gas | CA | 2,529 |
| 28 | Robert Moses Niagara Power Station | Hydro | NY | 2,515 |
| 29 | Bruce Mansfield Power Station | Coal | PA | 2,510 |
| 30 | W H Sammis Power Station | Coal | OH | 2,456 |
| 31 | Susquehanna Station | Nuclear | PA | 2,450 |
| 32 | Martin Lake Power Station | Coal | TX | 2,425 |
| 33 | Labadie Power Station | Coal | MO | 2,407 |
| 34 | Comanche Peak Station | Nuclear | TX | 2,406 |
| 35 | Salem Generating Station | Nuclear | NJ | 2,370 |
| 36 | Cross Generating Station | Coal | SC | 2,350. |
| 37 | Johnsonville Station | Coal | TN | 2,341 |
| 38 | Braidwood Generation Station | Nuclear | IL | 2,330 |
| 39 | J M Stuart Power Station | Coal | OH | 2,316. |
| 40 | Vogtle Station | Nuclear | GA | 2,302 |
| 41 | Byron Generating Station | Nuclear | IL | 2,300 |
| 42 | Sequoyah Station | Nuclear | TN | 2,277 |
| 43 | Sherburne County Station | Coal | MN | 2,275 |
| 44 | Limerick Station | Nuclear | PA | 2,264 |
| 45 | Fort Myers Power Station | Natural Gas | FL | 2,260 |
| 46 | Catawba Station | Nuclear | SC | 2,258 |
| 47 | Navajo Generating Station | Coal | AZ | 2,250 |
| 48 | Peach Bottom Station | Nuclear | PA | 2,244 |

| RANK | PLANT | FUEL | STATE | CAPACITY (MW) |
| --- | --- | --- | --- | --- |
| 49 | Diablo Canyon Power Plant | Nuclear | CA | 2,240 |
| 50 | LaSalle Generating Station | Nuclear | IL | 2,238 |

Since a major consideration in the continual operation of any of these power plants is a constant supply of fuel used to generate the plant, any type of disaster disrupting the supply of fuel could compromise the operation of the electric plants. Although all electrical generating stations across the country could be destroyed or damaged by natural disasters, a significant threat to our electrical grid comes from the possibility of terrorist attacks or even a nuclear war or land invasion.

The map below shows some of the *major* electrical power stations across the country.

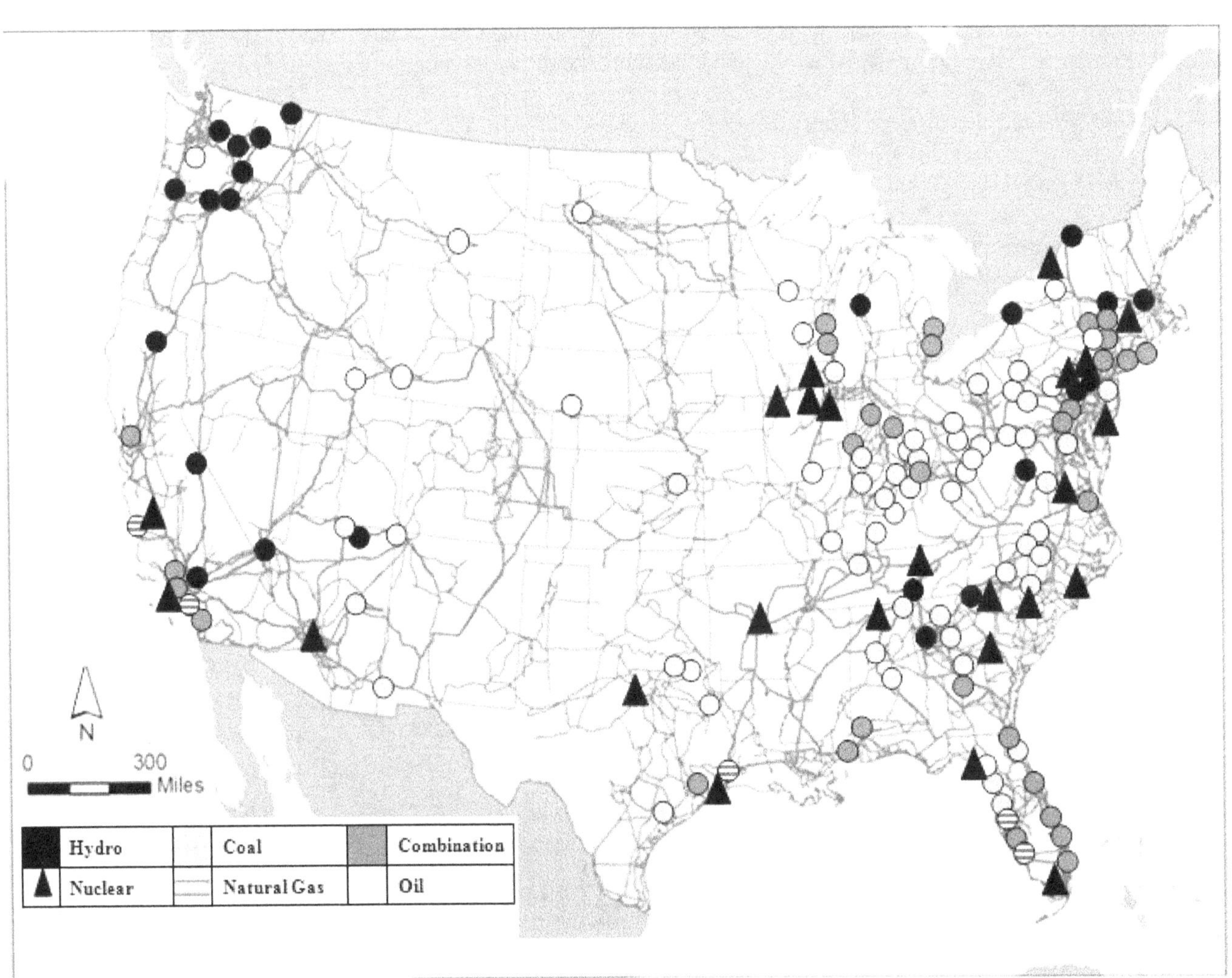


One of the principal national security issues at this time is the collapse of the electrical power grid - caused by either a natural disaster or a manmade terrorist act. In most cases, terrorists are interested in destroying critical and numerous buildings, structures, dams, bridges, power stations and population. But in the case of the electrical grid, a terrorist organization, rouge country or enemy nation would indeed focus on the destruction and/or damage to our electrical grid.

If you bring down the "power" of the United States - you have a good chance in bringing down the country as well. Electricity is the means by which we maintain our high standard of living. All citizens should recognize the vulnerability of the electrical grid across the nation and how susceptible these electrical power plants are to shortages in fuel and natural disasters but to manmade threats as well. Therefore, it is vital families **plan and protect** by purchasing, gathering and storing emergency supplies to support family members during a complete electrical shutdown of our power grid.

## NUCLEAR MELTDOWN

Nuclear power plants use heat generated from nuclear fission to convert water into steam which then powers generators to produce electricity.  Nuclear power plants operate in most states in the country and produce about twenty percent of the nation's power.  According to the United States Department of Energy, nearly three million Americans live within ten miles of an operating nuclear power plant.

All local and state governments, federal agencies, and electric utilities should have emergency response plans in the event of a nuclear power plant incident.  The plans generally define two emergency planning zones as follows: (1) zone covers an area within a ten-mile radius of the plant where people could be harmed by direct radiation exposure, and (2) zone covers a broader area, usually up to a fifty-mile radius from the plant where radioactive materials could contaminate water supplies, food crops and livestock.  <u>That does not mean in any way these plans are efficient or realistic</u>.  In fact, depending on when the plans were created, they could be outdated and may not include current factors or issues into the plan.  For example, in March of 2011, the country of Japan experienced a serious earthquake and tsunami where several nuclear power plants received significant damage.  It became obvious government agencies and the utility companies were <u>not</u> prepared or equipped to handle the disaster scenario of a possible nuclear meltdown.

In order to understand the disaster significance of a nuclear meltdown, it is wise to identify three periods which are common to all nuclear incident sequences: *initiation*, *intermediate* and *recovery* phases.  Although these phases cannot be represented by a precise period of time, they do provide a framework for emergency planning by family members.

- The **initiation** phase is the period at the beginning of a nuclear incident when the actual release of airborne materials has stopped and <u>immediate</u> decisions for protective actions are required based on the status of the nuclear facility (or other incident site) and the prospect for worsening conditions.  This phase may last for hours to several days.

- The **intermediate** phase is the period after the nuclear power plant and harmful releases are under control and <u>reliable</u> environmental data is available to make decisions on additional protective actions.  This phase extends until these additional protective actions are terminated, may overlap the initiation and recovery phases and may last for weeks to many months.

- The **recovery** phase is the period when recovery action to reduce radiation levels for unrestricted use in the environment to acceptable levels begins and ends when all recovery actions have been completed.  This period may take months to many years.

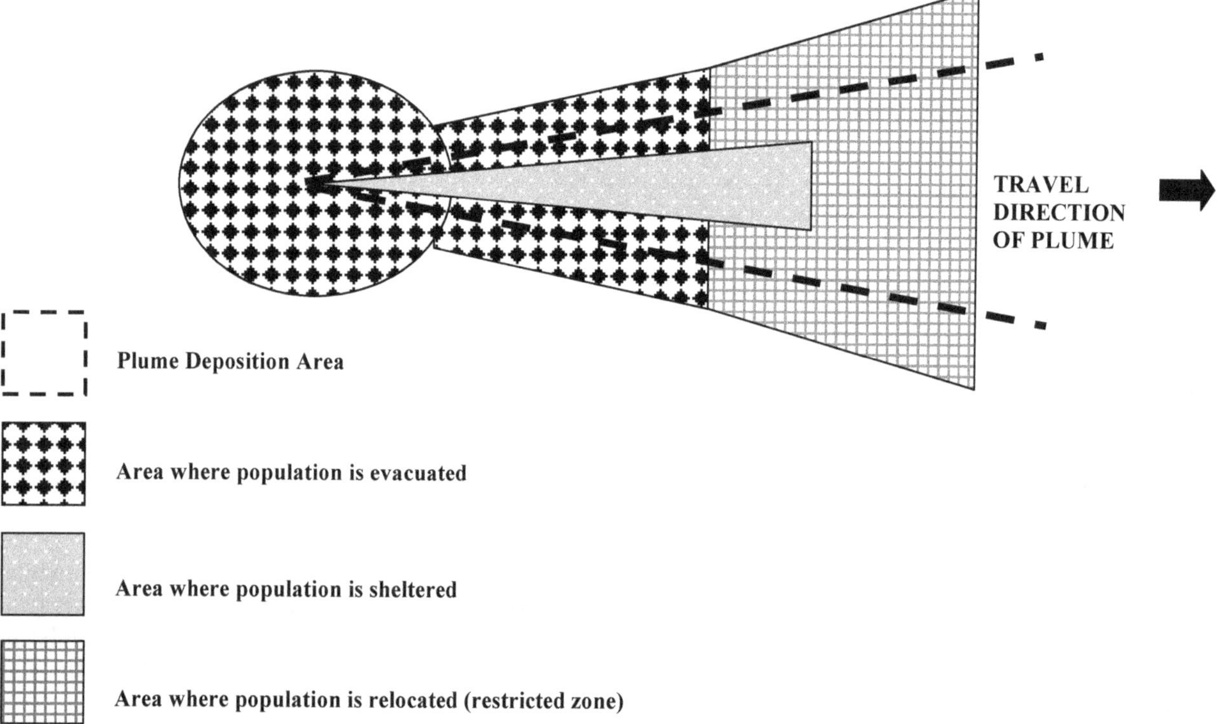

# INITIATION PHASE

During this early phase, the *first* exposure from airborne release of radioactive material will often be <u>direct exposure</u> by an overhead plume of radioactive materials carried by the wind. This plume contains radioactive gases, iodine and particulate materials depending on the nuclear source and conditions of the incident. In the immediate vicinity of the disaster, these materials would expose the entire body to gamma rays or radioactive particles.

A *second* exposure occurs when people are directly immersed in a radioactive plume, the radioactive material is <u>inhaled</u> and the skin and clothes are contaminated. These inhaled radioactive materials may remain in the lungs or move through the bloodstream to other organs. Many radioactive particles entering the bloodstream tend to be predominantly concentrated in a single organ. For example, if inhaled, a significant amount will rapidly move to the thyroid gland where much of the iodine will be deposited and most of the radiation dose will be delivered. Although particles deposited on the skin and clothing could be significant, it will be less in terms of cancer risk than a dose from inhalation, <u>providing</u> family members take early protective actions such as washing the exposed skin and changing contaminated clothing.

A *third* exposure occurs when the plume passes over an area and radioactive materials settle on the ground and other surfaces. Family members remaining in the area will continue to be exposed through ingestion, external radiation, and through inhalation of radioactive materials. The total dose from such deposited materials may be more dangerous because the term of exposure can be much longer than direct exposure from the plume.

The principal protective actions for use during the initiation phase are *evacuation* from the area to avoid or reduce high-level and short-term exposure from the plume or deposited activity OR *sheltering* inside a structure with doors and windows closed and exterior ventilation systems shut off to protect family members from exposure to direct radiation and inhalation from an airborne plume.

## <u>Evacuation</u>

When completed <u>before</u> the arrival of the radioactive plume, evacuation will provide total protection from any airborne release. Even if evacuation coincides with or follows plume passage, a large reduction of exposure may be possible. As a general rule, if family members receive a radiation dose of 1 REM, evacuation should be initiated.

There are some general guidelines regarding evacuation which may be useful for planning purposes as follows:

- *Advanced planning* is essential to identify potential problems that may occur during an evacuation.

- A place of refuge a long distance from the disaster site such as a cabin or the use of a motor home, camper, or trailer should be designated if family members are forced to evacuate the home. This alternate site should be <u>fully stocked</u> to support family members for the entire time of the disaster, including food, water, sanitary and medical supplies, fuel, money, documentation and other essential items.

- All family members should have their own individual evacuation kits.

- Plan on using personal transportation (including walking) or incorporate plans to use public transportation.

- Make arrangements for pets and livestock.

- Make sure arrangements are made for elderly, handicapped or disabled family members.

- Family members should *plan in advance* to avoid any possibilities of stress or alarm when evacuating the danger zone.

## <u>Shelter-In-Place</u>

Sheltering can be used as a protective measure against exposure to an <u>airborne plume</u>. A proper shelter could provide protection equal to or greater than evacuation and is less expensive and disruptive than evacuation. Sheltering can be rapidly implemented and may be the only choice if evacuation is impeded by health constraints or severe environmental conditions such as weather or floods.  However, sheltering is <u>not</u> appropriate where high doses of radiation are projected or for exposure lasting longer than two complete air exchanges in the shelter.

A shelter at the home may be more effective against inhalation of radioactive particulates whereas a large structure such as a shopping center, school, church or commercial building would generally provide greater protection against gamma radiation.  The degree of protection provided by structures is governed by the use of structural components and building materials such as the mass of walls and ceilings, and by the outside/inside air exchange rates to reduce gamma radiation.  If external dose from the plume or from deposited materials is the controlling factor, shelter construction and shelter size are the most important considerations and ventilation control and filtering are less important.

| STRUCTURE | PERCENT EFFECTIVENESS |
|---|---|
| *Wood frame house (first floor)* | 10 |
| *Wood frame house (basement)* | 40 |
| *Masonry house* | 40 |
| *Large Building* | 80 or better |

SOURCE:  Federal Emergency Management Administration

> **One of the major problems with sheltering is families may not leave the shelter as soon as the plume passes and as a result will receive exposure from radioactive gases trapped inside the home.**

According to FEMA, the main factors that reduce whole body exposure are:

- Wall materials, thickness and size of structure
- Number of overhead stories
- Use of a central location within the structure

When the primary exposure is inhalation, consideration should be given to the following:

- Ventilation control is essential for effective sheltering
- Reduce air exchange rates by sealing cracks and openings with cloth, weather stripping and tape
- Use wet towels, dust masks or handkerchiefs as a mask to filter the inhaled air
- After plume passage, open shelter to reduce airborne activity being trapped inside
- Administer potassium iodide as a thyroid-blocking agent directly *before* or *after* exposure

> **When sheltering in place and after confirmation the plume has passed, all family members should leave high exposure areas as soon as possible to avoid exposure of deposited radioactive material.**

## INTERMEDIATE PHASE

Contrary to the initiation phase when decisions have to be made quickly, the intermediate phase allows for decisions and actions to be delayed because of the reduced level of urgency for implementation of protective measures.  In some cases, families may have been prematurely evacuated and will be able to return home.  There may be groups who sheltered in place but because of high radiation doses, must now leave the area.  Decisions will now be made on whether specific areas or properties will be decontaminated and reoccupied, or condemned and the occupants permanently relocated.

The principal danger to family members occupying contaminated locations will be <u>external</u> exposure of the whole body by gamma radiation from deposited radioactive materials and <u>internal</u> exposure from the inhalation of radioactive materials.  For reactor incidents, external gamma radiation will be the dominant source.  Other potentially significant exposure includes beta radiation from surface contamination and direct ingestion of contaminated soil.

The two types of protective actions during the intermediate phase are *relocation* of people (households) from contaminated areas to avoid chronic radiation exposure and *decontamination* for protection from external body exposure due to deposit and inhalation of radioactive materials.

## Relocation

Relocation is the most effective protective action, but it is also the most costly and disruptive to individuals involved in leaving the area and is warranted only when the radiation dose is greater than 2 REM in the first year. After the restricted zone is established, families would more than likely be given permission to reenter the restricted zone under controlled conditions and secure their property and belongings. There may also be possible restrictions on the use of food and water due to contamination.

## Decontamination

As part of an extensive decontamination process, family members would need to establish a regiment of bathing themselves, pets, farm animals and livestock, changing and washing clothes, washing other exposed surfaces such as vehicles, machinery, equipment and any residential property, personal property or belongings that may have been contaminated. After the initial restriction zone is established, citizens would reenter the area for recovery activities, retrieval of property, security patrol, operation of vital services and in some cases, the care and feeding of pets, farm animals and livestock.

Simple dose reduction techniques could be used by persons receiving less than 2 REM such as (1) scrubbing and flushing surfaces, (2) soaking or plowing the soil, (3) removing and disposing of small areas of soil found to be highly contaminated, (4) spending more time in lower exposure rate areas, and (5) removal, disposal and replacement of contaminated surfaces. <u>Decontamination of areas outside the restricted area may be required during the first year.</u>

## RECOVERY PHASE

The recovery phase may take months to many years because so many populations (human, animal and plant), ecosystems, businesses and enterprises can be adversely affected by the meltdown and resulting radiation. There can be long-lasting affects on animals, plants, water supplies, agriculture, food supplies, invertebrates, aquatic organisms, marine and fresh water mammals, fish, forests, oceans and mountains.

The urban and rural communities, farms and manufacturing sites close to the meltdown could be compromised for long periods of time, and the population in the area would immediately feel the affect of unemployment, health problems and concerns in getting safe food and water for the family.

Many agriculture crops could be completely or partly excluded from cultivation and the ground in surrounding farms would need to take on extensive and expensive countermeasures to return the soil to a healthy condition. The economic spiral would continue to be felt by ranchers who raise cattle, sheep, horses, goats, chickens and pigs.

The massive financial implications to the government and individuals could be so overwhelming the entire local economic system may be at risk. The best example of demonstrating the consequences that occur with a nuclear meltdown is to merely utter two words – ***Chernobyl*** and ***Japan***.

The use of stored animal feed and uncontaminated water to limit the uptake of radioactive materials by domestic animals in the food chain can be applicable in any of the phases.

An effective plan to avoid nuclear contamination includes an (1) evacuation plan, (2) communication plan (between members) on how family members would communicate with one another in the event of a meltdown, and (3) logistical plan on where to meet and what to do based on possible scenarios and storage of appropriate emergency supplies.

All adult family members should understand the concepts and operations involved with nuclear power plants in their region including how they are operated, possible dangers and the procedures and plans outlined by the government agencies and plant officials in dealing with a nuclear meltdown or other situation that may occur at the plant.

In the United States, the state of *Illinois* leads the country with eleven nuclear plants followed closely by *Pennsylvania* with nine plants.  These nuclear plants are susceptible to both natural disasters and manmade dangerous events - a meltdown would have widespread consequences to the environment, the economy and the health and well-being of human, plant and animal populations.

The table below lists *major* nuclear plants and approximate population with specific radius miles from the plant.

| STATE | CITY | NAME OF REACTOR | POPULATION WITHIN "X" RADIUS MILES | | | | |
|---|---|---|---|---|---|---|---|
| | | | 0 | 5 | 10 | 20 | 50 |
| ALABAMA | Athens | *Browns Ferry* | 21,897 | 5,246 | 39,930 | 196,318 | 977,941 |
| | Columbia | *Farley* | 2,053 | 1,931 | 11,842 | 100,312 | 421,374 |
| ARIZONA | Wintersburg | *Palo Verde* | 136 | 808 | 4,255 | 42,427 | 1,990,846 |
| ARKANSAS | London | *Arkansas Nuclear* | 2,850 | 12,440 | 44,138 | 90,215 | 308,219 |
| CALIFORNIA | Avila Beach | *Diablo Canyon* | 1,627 | 1,622 | 26,123 | 144,068 | 465,521 |
| | San Clemente | *San Onofre* | 63,773 | 18,829 | 92,687 | 775,054 | 8,460,508 |
| CONNECTICUT | Waterford | *Millstone* | 16,288 | 48,608 | 123,482 | 317,466 | 2,996,756 |
| FLORIDA | Crystal River | *Crystal River* | 3,108 | 5,435 | 20,695 | 111,945 | 1,046,741 |
| | Homestead | *Turkey Point* | 60,512 | 10,322 | 161,555 | 698,751 | 3,476,981 |
| | Jensen Beach | *St. Lucie* | 26,342 | 30,548 | 206,595 | 420,273 | 1,271,947 |
| GEORGIA | Baxley | *Hatch* | 4,400 | 1,901 | 11,061 | 62,294 | 424,741 |
| | Waynesboro | *Vogtle* | 14,135 | 1,395 | 5,845 | 45,245 | 726,640 |
| ILLINOIS | Braceville | *Braidwood* | 793 | 14,887 | 33,910 | 192,904 | 4,976,020 |
| | Byron | *Byron* | 3,753 | 10,478 | 25,679 | 249,750 | 1,273,771 |
| | Clinton | *Clinton* | 7,225 | 1,234 | 14,677 | 67,764 | 813,658 |
| | Cordova | *Quad Cities* | 845 | 5,460 | 34,350 | 283,578 | 655,207 |
| | Marseilles | *LaSalle* | 5,094 | 2,924 | 17,643 | 107,520 | 1,902,775 |
| | Morris | *Dresden* | 13,636 | 20,302 | 83,049 | 490,473 | 7,305,482 |
| IOWA | Palo | *Duane Arnold* | 1,026 | 9,696 | 107,880 | 226,627 | 658,634 |
| KANSAS | Burlington | *Wolf Creek* | 2,674 | 1,477 | 5,466 | 12,979 | 176,656 |
| LOUISIANA | Killona | *Waterford* | 800 | 12,266 | 75,538 | 373,131 | 1,969,431 |
| | St. Francisville | *River Bend* | 5,930 | 5,188 | 23,466 | 124,642 | 951,103 |
| MARYLAND | Lusby | *Calvert Cliffs* | 19,442 | 13,197 | 48,798 | 181,324 | 2,890,702 |
| MASSACHUSETTS | Plymouth | *Pilgrim* | 56,468 | 20,890 | 75,835 | 307,399 | 4,737,792 |
| MICHIGAN | Bridgman | *Donald Cook* | 4,439 | 14,862 | 54,638 | 154,843 | 1,225,096 |
| | Monroe | *Fermi* | 20,733 | 16,109 | 92,377 | 420,241 | 4,799,526 |
| | Covert | *Palisades* | 2,462 | 6,330 | 28,644 | 113,037 | 1,326,618 |
| MINNESOTA | Monticello | *Monticello* | 12,759 | 18,956 | 62,976 | 237,360 | 2,977,934 |
| | Welch | *Prairie Island* | 1,863 | 5,931 | 27,996 | 127,891 | 2,945,237 |
| MISSISSIPPI | Port Gibson | *Grand Gulf* | 5,914 | 1,474 | 6,572 | 23,221 | 321,400 |
| MISSOURI | Fulton | *Calloway* | 12,790 | 1,375 | 10,092 | 49,917 | 546,292 |

| STATE | CITY | NAME OF REACTOR | POPULATION WITHIN "X" RADIUS MILES | | | | |
|---|---|---|---|---|---|---|---|
| | | | 0 | 5 | 10 | 20 | 50 |
| NEBRASKA | Brownville | *Cooper* | 132 | 744 | 4,414 | 16,056 | 163,610 |
| | Ft. Calhoun | *Ft. Calhoun* | 2,085 | 8,346 | 20,639 | 386,061 | 953,410 |
| NEW HAMPSHIRE | Seabrook | *Seabrook* | 8,323 | 40,096 | 118,747 | 464,872 | 4,315,571 |
| NEW JERSEY | Forked River | *Oyster Creek* | 5,244 | 36,916 | 133,609 | 485,719 | 4,482,261 |
| | Hancocks Bridge | *Hope Creek* | 124 | 5,294 | 53,811 | 571,729 | 5,523,010 |
| | Hancocks Bridge | *Salem* | 124 | 5,237 | 52,091 | 545,820 | 5,482,329 |
| NEW YORK | Buchanan | *Indian Point* | 2,230 | 78,806 | 272,539 | 1,187,284 | 17,220,895 |
| | Ontario | *Ginna* | 10,136 | 12,581 | 66,847 | 593,425 | 1,269,589 |
| | Scriba | *FitzPatrick* | 6,840 | 4,850 | 35,136 | 100,830 | 909,798 |
| | Scriba | *Nine Mile Point* | 6,840 | 5,565 | 35,631 | 100,372 | 909,523 |
| NORTH CAROLINA | Huntersville | *McGuire* | 46,773 | 50,660 | 199,869 | 1,013,135 | 2,850,782 |
| | New Hill | *Shearon Harris* | 1,681 | 9,220 | 96,401 | 615,304 | 2,562,573 |
| | South Port | *Brunswick* | 16,126 | 11,762 | 36,413 | 174,599 | 468,953 |
| OHIO | Oak Harbor | *Davis Besse* | 9,416 | 3,426 | 18,635 | 106,294 | 1,791,856 |
| | Perry | *Perry* | 36,058 | 20,647 | 83,410 | 281,831 | 2,281,531 |
| PENNSYLVANIA | Delta | *Peach Bottom* | 728 | 10,189 | 46,536 | 482,686 | 5,526,342 |
| | Limerick | *Limerick* | 18,074 | 91,939 | 252,196 | 1,168,871 | 8,027,924 |
| | Middleton | *Three Mile Island* | 22,314 | 42,581 | 211,261 | 880,820 | 2,803,322 |
| | Salem | *Susquehanna* | 4,271 | 11,842 | 54,842 | 332,040 | 1,765,761 |
| | Shippingport | *Beaver Valley* | 198 | 15,149 | 114,514 | 450,649 | 3,140,766 |
| SOUTH CAROLINA | Hartsville | *Robinson* | 7,764 | 11,041 | 32,675 | 92,365 | 893,536 |
| | Jenkensville | *Summer* | 677 | 2,477 | 17,599 | 162,243 | 1,187,553 |
| | Seneca | *Oconee* | 35,003 | 119,51 | 66,307 | 207,938 | 1,404,690 |
| | York | *Catawba* | 29,490 | 40,896 | 213,407 | 921,811 | 2,559,394 |
| TENNESSEE | Soddy-Daisy | *Sequoyah* | 12,714 | 26,307 | 99,664 | 473,436 | 1,079,868 |
| | Spring City | *Watts Bar* | 8,855 | 4,276 | 18,452 | 110,594 | 1,186,648 |
| TEXAS | Bay City | *South Texas* | 17,614 | 1,136 | 5,651 | 29,344 | 254,049 |
| | Glen Rose | *Comanche Peak* | 2,444 | 5,764 | 30,653 | 74,272 | 1,755,258 |
| VERMONT | Vernon | *Vermont Yankee* | 2,206 | 11,181 | 35,284 | 147,109 | 1,533,472 |
| VIRGINIA | Louisa | *North Anna* | 12,464 | 4,994 | 21,396 | 148,048 | 1,912,015 |
| | Surry | *Surry* | 2,551 | 13,518 | 127,041 | 440,190 | 2,292,642 |
| WASHINGTON | Richland | *Columbia* | 48,058 | 279 | 10,055 | 169,362 | 445,416 |

| STATE | CITY | NAME OF REACTOR | POPULATION WITHIN "X" RADIUS MILES | | | | |
|---|---|---|---|---|---|---|---|
| | | | 0 | 5 | 10 | 20 | 50 |
| WISCONSIN | Kewaunee | *Kewaunee* | 6,276 | 2,557 | 10,292 | 78,879 | 776,954 |
| | Two Rivers | *Point Beach* | 11,712 | 2,730 | 19,975 | 81,186 | 777,556 |

SOURCE: United States Department of Energy, Nuclear Regulatory Commission

**IT IS IMPORTANT FOR FAMILY MEMBERS WHO LIVE NEAR A NUCLEAR REACTOR TO BECOME INFORMED AS TO WHAT ACTION TO TAKE IN THE EVENT OF A NUCLEAR DISASTER. CONTACT LOCAL OFFICIALS AND FIND OUT WHAT PLAN IS IN PLACE FOR EVACUATION OF THE SURROUNDING POPULATION.**

The following map outlines the locations of most nuclear reactors located in the continental United States. As you can quickly observe, a majority of the sites are located in the eastern and mid regions of the country and many of these sites are in the direct path of several common natural disasters including earthquakes, tornadoes and hurricanes.

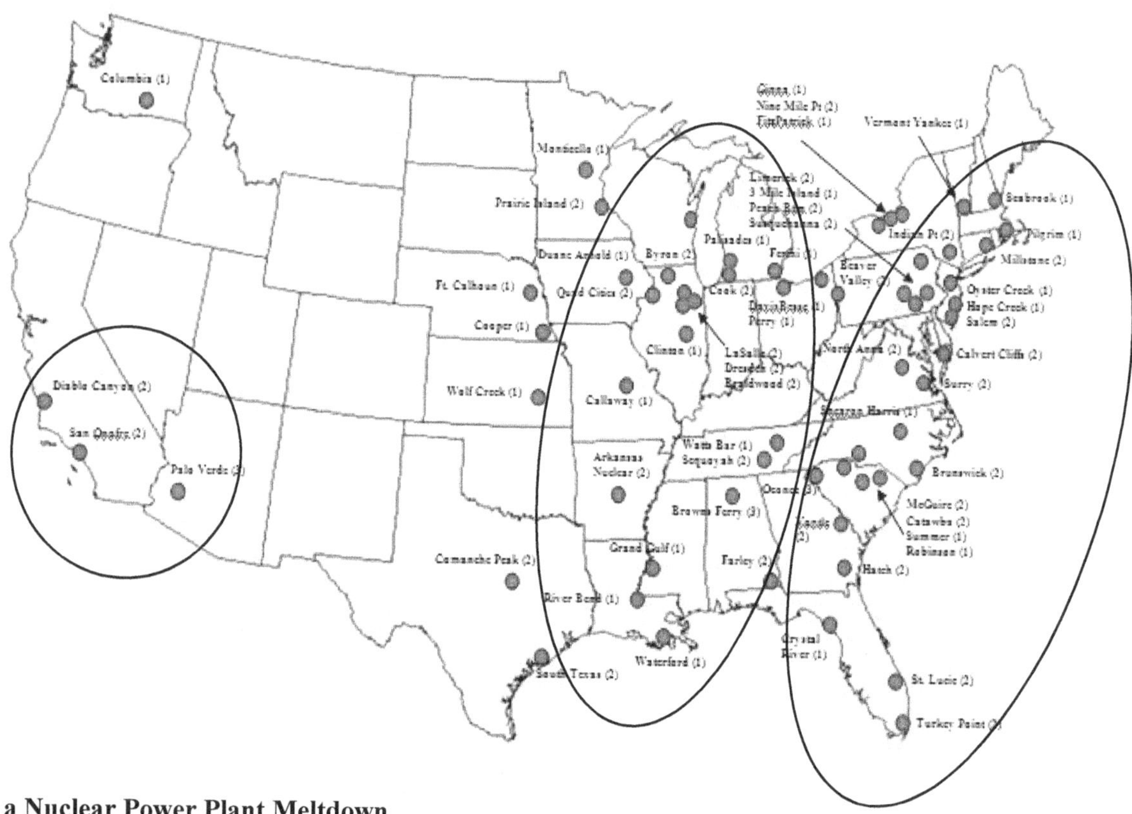


## Before a Nuclear Power Plant Meltdown

Gather public emergency information materials from the power company operating the local nuclear power plant or the local emergency services office. If you live within ten miles of the power plant, you should receive the materials yearly from the utility company or state and local government. Make sure the family has a comprehensive emergency evacuation plan that includes all family members, pets and livestock. Living near a nuclear power plant poses a serious threat if a natural or manmade disaster occurs causing the plant to become unstable. It is critical that evacuation kits are fully stocked and ready for evacuation.

## During a Nuclear Power Plant Meltdown

If an accident at a nuclear power plant were to release radiation in the area of the home, local authorities should activate warning sirens or another approved alert method and provide instructions to citizens through the Emergency Alert System (EAS) on local television and radio stations. If advised to remain indoors, turn off the air conditioner, ventilation fans, furnace and other air intakes.  Place heavy, dense material between family members and pets to shield from the radiation source.  Go to a basement or other underground area.

Unfortunately, recent past history has shown politicians and government officials are not <u>willing</u> or <u>able</u> to determine the proper response for citizens in the event of a nuclear disaster.  The decision to advise the public to take action to protect them from a nuclear incident involves a complex judgment in which the risk avoided by the protective action must be weighed in the context of the risks involved in taking the action.  If you even <u>suspect</u> a local nuclear plant has been compromised in <u>any</u> way – immediately evacuate the area – regardless of the claim of so-called experts or government employees.  Corporate executives and politicians in the government LIE and knowledgeable scientists and experts are forced to LIE by corporate executives and politicians.  Secure the home, arrange for livestock, gather family members and pets and evacuate the area.  Keep car windows and vents closed and use re-circulating air.  Stay away from the incident zone.

### After a Nuclear Power Plant Meltdown

Do <u>not</u> return to the home until <u>legitimate</u> and <u>trusted</u> sources have indicated the area is safe.  Remain away from the incident zone until the *scientific* community has analyzed the data and concluded there is no danger to human and animal life.  Family members must recognize it could take weeks, months or even years before the area would be safe to inhabit again.

## EXPLOSIONS

Terrorists have frequently used explosive devices as one of their most common and lethal weapons.  It is relatively simple to learn how to make explosive devices - the information is readily available in books, the Internet and other information sources.  Explosive devices can be highly portable by using vehicles and humans as a means of transport and they are easily detonated from remote locations or by suicide bombers.

### Bomb Threat

If at work and you receive a telephone bomb threat, get as much information from the caller as possible.  Try to ask the following questions:

- **When is the bomb going to explode?**
- **Where is it right now?**
- **What does it look like?**
- **What kind of bomb is it?**
- **What will cause it to explode?**
- **Did you place the bomb?**

> **Keep the caller on the line and record everything that is said by the caller.  Notify the police and building management immediately.**

### Suspicious Packages

Terrorists have been known to send bombs and other explosive or hazardous materials through the mail – generally to a government agency, corporate building or private individuals.  Be cautious of suspicious packages and letters that could contain explosives and chemical or biological agents.

Some typical characteristics of envelopes and parcels that <u>may</u> be dangerous are as follows:

- Addressed to individual no longer with organization or otherwise outdated
- City or state in the postmark does not match return address
- Excessive postage or packaging material (masking tape and string)
- Hand-written or poorly typed addresses
- Inappropriate or unusual labeling
- Incorrect titles or titles without a name
- Lopsided or oddly shaped package
- Marked with restrictive endorsements e.g. "Personal," "Confidential," or "Do Not X-ray"
- Marked with threatening language

- Misspelled words
- No return address or a return address that cannot be verified as legitimate
- Not addressed to a specific person
- Protruding wires or aluminum foil
- Strange odors or stains
- Unexpected delivery or from someone unfamiliar
- Unusual weight given size of item

With suspicious envelopes and packages that could contain biological and chemical agents, **the unfortunate individual who handles or opens the package and those persons who are in the room at the time should not leave the area**.

By doing so, the contaminant could easily be spread to other persons in the building. Instead, place the package in a plastic bag or some other type of container to prevent leakage of contents. If you do not have a container, then cover the package with anything available e.g. clothing, paper, trash can, and do move as far away as possible (while still remaining in the room) from the package.

Close all outside doors and windows. Attempt to communicate the situation to someone outside of the area using a phone, a written note or a loud voice. Keep hands and arms away from face, refrain from eating or drinking and if possible wash hands with soap and water to prevent spreading any powder to the face.

### Before an Explosion

Make sure your employer or building management personnel has personal medical information and contact information on file. Understand the company plan to deal with explosions and what is expected of you.

### During an Explosion

During an explosion, attempt to get under a sturdy table or desk in order to avoid falling debris and objects.

### After an Explosion

After the explosion, leave the building, watch for weakened floors and stairways and check for fire and other hazards. Upon exiting the building, do not use elevators. Do not stop to retrieve personal possessions or make phone calls. Once out of the building, do not stand in front of windows, glass doors or other potentially hazardous areas and move away from sidewalks or streets to be used by emergency officials or others still exiting the building.

If trapped in debris, use a flashlight or whistle (if possible) to signal your location to rescuers or tap on a pipe or wall so rescuers can hear where you are located. Shout only as a last resort since shouting can cause a person to inhale dangerous amounts of dust. Attempt to cover the nose and mouth with cotton material and try to breathe through the material. Avoid unnecessary movement to avoid kicking up dust.

There can be a significant number of casualties and/or damage to buildings and infrastructure. There will be increased law enforcement following a terrorist attack due to the event's criminal nature. Health and mental health resources in the affected communities can be strained to their limits and may even be overwhelmed.

As with all terrorist acts, there will be extensive media coverage, strong public fear and international implications and consequences that can continue for a prolonged period. Businesses, government offices and schools may be closed and there may be restrictions on domestic and international travel. Depending on the extent of the damage, clean-up could take weeks, months or even years.

## BIOLOGICAL THREATS

Biological <u>agents</u> are organisms or toxins that kill or incapacitate people, animals, livestock and crops and a biological <u>attack</u> is a deliberate release of germs or other biological substances that cause illness and death. Biological <u>warfare</u> (BW) or germ warfare is bacteria, viruses, fungi, or biological toxins used to kill or incapacitate humans, animals or plants as an act of war. Biological <u>weapons</u> are living organisms or viruses that reproduce or replicate within their host victims. Entomological (insect) warfare is also considered a type of biological warfare.

There are three basic groups of biological agents used as weapons - *bacteria*, *viruses* and *toxins*. Most biological agents are difficult to grow and maintain because many quickly break down when exposed to sunlight and other environmental factors, while others, such as anthrax spores, are very long lived.

Biological agents are dispersed using four delivery methods as follows:

- **Aerosols** - dispersed into the air forming a fine mist that may drift for miles
- **Animals** - spread by insects and animals e.g. fleas, mice, flies, bees, mosquitoes and livestock
- **Food and Water** - spread by food and water sources
- **Person-to-Person** - spread by humans e.g. smallpox, plague, and the Lassa viruses

Biological weapons are employed to gain a strategic or tactical advantage over an enemy either by threat or by actual deployment. These agents may be lethal or non-lethal, and could be targeted against a single individual, a group of people or even an entire population. They could be developed, acquired, stockpiled or deployed by countries, nation states or by non-national groups such as a terrorist organization. A biological attack could take place on the street, in the subway, public transportation, or at a stadium or shopping mall.

The **offensive** use of biological warfare, including mass production, stockpiling and use of biological weapons was outlawed by the Biological Weapons Convention (BWC) in 1972 to prevent biological attacks resulting in civilian fatalities and disruption to economic and societal infrastructure. However, a nation or group that selects to produce and threatens to use such a weapon can pose a real threat to other countries around the world.

As a **tactical** weapon for military use, the difficulty of using biological weapons is the weaponization, storage and delivery of the biological weapon to a vulnerable target. In addition to targeting the human population, biological warfare can target plants to destroy crops or defoliate vegetation, target fisheries, water-based vegetation, and attack animals to eliminate animal resources for transportation and food.

### Before a Biological Threat

A biological attack may or may not be immediately obvious to the general population. For example, with the anthrax mailings, local health care workers reported a pattern of unusual illness and a wave of sick people seeking emergency medical attention. Most citizens will learn of the danger through an emergency radio or television broadcast or some other signal used in the community.

**It is extremely difficult if not impossible to** *prepare in advance* **for the possibility of a biological attack**. Children and older adults are particularly vulnerable to biological agents. The best defense - have the home stocked with emergency supplies, try to avoid public areas where large numbers of people regularly congregate, keep immunizations up to date and always carry a high-quality dust mask in the purse or briefcase.

As a precaution, consider installing a High Efficiency Particulate Air (HEPA) filter in the furnace return duct of the home and homes of family members. These filters remove particles in the 0.3 to 10 micron range and will filter out most biological agents entering the house. If there is no central heating or cooling system in the house, a stand-alone portable HEPA filter could be used.

> *The scenarios of biological and chemical warfare painted by the American media during the months after September 11 only betray the inability of the government to determine the magnitude of the danger.*
>
> - **Jurgen Habermas**

### During a Biological Threat

In the event of a biological attack, public health officials may not immediately be able to provide information since it will take time to determine the type and severity of the illness and treatment. Family members should watch television broadcasts, listen to the radio or check the Internet for official news and information including signs and symptoms of the disease, areas in danger, if medications or vaccinations are being distributed and where family members can seek medical attention.

If exposed to a biological agent, protect yourself by covering mouth and nose with a high-quality dust mask or layers of fabric that can filter the air but still allow breathing.  Examples include two to three layers of cotton such as a T-shirt, handkerchief, towel, tissues or paper towels.  <u>It is very important that most of the air you breathe comes *through* a mask or cloth and not around it</u>.

Adults should do whatever they can to make the best fit possible for children.  There are also a variety of face masks readily available in hardware stores and are rated based on how small a particle they can filter in an industrial setting.  Simple cloth face masks can filter some of the airborne contaminants or germs you might breathe into your body, but will probably not protect from chemical gases.  If possible, remove and bag your clothes and personal items and follow official instructions for disposal of contaminated items.

If a family member develops any of the symptoms below while a biological alert is in force, keep them separated from others and practice good hygiene and cleanliness to avoid spreading germs.

- Cough
- Decreases in activity
- Diarrhea
- Earache
- Headache
- Loss of appetite
- Loss of energy
- Nausea and vomiting
- Pale or flushed face
- Rash or infection of the skin
- Red or pink eyes
- Sore throat
- Stomach ache
- Temperature of more than 100 degrees
- Thick discharge from nose

> *There is such a thing as legitimate warfare: war has its laws; there are things which may fairly be done, and things which may not be done.*
>
> **-John Henry Newman**

### <u>After a Biological Threat</u>

Stay indoors and pay close attention to all official warnings and instructions on how to proceed.  The basic public health procedures and medical protocols for handling exposure to biological agents are the same as for any infectious disease, but the delivery of medical services for a biological event may be handled differently in order to respond to increased demand.

## CHEMICAL WARFARE

Chemical warfare involves using the toxic properties of chemical substances as weapons and is classified as weapons of mass destruction.  Family members should not be so naïve as to believe it could not happen in our country - either by a hostile nation, terrorist organization or released inadvertently by our own government.  Chemical warfare does <u>not</u> depend upon explosive force to achieve an objective but instead depends upon the unique properties of the chemical agent weapon.  A lethal agent is designed to injure or incapacitate the enemy or deny use of a particular area of terrain.  Defoliants are used to quickly kill vegetation and deny its use for cover and concealment.  It can also be used against agriculture and livestock to promote hunger and starvation.

These chemical agents are poisonous vapors, aerosols, liquids and solids that have toxic affects on people, animals or plants.  Some chemical agents may be odorless and tasteless and can be released by bombs or sprayed from aircraft, boats and vehicles.  They can have an immediate affect (a few seconds to a few minutes) or a delayed affect between two and forty-eight hours.

<u>It is also extremely difficult if not impossible to *prepare in advance* for the possibility of a chemical attack</u>.  A chemical attack could come without warning.  Again, the best defense is to have the home stocked with emergency supplies, try to avoid public areas where large numbers of people regularly congregate, and always carry a high-quality dust mask in the purse or briefcase.

While potentially lethal, chemical agents are difficult to deliver in lethal concentrations because they are difficult to produce and once outdoors, the agents often dissipate rapidly.  Signs of a chemical release include people having difficulty breathing; eye irritation; loss of coordination; nausea or having a burning sensation in the nose, throat and lungs.  The presence of many dead insects, birds or animals may also indicate the release of a chemical agent.

The Geneva Protocol, known as the *Protocol for the Prohibition of the Use in War of Asphyxiating, Poisonous or other Gases, and of Bacteriological Methods of Warfare* entered into force on 8 February 1928 and is an international treaty prohibiting the use of chemical and biological weapons.  There are over 133 nations listed as state parties to the treaty which states that chemical and biological weapons are "justly condemned by the general opinion of the civilized world."  While the treaty prohibits the use of chemical and biological weapons, it does not address the production, storage or transfer of these weapons nor does it take into account rouge nations or terrorist groups.

The Chemical Weapons Convention (CWC) is an arms control agreement with the force of international law.  This agreement outlaws the production, stockpiling and use of chemical weapons.  There are 188 signatories which represent 98% of the global population.

The nations included in the Chemical Weapons Convention are shown in dark and light colors.  The light colored territories are nations having declared stockpiles of chemical weapons and/or have known production facilities for chemical weapons.  These include (but not limited to) the United States, Russia, India and China.

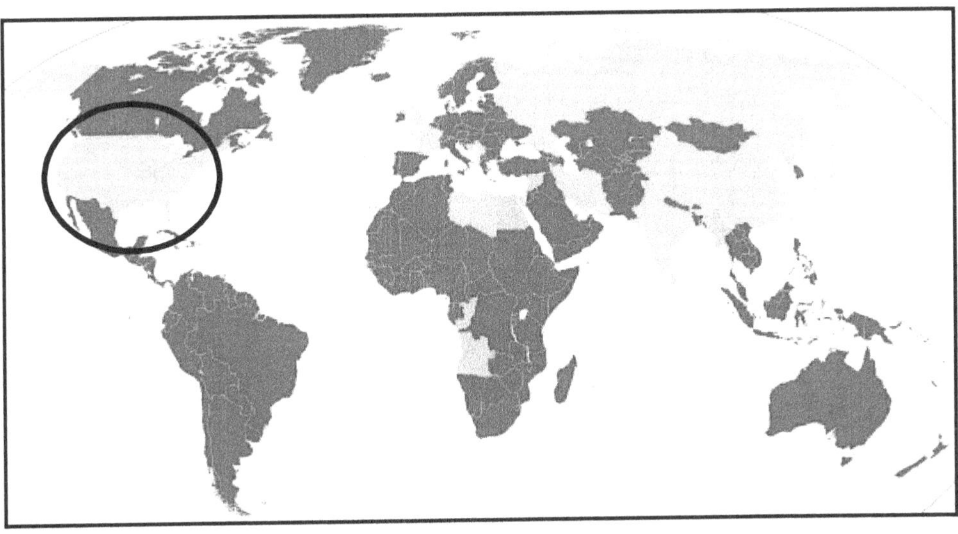

There are three basic methods in which chemical agents are stored including:

- **Self-Contained Munitions** – weapons ready for intended use such as projectiles, cartridges, and rockets
- **Aircraft-Delivered Munitions** – weapons ready for their intended use without an explosive component
- **Raw Agent** - weapons housed in one-ton containers

These tables provide a list of chemical agents designated for use in chemical warfare.  ***It will be enlightening to thoroughly read the description for each agent and the affects the chemicals have on human and animal life***.  It becomes apparent if family members come in contact with any of these agents - death would occur within a short period of time.

| BLOOD AGENTS | |
| --- | --- |
| **Diphosgene** | Colorless liquid that has a relatively high vapor pressure.  Exposure to diphosgene is similar in hazard to phosgene.  Poison that has an odor which may not be noticed and symptoms may be slow to appear.  Diphosgene can be detected in extremely minute amounts and is four times the Threshold Limit Value.  Its high toxicity disrupts the blood-air barrier causing choking and suffocation.  Sodium bicarbonate may be used to neutralize liquid spills of diphosgene.  Gaseous spills may be mitigated with ammonia. |

| | |
|---|---|
| **Cyanogen Chloride** | Blood agent and an easily condensed colorless gas causing immediate injury upon contact with the eyes or respiratory organs. Symptoms of exposure may include drowsiness, runny nose, sore throat, coughing, confusion, nausea, vomiting, edema, loss of consciousness, convulsions, paralysis and death. It is especially dangerous because it is capable of penetrating the filters in gas masks. It is unstable due to polymerization, sometimes with explosive violence. |
| **Phosgene** | Poison that has an odor which may not be noticed and symptoms may be slow to appear. Phosgene can be detected in extremely minute amounts and is four times the Threshold Limit Value. Its high toxicity disrupts the blood-air barrier causing choking and suffocation. Sodium bicarbonate may be used to neutralize liquid spills of phosgene. Gaseous spills may be mitigated with ammonia. |
| **Hydrogen Cyanide** | Blood agent that is a colorless and extremely poisonous liquid that boils slightly above room temperature at 79 °F. A minute concentration of hydrogen cyanide in the air will kill a human within ten minutes by halting cellular respiration. Hydrogen cyanide was used by Nazi Germany in the concentration camps and is also used in the United States in gas chambers employed in judicial execution. |

**CHOKING AGENTS**

| | |
|---|---|
| **Chloropicrin** | Colorless and highly toxic liquid that is insoluble in water with which it is stable. Chloropicrin is a severe irritant of the respiratory system in humans. It is severely irritating to the lungs, eyes, and skin. Chloropicrin causes humans to shut their eyes involuntarily and if splashed into the eye will cause corneal oedema and liquification of the cornea. It can be absorbed systemically through inhalation, ingestion, and the skin. Exposure to small concentrations cannot be tolerated for more than one minute, and exposure for only a few seconds is temporarily disabling. <br><br> With higher concentrations of three to thirty seconds, there is tearing and eye pain, respiratory tract injury and with exposure in the air for thirty minutes, the result is death caused by pulmonary oedema. Because of chloropicrin's stability, protection requires highly effective absorbents such as activated charcoal. Chloropicrin is absorbed readily at any temperature which may pose a threat in low or high temperature climates. |
| **Chlorine** | Toxic gas that irritates the respiratory system. It is a yellow-green gas that has a distinctive strong smell of pepper and pineapple or common household bleach. It tastes metallic and stings the back of the throat and chest. Because it is heavier than air, it tends to accumulate at the bottom of poorly ventilated spaces. Chlorine gas is a strong oxidizer and may react with flammable materials. Chlorine can react with water in the mucosa of the lungs to form hydrochloric acid, an irritant that can be lethal. In small doses, coughing, vomiting and lung damage may occur and in larger doses, exposure can be fatal after a few deep breaths of the gas. The damage done by chlorine gas can be prevented by using a gas mask or other filtration method which makes the overall chance of death by chlorine gas much lower than those of other chemical weapons. |

**NERVE AGENTS**

| | |
|---|---|
| **Cyclosarin** | Extremely toxic substance. When at room temperature is a colorless liquid whose odor has been described as sweet and musty or resembling peaches or shellac. Unlike sarin, cyclosarin has a low vapor pressure and evaporates about 69 times slower than sarin and 20 times slower than water. Cyclosarin is flammable with a flash point of 201 °F. |
| **Soman** | Extremely toxic nerve agent interfering with normal functioning of mammalian nervous system. In pure form, it is a volatile, corrosive, and colorless liquid with a faint odor. More commonly, it is a yellow/brown color and has a strong odor described as similar to camphor. |

| | |
|---|---|
| **VX** | The most toxic nerve agent ever synthesized whose only application is in chemical warfare as a nerve agent.  With its high viscosity and low volatility, VX has the texture and feel of motor oil.  This makes it especially dangerous as it has a high persistence in the environment.  It is odorless and tasteless, and can be distributed as a liquid, both pure and as a mixture with a polymer in the form of a thickened agent or aerosol.  It works as a nerve agent by the flaccid paralysis of all the muscles in the body.  Sustained paralysis of the diaphragm muscle causes death by asphyxiation.  The lethal dose for humans is minute through skin and for inhalation.<br><br>Early symptoms of skin contact may be local muscular twitching or sweating at the area of exposure followed by nausea or vomiting.  Some of the early symptoms of a VX vapor exposure may be runny nose and/or tightness in the chest with shortness of breath. Primary consideration should be given to removal of the liquid agent from the skin before removal of the individual to an uncontaminated area or atmosphere.  An antidote drug of atropine or pralidoxime must be immediately injected. |
| **Sarin** | Colorless and odorless liquid attacks the nervous system and has a high volatility relative to similar nerve agents.  Initial symptoms following exposure to sarin are a runny nose, tightness in the chest and constriction of the pupils.  The victim then has difficulty breathing and experiences nausea and drooling.  As the victim continues to lose control of bodily functions, the victim vomits, defecates and urinates.  This phase is followed by twitching and jerking.  Ultimately, the victim becomes comatose and suffocates in a series of convulsive spasms.  Inhalation and absorption through the skin pose a great threat as vapor concentrations immediately penetrate the skin.  People who absorb a non-lethal dose but do not receive immediate medical treatment may suffer permanent neurological damage.  Even at very low concentrations, sarin can be fatal.  Death may follow in one minute after direct ingestion of a lethal dose if antidotes such as atropine and pralidoxime are not quickly administered.  Sarin is estimated to be over 500 times more toxic than cyanide. |
| **Tabun** | Extremely toxic chemical substance that is a clear, colorless, and tasteless liquid with a faint fruity odor.  Although pure tabun is clear, less-pure tabun may be brown.  Tabun is toxic even in minute doses and fatally interferes with normal functioning of the mammalian nervous system.  It is a volatile chemical that can be used to contaminate water.  Tabun can be destroyed with bleaching powder though the poisonous gas cyanogen chloride is produced.  The symptoms of exposure include nervousness, restlessness, contraction of the pupil, runny nose, excessive salivation, difficulty breathing due to bronchial constriction/secretions, sweating, slow heartbeat, loss of consciousness, convulsions, flaccid paralysis, loss of bladder and bowel control and lung blisters.<br><br>Tabun breaks down slowly which after repeated exposure can lead to build up in the body and the affects appear slowly when absorbed through the skin rather than inhaled.  Inhaled lethal dosages kill in one to ten minutes and liquid absorbed through the eyes kills equally as fast.  Individuals who experience mild to moderate exposure to tabun can recover completely, if treated as soon as exposure occurred.  Treatment for suspected tabun poisoning is often three injections of a nerve agent antidote such as atropine or pralidoxime chloride. |



| | |
|---|---|
| **Nitrogen Mustard** | Cytotoxic chemotherapy agents similar to mustard gas.  Although their common use is medicinal, in principle these compounds can also be deployed as chemical warfare agents.  Nitrogen mustards are nonspecific DNA alkylating agents. |
| **Phosgene Oximine** | Poison with odor that may not be noticed and symptoms may be slow to appear.  Phosgene can be detected in extremely minute amounts and is four times the Threshold Limit Value.  Its high toxicity disrupts the blood-air barrier causing suffocation.  Sodium bicarbonate may be used to neutralize liquid spills of phosgene. Gaseous spills may be mitigated with ammonia. |

| | |
|---|---|
| **Sulfur Mustard** | The sulfur mustards have the ability to form large blisters on exposed skin.  Pure sulfur mustards are colorless and viscous liquids at room temperature.  When used in impure form, such as warfare agents, they are usually yellow-brown in color and have an odor resembling mustard plants, garlic or horseradish.  The compound readily eliminates a chloride ion which prevents cellular division and generally leads directly to programmed cell death, or, if cell death is not immediate, damaged DNA may lead to the development of cancer.  It is not easily soluble in water but is very soluble in fat, contributing to its rapid absorption into the skin.<br><br>Mustard gas has extremely powerful blistering affects on its victims.  It is strongly mutagenic, carcinogenic and lipophilic due to its alkylation properties.  People exposed to mustard gas rarely suffer immediate symptoms, and mustard-contaminated areas may appear completely normal.  Within twenty-four hours of exposure, victims experience intense itching and skin irritation which gradually turns into large blisters filled with yellow fluid wherever the mustard agent contacted the skin.  These are chemical burns and are very debilitating.  Mustard gas vapor easily penetrates clothing fabrics such as wool or cotton.  If the victim's eyes were exposed, they become sore beginning with conjunctivitis, after which the eyelids swell, resulting in temporary blindness.<br><br>At very high concentrations, if inhaled, mustard agent causes bleeding and blistering within the respiratory system, damaging mucous membranes and causing pulmonary edema.  Depending on the level of contamination, mustard gas burns can vary between first, second and third degree burns.  Mild or moderate exposure to mustard agent is unlikely to kill though victims invariably require lengthy periods of medical treatment and convalescence before recovery is complete.  The mutagenic and carcinogenic affects of mustard agent mean that victims who recover from mustard gas burns have an increased risk of developing cancer in later life.  Severe mustard gas burns (e.g. where more than 50% of the victim's skin has been burned) are often fatal with death occurring within days or even weeks.  Skin damage can be reduced if povidone-iodine, (Betadine) in a base of glycofurolis is rapidly applied, but since mustard agent initially has no symptoms, exposure is usually not recognized until skin irritation begins, at which point it is too late for countermeasures. |

**SOURCE:  United States Department of Defense**

## Before a Chemical Threat

All families should follow steps to create a shelter-in-place location in the home.  Make sure the designed area is fully stocked with emergency items including food, water, sanitary and medical supplies, hand-crank radio, etc.

## During a Chemical Threat

Attempt to define the impacted area or where the chemical is coming from and take *immediate* action to move away from the area and in a direction upwind of the source.  Once out of the vicinity, find shelter as quickly as possible.  If at the home, immediately go to the designated shelter-in-place location in the home and be sure to take pets with you.  Close doors and windows and turn off all ventilation, including furnaces, air conditioners, vents, and fans and seal the room with duct tape and plastic sheeting.

Listen to the radio for instructions from authorities.  If the chemical is inside a building, get out of the building without passing through the contaminated area, if possible.  If you cannot exit the building or find clean air without passing through the contaminated area, move as far away as possible and shelter-in-place.

## After a Chemical Threat

Decontamination is needed <u>within minutes</u> of exposure to minimize health risks.  Flush eyes with water and decontaminate hands using soap and water.  Gently wash face and hair with soap and water before thoroughly rinsing with water.  Decontaminate other body areas likely to have been contaminated by blotting (do not swab or scrape) with a cloth soaked in soapy water and rinse with clear water.

Family members who wear glasses or contact lenses should remove them.  Put glasses in a pan of household bleach and then rinse and dry.  Remove all clothing and other items in contact with the body and place contaminated clothing and items into a plastic bag and seal it.  Contaminated clothing normally removed over the head should be cut off to avoid contact with the eyes, nose and mouth.  Clothing stored in drawers or closets is likely to be safe to wear.

Bleach solutions, concentrated or diluted, should <u>not</u> be used to clean the body; however, diluted bleach (1 part household bleach to 9 parts water) can be used on equipment and other hard surfaces.  Because bleach solutions irritate the eyes, skin and respiratory tract, they must be handled with caution and used with adequate ventilation.

**A PERSON AFFECTED BY A NERVE, BLOOD, BLISTER OR CHOKING AGENT REQUIRES <u>IMMEDIATE</u> MEDICAL ATTENTION AND THE APPROPRIATE ANTIDOTE.  DURING A <u>MAJOR</u> CHEMICAL ATTACK (OR EVEN THE UNINTENDED RELEASE OF THESE AGENTS), MEDICAL ATTENTION AND ANTIDOTES FOR THE GENERAL PUBLIC WOULD NOT BE AVAILABLE IN TIME. KNOW IT. ACCEPT IT. DEAL WITH IT.**

## TERRORIST THREATS

There is a major difference between an act of war and a terrorist threat.  Most citizens have been led to believe a terrorist simply acts out of hatred.  How ridiculous!  There are countless reasons why an individual or group of individuals would commit a so-called terrorist act.  For example, when Timothy McVeigh blew up the Murrow Building in Oklahoma City, his motive was not hatred but frustration with corruption in government.

England considered the Boston Tea Party to be a terrorist act, yet the Americans who were struggling to pay tax to the English considered it a justified and patriotic act of defiance against oppression.  Citizens who support the far left political platform in this country and who continue to riot in the streets - sometimes just for the fun and joy it gives them - destroying property and injuring innocent people could also be considered as terrorists.  There are countless other so-called terrorist acts around the world instigated by a group of individuals who have strong religious, economic or philosophical beliefs.  **<u>It appears that accusing someone of being a terrorist and being labeled a terrorist depends on which side of the bullet or explosion you are on in the debate</u>**.

Whatever the real reasons or motivations for a so-called terrorist act, and whether or not the "terrorists" are justified or not justified in their actions, the point to be made is the ultimate goal of the terrorist is to generally destroy the target including people, animals, natural resources, infrastructure and property – and to cause as much fear in the general population as possible.

At least for the *present* time, a terrorist or terrorist organizations appear <u>not</u> to have sufficient funds, expertise, materials and/or manpower to initiate a *massive* attack or *large-scale* assault that could <u>cripple an entire nation</u>.  We have learned from experience it *is* possible for a terrorist group to successfully bring down the twin towers in New York City which did indeed have a devastating ripple affect throughout the country.  The citizens who were obviously impacted the most were the families of those who died in the explosions and those who lost their jobs in the vicinity.  The point to be made is although the incident was tragic, heartbreaking and disastrous; it did NOT bring down and cripple our entire country.

A terrorist act can take place anywhere, under any circumstance and at any time.  It can involve a group of political, religious or environmental zealots, a mentally ill person who believes someone is out to get him or a bunch of silly teenagers out for a good time.  Family members should <u>not</u> be naïve enough to believe claims by the government that they can protect us from every possible terrorist scenario - the arithmetic is simply not there.  There is not enough expertise, experience, knowledge, time, money, computer processing power or manpower to make every <u>thing</u> and every <u>one</u> safe all the time - or for that matter - <u>at any time</u>.

<u>A terrorist act can not only include the use of bombs or explosions in public locations but can also involve acts of damage and destruction such as the derailment of railroad tracks, poisoning of water sources, destruction of a major electrical grid, sabotage to transportation systems (airlines, cruise ships or pipelines) or damage to an important hydro-electric dam</u>.

There is a fine line between being *reasonably* vigilant and attentive or *overly* obsessed and paranoid when attempting to control or at least manage your surroundings to avoid a possible terrorist act.  Remember - <u>not everyone is out to get</u>

you, but at the same time, by watching the appearance and behavior of others, and by using past experiences and intuition - most people can recognize or feel when something isn't right about a situation.

As a means to *plan in advance* in the event of terrorist act, use *logic*, *reason* and *common sense* when following these recommendations:

- Always remain vigilant and observant when in **public places** with a large population such as a shopping mall, movie theatre, large department store, school, stadium, restaurant, park, military base, seaport, airport, train or bus station, zoo, post office, financial institution, government building, church or synagogue, transportation system (subway, train, airplane, boat, etc.) and the corporate headquarters of large companies.

- Remain alert if attending any type of **public event** including marathons, fairs, parades, holiday celebrations, sporting events, exhibits, concerts and political or environmental speeches.

- Carry a high quality **dust mask** in the purse or briefcase in the event of an explosion, biological or chemical attack.

- Be observant of your **surroundings** and **individuals** in your immediate area including:

  - Individuals who tend to wear clothing that may conceal any recognizable marks on their body (tattoo or body piercing) or covers their face (hoodie or hat)

  - Individuals wearing a backpack, carrying large bags or packages

  - Individuals who may drop a package or bag on the ground and then hurry away from the site

  - Individuals who exhibit unusual behavior such as anger, irritation, aggravation, frustration, distraction or disorientation

  - Individuals who are carrying any type of weapon, e.g. gun, knife, bomb or grenade

  - Individuals who do not "fit in" or seem out of place in the surrounding environment, e.g., known gang members entering an elementary school

  - Individuals who are overheard talking about committing a terrorist act

  - Individuals who are known criminals, extremists or gang members congregating in one area

If something doesn't feel right about whom or what you have observed, contact law enforcement and describe your observations. If possible, move away from the general area until investigated by local officials.

## WARFARE

Over the course of the past thirty years as I have researched and studied emergency preparation, I have encountered a wide assortment of opinions on whether or not the citizens of the world would ever experience World War III and if it would take place on our own soil. In the past several years, the general consensus a major world war is possible has increased but family members will have to decide for themselves.

Regardless of the opinions, however, it is always prudent to *plan for the worst case scenario* and *prepare in advance* to be ready for this drastic and dramatic scenario. It then becomes a win/win scenario. If there **is** a World War III and you have *prepared in advance* - you win. If there **is not** a World War III and you have *planned in advance* - you still win. Although many experts claim to have plausible scenarios and culprits who may start another war – no one is certain **why – who – what – where** – or **when** the world would experience this event.

Let's look at several countries in the world and see what they offer in the way of military might and machinery.

## Worlds Largest Military Forces

| RANK | COUNTRY | CONTINENT | ACTIVE TROOP STRENGTH | RESERVE TROOP STRENGTH | TOTAL TROOP STRENGTH |
|---|---|---|---|---|---|
| 1 | *North Korea* | **Europe** | **1,082,000** | **4,700,000** | **5,782,000** |
| 2 | *China* | Asia | 3,750,000 | 550,000 | 4,300,000 |
| 3 | *Russia* | Europe | 1,160,000 | 2,400,000 | 3,560,000 |
| 4 | India | Asia | 2,414,000 | 535,000 | 2,949,000 |
| *5* | *United States* | *North America* | *1,414,000* | *1,259,000* | *2,673,000* |

**SOURCE:  United States Department of Defense**

## World's Largest Army Forces

| RANK | COUNTRY | CONTINENT | TOTAL TROOP STRENGTH |
|---|---|---|---|
| 1 | *China* | **Asia** | **1,600,000** |
| 2 | India | Asia | 1,100,000 |
| 3 | *North Korea* | Asia | 950,000 |
| 4 | South Korea | Asia | 560,000 |
| 5 | Pakistan | Asia | 550,000 |
| *6* | *United States* | *North America* | *477,800* |
| 7 | Vietnam | Asia | 412,000 |
| 8 | Turkey | Asia/Europe | 402,000 |
| 9 | Iraq | Asia | 375,000 |
| 10 | *Russia* | Europe | 321,000 |

**SOURCE:  United States Department of Defense**

## World's Largest Naval Forces

| RANK | COUNTRY | CONTINENT | TOTAL TROOP STRENGTH |
|---|---|---|---|
| *1* | *United States* | *North America* | *332,000* |
| 2 | *China* | Asia | 250,000 |
| 3 | *Russia* | Europe | 142,000 |
| 4 | South Korea | Asia | 68,000 |
| 5 | India | Asia | 64,000 |
| 6 | France | Europe | 57,500 |
| 7 | Mexico | North America | 56,000 |
| 8 | Taiwan | Asia | 53,000 |
| 9 | Turkey | Asia/Europe | 48,600 |
| 10 | *North Korea* | Asia | 46,000 |

**SOURCE:  United States Department of Defense**

## World's Largest Combat Aircraft Arsenal

| RANK | COUNTRY | CONTINENT | FIGHTERS | BOMBERS | ATTACK | TOTAL |
|---|---|---|---|---|---|---|
| *1* | *United States* | *North America* | *3,043* | *171* | *1,185* | *4,399* |
| 2 | *China* | Asia | 901 | 91 | 110 | 1,102 |
| 3 | *Russia* | Europe | 1,264 | 166 | 1,267 | 2,697 |
| 4 | India | Asia | 1,120 | 118 | 370 | 1,608 |
| 5 | *North Korea* | Asian | 899 | 60 | 211 | 1,170 |

| RANK | COUNTRY | CONTINENT | FIGHTERS | BOMBERS | ATTACK | TOTAL |
|---|---|---|---|---|---|---|
| 6 | South Korea | Asia | 648 | 60 | 352 | 1,060 |
| 7 | Pakistan | Asia | 325 | 30 | 250 | 605 |
| 8 | Israel | Europe | 233 | 10 | 264 | 507 |
| 9 | Egypt | Africa | 644 | 25 | 0 | 669 |
| 10 | United Kingdom | Europe | 345 | 50 | 209 | 604 |

**SOURCE:  United States Department of Defense**

## World's Largest Submarine Arsenal

| RANK | COUNTRY | CONTINENT | TOTAL |
|---|---|---|---|
| *1* | *United States* | *North America* | *74* |
| 2 | *China* | Asia | 62 |
| 3 | *Russia* | Europe | 57 |
| 4 | *North Korea* | Asia | 26 |
| 5 | South Korea | Asia | 18 |

**SOURCE:  United States Department of Defense - totals do not include secret submarines**

## World's Largest Nuclear Warhead Arsenal

| RANK | COUNTRY | CONTINENT | LONG RANGE MISSLES | LONG RANGE AIRCRAFT | MID/SHORT RANGE SYSTEMS | TOTAL DEPLOYED WARHEADS | WAR HEADS HELD IN RESERVE | TTL |
|---|---|---|---|---|---|---|---|---|
| **1** | **Russia** | **Europe** | **1,666** | **838** | **2,000** | **4,504** | **7,950** | **15,104** |
| *2* | *USA* | *N America* | *1,702* | *500* | *500* | *2,702* | *2,500* | *5,202* |
| 3 | France | Europe | 240 | - | 60 | 300 | - | 300 |
| 4 | China | Asia | 26 | - | 150 | 176 | 65 | 240 |
| 5 | UK | Europe | 150 | - | - | 150 | 50 | 200 |
| 6 | Israel | Middle East | - | - | - | - | - | 80 |
| 7 | India | Asia | - | - | - | - | - | 50 |
| 8 | Pakistan | Middle East | - | - | - | - | - | 60 |
| 9 | North Korea | Asia | - | - | - | - | - | 5-15 |

**SOURCE: Union of Concerned Scientists – all numbers are estimates**

## MILITARY INSTALLATIONS

There are hundreds of military installations in the United States and around the world.  Every one of the installations controlled by the United States is important and the military and civilian personnel assigned to these sites provide a critical role to the overall safety and security of our country and allies.

During these volatile times, the opening and closing of installations, the reorganization and reassignment of military personnel, weapons, artillery and equipment and the birth of new and improved technology takes place on a continual basis, depending on the current political climate of countries around the globe.

As part of *advanced emergency planning*, it is important to recognize the significance of our military installations in the overall strategy of nations who may elect to declare war.  There are several military installations in the United States

*In peace, sons bury their fathers. In war, fathers bury their sons.*

**- Herodotus**

considered as probable strategic nuclear targets and are referred to as **POWER PROJECTION PLATFORMS** - a term used by the military to refer to the ability of a nation to conduct expeditionary warfare, e.g. to intimidate or threaten other nations in an area distant from its own territory. The United States definitely can conduct expeditionary warfare – and so can Russia and China and many other countries around the world.

While traditional measures of power projection generally focus on hard and heavy power *assets* (tanks, artillery, soldiers, aircraft and naval vessels) and while long-range weapons including intercontinental ballistic missiles (ICBMs) and cruise missiles project deadly force, power projection also revolves around military *logistics* – the ability to transport troops and weapons from current location in the country to the enemy. This is where designated sea port and aerial port of embarkation is important because airlift and sealift facilities provide our country with the means to deploy units of soldiers or weapons to distant destinations.

Family members should analyze the strategic importance of military bases designated as Power Projection Platforms and designated sea ports and aerial ports of embarkation. As you examine the table below, you will notice the Port of Beaumont/Corpus Christi in Texas is listed SIX times as the designated seaport of embarkation for many of these major military installations. Likewise, there are other sea and aerial ports located on the east coast.

In addition to the actual military installation, it makes sense an enemy would target the sea and aerial ports of embarkation as part of their first attack in order to hamper our forces from being able to transport to enemy soil. Families living near these sites should take special precautions.

Listed below are installations most military commanders consider to be Power Projection Platforms:

| UNITED STATES MILITARY POWER PROJECTION PLATFORMS | | |
|---|---|---|
| **INSTALLATION** | **DESIGNATED SPOE** <br> **(Sea Port/Embarkation)** | **DESIGNATED APOE** <br> **(Aerial Port/Embarkation)** |
| *Camp Pendleton* <br> **OCEANSIDE, CALIFORNIA** | *Port of San Diego* <br> **SAN DIEGO** <br> **CALIFORNIA** | *March Air Force Base* <br> **RIVERSIDE** <br> **CALIFORNIA** |
| *Camp Lejeune* <br> **JACKSONVILLE, NORTH CAROLINA** | *Port of Morehead City* <br> **MOREHEAD** <br> **NORTH CAROLINA** | *Marine Corps Air Station* <br> *Cherry Point* <br> **HAVELOCK** <br> **NORTH CAROLINA** |
| *Fort Stewart* <br> **HINESVILLE, GEORGIA** | *Port of Savannah* <br> **SAVANNAH** <br> **GEORGIA** | *Hunter Army Airfield* <br> **SAVANNAH** <br> **GEORGIA** |
| *Fort Bragg* <br> **FAYETTEVILLE, NORTH CAROLINA** | *Port of Wilmington* <br> **WILMINGTON** <br> **NORTH CAROLINA** | *Pope Air Force Base* <br> **FAYETTEVILLE** <br> **NORTH CAROLINA** |
| *Fort Hood* <br> **KILLEEN, TEXAS** | *Port of Beaumont/Corpus Christi* <br> **BEAUMONT** <br> **TEXAS** | *Robert Gray Army Airfield* <br> **KILEEN** <br> **TEXAS** |
| *Fort McCoy* <br> **TORNAH, WISCONSIN** | *Port of Hampton Roads* <br> **HAMPTON ROADS** <br> **VIRGINIA** | *Volk Field* <br> **ORANGE** <br> **WISCONSIN** |
| *Fort Drum* <br> **WATERTOWN, NEW YORK** | *Port of New York/New Jersey* <br> **NEW YORK** <br> **NEW JERSEY** | *Wheeler-Sack Army Airfield* <br> **WATERTOWN** <br> **NEW YORK** |

| UNITED STATES MILITARY POWER PROJECTION PLATFORMS | | |
| --- | --- | --- |
| **INSTALLATION** | **DESIGNATED SPOE**<br>(Sea Port/Embarkation) | **DESIGNATED APOE**<br>(Aerial Port/Embarkation) |
| *Fort Lewis*<br>**TACOMA, WASHINGTON** | *Port of Tacoma*<br>**TACOMA**<br>**WASHINGTON** | *McChord Air Force Base*<br>**TACOMA**<br>**WASHINGTON** |
| *Fort Campbell*<br>**HOPKINSVILLE, KENTUCKY** | *Port of Jacksonville*<br>**JACKSONVILLE**<br>**FLORIDA** | *Campbell Army Airfield*<br>**CLARKSVILLE**<br>**TENNESSEE** |
| *Fort Riley*<br>**JUNCTION CITY, KANSAS** | *Port of Beaumont/Corpus Christi*<br>**BEAUMONT**<br>**TEXAS** | *Forbes Field*<br>**TOPEKA**<br>**KANSAS** |
| *Fort Carson*<br>**COLORADO SPRINGS, COLORADO** | *Port of Beaumont/Corpus Christi*<br>**BEAUMONT**<br>**TEXAS** | *Peterson Air Force Base*<br>**COLORADO SPRINGS**<br>**COLORADO** |
| *Fort Polk*<br>**LEESVILLE, LOUISIANA** | *Port of Beaumont/Corpus Christi*<br>**BEAUMONT**<br>**TEXAS** | *Alexandria International Airport*<br>**ALEXANDRIA**<br>**LOUISIANA** |
| *Fort Dix*<br>**NEW HANOVER, NEW JERSEY** | *Port of New York/New Jersey*<br>**NEW YORK**<br>**NEW JERSEY** | *McGuire Air Force Base*<br>**WRIGHTSTOWN**<br>**NEW JERSEY** |
| *Fort Bliss*<br>**EL PASO, TEXAS** | *Port of Beaumont/Corpus Christi*<br>**BEAUMONT**<br>**TEXAS** | *Biggs Air Force Base*<br>**EL PASO**<br>**TEXAS** |
| *Fort Sill*<br>**LAWTON, OKLAHOMA** | *Port of Beaumont/Corpus Christi*<br>**BEAUMONT**<br>**TEXAS** | *Lawton/Ft. Sill Regional Airport*<br>**LAWTON**<br>**OKLAHOMA** |
| *Fort Benning*<br>**COLUMBUS, GEORGIA** | *Port of Savannah*<br>**SAVANNAH**<br>**GEORGIA** | *Lawson Army Airfield*<br>**COLUMBUS**<br>**GEORGIA** |
| *Fort Eustis*<br>**NEWPORT NEWS, VIRGINIA** | *Port of Hampton Roads*<br>**HAMPTON ROADS**<br>**VIRGINIA** | *Langley Air Force Base*<br>**HAMPTON**<br>**VIRGINIA** |

**SOURCE: US DEPARTMENT OF TRANSPORTATION/FEDERAL HIGHWAY ADMINISTRATION**

There are other military installations, garrisons and command centers in the country and around the world that may also be considered as <u>primary</u> and/or <u>strategic</u> nuclear targets including:

## ARMY

|  | |
|---|---|
| **COMMAND**<br>United States Army *Central*<br>**Fort McPherson, Georgia** | Provides continuous oversight and control of Army operations throughout **Afghanistan**, Bahrain, Egypt, **Iran**, **Iraq**, Jordan, Kazakhstan, Kuwait, Kyrgyzstan, **Lebanon**, Oman, **Pakistan**, Qatar, Saudi Arabia, **Syria**, Tajikistan, Turkmenistan, United Arab Emirates, Uzbekistan and **Yeman**. |
| **COMMAND**<br>United States Army *North*<br>**Fort Sam Houston, Texas** | Provides continuous oversight and control of Army operations throughout the continental United States, Alaska, Canada, Mexico, Gulf of Mexico, Straits of Florida, Bahamas, Puerto Rico and the US Virgin Islands. |
| **COMMAND**<br>United States Army *South*<br>**Fort Sam Houston, Texas** | Provides continuous oversight and control of Army operations throughout Antigua, Barbuda, Argentina, Aruba, Barbados, Belize, Bermuda, Bolivia, Brazil, Cayman Islands, Chile, Colombia, Costa Rica, Curacao, Dominica, Dominican Republic, Ecuador, El Salvador, Grenada, Guatemala, Guyana, Haiti, Honduras, Jamaica, Nicaragua, Panama, Paraguay, Peru, Uruguay, Venezuela, Suriname, Trinidad, Tobago, St. Kitts, St. Nevis, St. Lucia, St. Vincent, and the Grenadines. |
| **COMMAND**<br>United States Army *Pacific*<br>**Fort Shafter, Hawaii** | Provides continuous oversight and control of Army operations throughout Australia, Bangladesh, Bhutan, Brunei, Cambodia, **China**, Fiji, India, Indonesia, Japan, Kiribati, Laos, Malaysia, Maldives, Marshall Islands, Micronesia, Mongolia, Myanmar, Nauru, Nepal, New Zealand, **North Korea**, (less the Korean Peninsula) Palau, Papua New Guinea, Philippines, **Russia (limited)**, Samoa, Singapore, Solomon Islands, **South Korea**, Sri Lanka, Thailand, Timor-Leste, Tonga, Tuvalu, Vanuatu, and Vietnam. |
| **COMMAND**<br>United States Army *African*<br>Kelley Barracks<br>**Stuttgart, Germany** | Provides continuous oversight and control of Army operations throughout Africa except Egypt, Cape Verde, Sao Tome, Principe, Comoros, Madagascar, Mauritius and, Seychelles. |
| **COMMAND**<br>Unites States Army *European*<br>**Stuttgart, Germany** | Provides continuous oversight and control of Army operations throughout all European countries, **Russia**, Iceland, Greenland and **Israel.** |
| **COMMAND**<br>US Deployment and Distribution<br>**Alexandria, Virginia** | Assigned Army Command to the United States **Transportation** Command |
| **COMMAND**<br>United States Army Space &<br>Missile Defense Army<br>Strategic Forces<br>**Huntsville, Alabama** | Provides continuous oversight, control, integration and coordination of Army forces supporting USSTATCOM |
| **COMMAND**<br>United States Army Installation<br>Management<br>**Arlington, Virginia** | Manages Army installations to support readiness and mission execution, provide equitable services and facilities and optimized resources. |

| COMMAND<br>United States Army Network Enterprise Technology<br>**Fort Huachuca, Arizona** | Single Army authority to operate, control and defend the Army's information structure at the enterprise level. |
|---|---|
| COMMAND<br>United States Army Intelligence/Security<br>**Fort Belvoir, Virginia** | Synchronizes the operations of all assigned units to produce intelligence in support of the Army, Combatant Commands and the National Intelligence community. |
| COMMAND<br>US Army Corps of Engineers<br>**Washington DC**<br>**District of Columbia** | Provides engineering services and capabilities in support of national interests. |
| COMMAND<br>United States Army Reserve<br>**Fort McPherson, Georgia** | Provides trained and ready units that are prepared to mobilize and support armed services during time of war or national emergency |

**SOURCE: United States Department of Defense**

## AIR FORCE

| COMMAND<br>Air Combat Command<br>*Langley Air Force Base*<br>Virginia | Primary provider of combat airpower to country's war fighting commands. Air Combat Command consists of more than 109,000 <u>active duty</u> members and <u>civilians</u>. When mobilized, more than 63,000 members of the <u>Air National Guard</u> and <u>Air Force Reserve</u>, along with over 600 aircraft, are assigned to ACC. In total, ACC and ACC units consist of 1,750 aircraft. |
|---|---|
| COMMAND<br>US Air Force Warfare Center<br>*Nellis Air Force Base* - Nevada | The Air Warfare Center oversees operations of the host units of the 57th Wing, 98th Range Wing and 99th Air Base Wing. Home of B61/ALCM Storage (750) and B61 Mods (600). |
| COMMAND<br>Air Force Northern Command<br>*Peterson Air Force Base*<br>Colorado Springs, Colorado | Responsible for military support for <u>civil authorities</u> in the United States and protecting the territory and <u>national interests</u> of the United States within the <u>contiguous United States</u>, <u>Alaska</u>, Canada, <u>Mexico</u> (and the air, land and sea approaches to these areas). |
| **Barksdale Air Force Base**<br>Bossier City, Louisiana | Host unit is the 2nd Bomb Wing. Home of B62H Bombers (140); and W80 ALCM/ACM (400). |
| **Eglin Air Force Base**<br>Valparaiso, Florida | Host unit is the 96th Air Base Wing. The Air Warfare Center oversees the 53rd Air Base Wing. Eglin is the home of the Air Armament Center (AAC) and is one of three product centers in the Air Force Materiel Command. Serving as the focal point for all Air Force armaments, the AAC is the center responsible for the development, acquisition, testing, deployment and sustainment of all air-delivered weapons. |
| **Fairchild Air Force Base**<br>Spokane, Washington | Host unit is the 92nd Air Refueling Wing responsible for providing air refueling, passenger and cargo airlift and evacuation missions. Home of B61 Bombers (25) and B83 Bombers (60). |
| **Grand Forks Air Force Base**<br>Emerado, North Dakota | Host unit is the 319th Air Base Wing. Home of B61 Bombers (25), B83 Bombers (60) and Minuteman III Silos (60). |
| **Kirtland Air Force Base**<br>Albuquerque, New Mexico | Host units include 377th Air Base Wing, 498th Nuclear Systems Wing and 58th Special Operations Wing. Home of the Air Force Material Command Nuclear Weapons Center responsible for maintaining reliable nuclear weapons. Home of B61/ALCM Storage (450); B61 Mods (600); W84 GLCM (400); Minuteman II (450) and W6 SRAM (550). |

| | |
|---|---|
| **Malmstrom Air Force Base**<br>Great Falls, Montana | Host unit is the 341st Missile Wing and the 819th Red Horse Squadron. Home of Minuteman III ICBM Silos (550). |
| **Minot Air Force Base**<br>Minot, North Dakota | Host units include the 5th Bomb Wing and the 91st Missile Wing. Home  of Minuteman III ICBM Silos (455); W80 ALCM (100); W80 ACM (300); B52H Bombers; B61 Bombers (50); B83 Bombers (90); UH-1N Twin Huey helicopters. |
| **Seymour-Johnson**<br>**Air Force Base**<br>Goldsboro, North Carolina | Host unit is the 4th Fighter Wing, 916th Air Refueling Wing, and the 414th Fighter Group.  Home of F25E's for 4th Fighter Wing. |
| **Warren Air Force Base**<br>Cheyenne, Wyoming | Hose unit is the 90th Missile Wing.  Home of Twentieth Air Force which commands all US Air Force ICBM's.  Home of Minuteman III ICBM Silos (460) and MX ICBM Silos (525). |
| **Whiteman Air Force Base**<br>Knob Noster, Missouri | Host unit is the 509th Bomb Wing that operates the B2 Spirit Stealth Bombers employed to strike high value targets that are either out of range of conventional aircraft or considered to be too heavily defended for conventional aircraft to strike without high risk of loss.  Home of B2 Bombers (550). |

**SOURCE:  United States Department of Defense**

**MARINES**

| | |
|---|---|
| **COMMAND**<br>Quantico, Virginia | Headquarters for the United States Marine Corps. |
| **Marine Corps Air Ground**<br>**Combat Center**<br>Twenty Nine Palms, California | Host units include the 7th Marine Regiment, and several tank, combat and assault amphibian battalions.  Home to the largest military training area in the nation and largest US base in the world. |
| **Marine Corps Logistics Base**<br>Barstow, California | Supply and maintenance installation to rebuild and repair ground combat and combat support equipment and to support installation on the west coast. |
| **Marine Corps Recruit Depot**<br>San Diego, California | Trains enlisted male recruits living west of the Mississippi River. |
| **Marine Corps Logistics Base**<br>Albany, Georgia | Supply and maintenance installation to rebuild and repair ground combat and combat support equipment and to support installation on the east coast. |
| **Marine Corps Base**<br>Kane'ohe Bay, Oahu, Hawaii | Host units include the 3rd Marine Regiment and several aircraft groups and battalions. |

**SOURCE:  United States Department of Defense**

**NAVY**

| | |
|---|---|
| **COMMAND**<br>United States Navy<br>Arlington, Virginia | Headquarters for the United State Naval Forces |
| **Yorktown Weapons**<br>**Naval Station**<br>Hampton Roads, Virginia | Provides weapons and ammunition storage and a loading facility for ships of the US Atlantic Fleet.  Home of W80 SLCM (160). |
| **Kitsap Naval Base**<br>Kitsap Peninsula, Washington | Home of Nuclear Submarine Arsenal and Trident I C4 (1600) 3RD LARGEST NAVY BASE IN USA.  One of Navy's four nuclear shipyards, one of two nuclear weapons facilities, the only West Coast dry dock capable of handling a Nimitz class aircraft carrier, Navy's largest fuel depot. |

| | |
|---|---|
| **North Island Naval Air Station**<br>San Diego, California | Headquarters for four major military commands including Naval Air Forces (maintenance and training of all naval aircraft and aircraft carriers in the Atlantic and Pacific Fleets, Naval Air Reserve and Naval Air Training Command), Carrier Strike Group One and Seven and Cruiser Destroyer Group One; Home to the USS Carl Vinson and USS Ronald Reagan aircraft carriers and to over 230 other stationed aircraft. Home of W80 SLCM (160). |
| **Kings Bay Naval Base**<br>Jacksonville, Georgia<br>Atlantic Ocean Theater | Host is US Second Fleet. Home of Strategic Weapons Facility & Submarine Launched Ballistic Missiles; Trident I C4 (1600) and Trident II D5 (400). |
| **Norfolk Naval Station**<br>Norfolk, Virginia | Supports navy forces in the United States Fleet Forces Command and those operating in the Atlantic, Ocean, Mediterranean Sea and Indian Ocean. It is the world's largest naval station supporting 75 ships and 134 aircraft in 14 piers and 11 aircraft hangars. Houses largest concentration of Navy forces. |
| **3<sup>rd</sup> Fleet, Navy**<br>San Diego, California<br>Eastern and Northern Pacific Theater | Flagship is *USS Coronado* operating from San Diego, California. Responsible for defense of west coast. Third Fleet is responsible for the operational readiness of Carrier Task Forces and Amphibious Ready Groups using the *USS Nimitz*, *USS Carl Vinson*, *USS Abraham Lincoln*, *USS John Stennis* and *USS Ronald Reagan* aircraft carriers. |
| **5<sup>th</sup> Fleet, Navy**<br>Persian Gulf Theater | Operates in Arabian (Persian) Gulf, Red Sea, Arabian Sea and coast off East Africa. These forces normally consist of an Aircraft Carrier Battle Group, an Amphibious Ready Group, surface combatants, submarines, maritime patrol and reconnaissance aircraft, and logistics vessels. |
| **6<sup>th</sup> Fleet, Navy**<br>Naples, Italy<br>African – European Theater | Flagship is the *USS Mount Whitney* in Gaeta, Italy on the Mediterranean and is the major operational component of Naval Forces Europe and Naval Forces Africa. The principal striking power of the Sixth Fleet resides in its aircraft carriers and the modern jet aircraft, its submarines, and its reinforced battalion of US Marines on board amphibious ships deployed in the Mediterranean. |
| **7<sup>th</sup> Fleet, Navy**<br>Yokosuka, Japan<br>Western Pacific/Indian Ocean Arabian Gulf Theater | Flagship is the *USS Blue Ridge* in Yokosuka, Japan. The largest of the forward-deployed U.S. fleets, with 50-60 ships, 350 aircraft and 60,000 Navy and Marine Corps personnel. |
| **10<sup>th</sup> Fleet, Navy**<br>Fort Mead, Maryland | Responsible for cyber warfare programs supporting information, computer and electronic warfare and space operations. |

**SOURCE: United States Department of Defense**

## MULTIPLE SERVICES

| | |
|---|---|
| **COMMAND**<br>United States *Central* Command<br>**MacDill Air Force Base**<br>Tampa, Florida | Responsibility includes countries in the <u>Middle East</u>, <u>North Africa</u>, and <u>Central Asia</u>, most notably <u>Afghanistan</u> and <u>Iraq</u>. Components include United States Army Forces Central Command, Air Forces Central Command, Marine Forces Central Command, Naval Forces Central Command and Special Operations Command Central. |
| **COMMAND**<br>United States *Southern* Command<br>Miami, Florida | Responsible for providing contingency planning and operations in <u>Central</u> and South America, the <u>Caribbean</u> (except U.S. commonwealths, territories, and possessions), <u>Cuba</u>, their territorial waters, and for the force of U.S. military resources at these locations. |
| **COMMAND**<br>United States *Strategic* Command<br>**Offutt Air Force Base**<br>Omaha, Nebraska | Responsible for military satellites, information missile defense, global command and control, intelligence, surveillance, and reconnaissance, global strike and strategic deterrence (the United States nuclear arsenal) and combating weapons of mass destruction. |

|  | |
| --- | --- |
| **COMMAND**<br>United States *European* Command - Stuttgart, Germany | Responsibility covers fifty-one countries and territories, including <u>Europe</u>, *Russia*, <u>Iceland</u>, <u>Greenland</u>, and *Israel*. |
| **COMMAND**<br>United States *Pacific* Command<br>**Camp H.M. Smith**<br>Halawa Heights, Hawaii | Responsibility covers Pacific Ocean with <u>U.S. Army Pacific</u>, <u>Marine Forces Pacific</u>, <u>U.S. Pacific Fleet</u>, and <u>Pacific Air Forces</u>, headquartered in Honolulu with component forces stationed throughout the region. |

**SOURCE: United States Department of Defense**

A good rule of thumb for family members is to pay close attention to any military bases located in the general vicinity of the home and/or individual households. Find out what type of military personnel are stationed at the base and what type of arsenal and/or equipment is housed there as well. An enemy would attempt to destroy target sites having personnel, arsenal, weapons and equipment that could be used as a counter-strike against <u>them</u>. For example, if you learn the 3rd Infantry Division, the 101st Airborne Division, the 1st Armored Division and a large number of bombers have now been assigned to a base in your area – you would have cause for serious concern! **PREPARE**!

## NUCLEAR WAR

Wars have been started over a simple misunderstanding, lying by government politicians, inaccurate information or desires of men to increase their own wealth and power at the expense of the population. Many wars have begun over the rights, control and power over natural resources, economic issues or religious beliefs. A government may defend their right to attack another country as a preemptive strike or to secure their own borders. In war, a common goal is to quickly force the surrender of the target country as dictated by the new regime.

These two maps display the Power Projection Platforms (PPP) and other military installations located throughout the continental United States and the military installations where a majority of our nuclear arsenal is located.

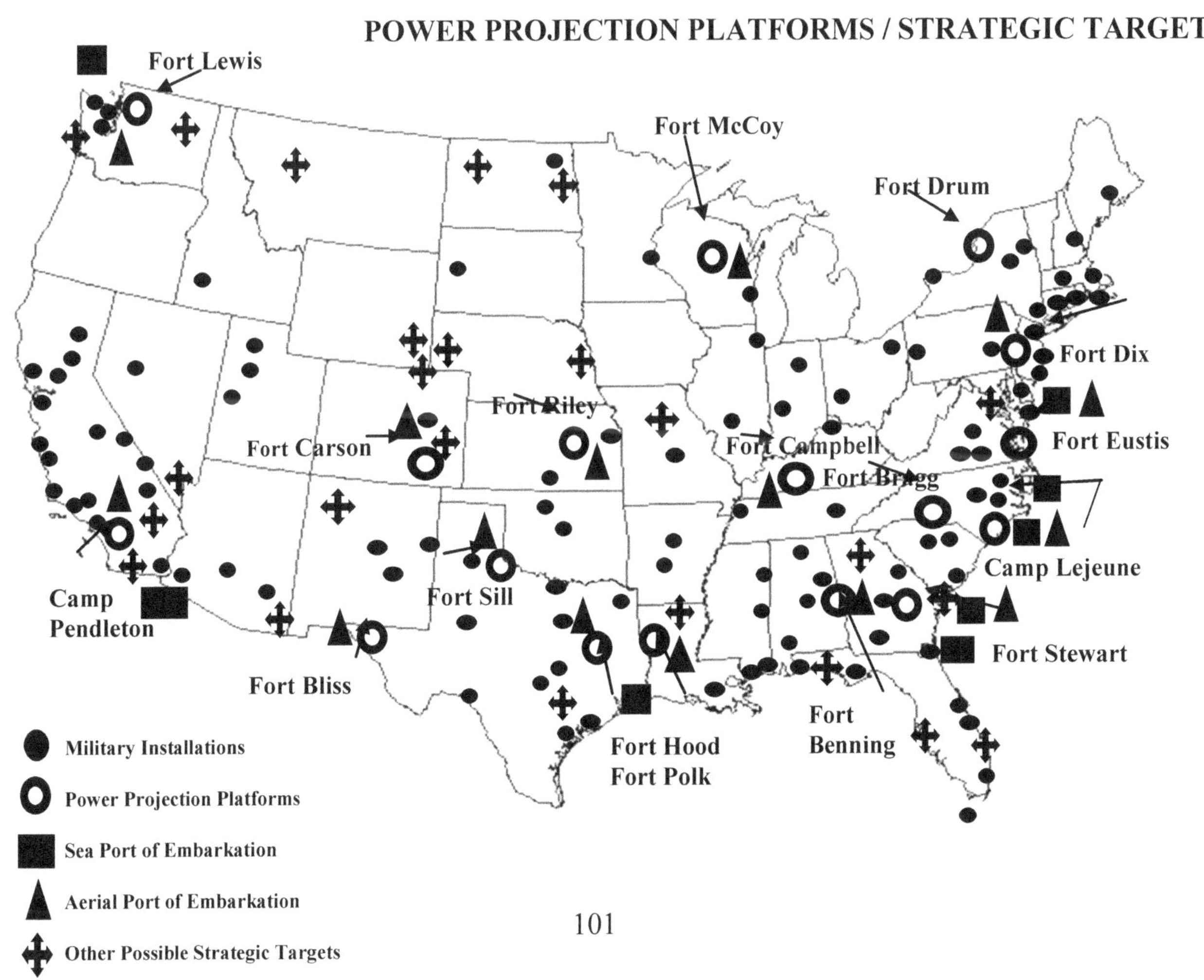

The map below identifies the location of some of the major nuclear weapon arsenals in the United States:

| NO | NUCLEAR WEAPON BASE AND ARSENAL |
|---|---|
| 1 | **KITSAP NAVAL BASE, WASHINGTON**<br>**Nuclear Submarine Arsenal**<br>Trident I C4 – 1,600 |
| 2 | **NELLIS AIR FORCE BASE, NEVADA**<br>B61/ALCM Storage – 750 and B61 Mods - 600 |
| 3 | **NORTH ISLAND NAVAL AIR STATION- CALIFORNIA**<br>W80 SLCM - 160 |
| 4 | **FAIRCHILD AIR FORCE BASE, WASHINGTON**<br>B41 Bombers - 25, B83 Bombers - 60 |
| 5 | **MALMSTROM AIR FORCE BASE, MONTANA**<br>Minuteman III ICBM Silos -550 |
| 6 | **MINOT AIR FORCE BASE, NORTH DAKOTA**<br>Minuteman III ICBM Silos – 455<br>W80 ALCM – 100,  W80 ACM - 300,  B61 - 50,  B83 - 90 |
| 7 | **WARREN AIR FORCE BASE – COLORADO/WYOMING/NEBRASKA**<br>Minuteman III ICBM Silos – 460,  MX  ICBM Silos - 525 |
| 8 | **KIRTLAND AIR FORCE BASE - NEW MEXICO**<br>B61/ALCM Storage–450, B61 Mods–600, W84 GLCM– 00, Minuteman II-450, W69SRAM-550 |
| 9 | **GRAND FORKS AIR FORCE BASE, NORTH DAKOTA**<br>B61 Bombers - 25, B83 Bombers - 60, Minuteman III Silos - 60 |

| NO | NUCLEAR WEAPON BASE AND ARSENAL |
|---|---|
| 10 | **PANTEX PLANT – AMARILLO, TEXAS**<br>3,000 warheads awaiting disarmament |
| 11 | **WHITEMAN AIR FORCE BASE - MISSOURI**<br>B2 Bombers - 550 |
| 12 | **BARKSDALE AIR FORCE BASE, LOUISIANA**<br>B52H Bombers – 140,  W80 ALCM/ACM - 400 |
| 13 | **YORKTOWN NAVAL WEAPONS STATION VIRGINIA**<br>W80 SLCM - 160 |
| 14 | **SEYMOUR-JOHNSON AIR FORCE BASE, NORTH CAROLINA**<br>F25E's for 4th Fighter Wing |
| 15 | **STRATEGIC WEAPONS FACILITY – Kings Bay, GEORGIA**<br>Submarine Launched Ballistic Missiles, Trident I C4 – 1,600,  Trident II D5 - 400,  Warhead Storage |

**SOURCE:** United States Department of Defense

---

**Did you know that after the Japanese destroyed our fleet in Pearl Harbor on 7 December 1941, they could have sent troop ships and carriers directly into California and finish what they started?**

**The prediction from our military generals at the time was that we would not be able to stop a massive invasion until they reached the Mississippi River. Keep in mind that after we were attacked at Pearl Harbor, the United States entered the war and also had a two million man army and war ships fighting the Germans.  So, why did Japan not invade our country?  After the war, the remaining Japanese generals and admirals were asked that question.  Their answer?  They know that almost every home  in America had guns and the Americans knew how to use them. The world's largest army was America's hunters.  A blogger added up the deer license sales in just a handful of states and arrived at a striking conclusion.  There were over 600,000 hunters in one season in the state of Wisconsin.  During those months, Wisconsin's hunters became the eighth largest army in the world with more men having guns than in Iran, France and Germany combined.  That number pales in comparison to the 750,000 who hunted in the woods of Pennsylvania or the 700,000 who hunted in Michigan.  There were also a quarter million hunters in West Virginia.  When you add up the totals, it demonstrates hunters in those <u>four states</u> alone would comprise the largest army in the world.**

# NEVER - EVER - GIVE UP YOUR GUNS!  NEVER!

As a general rule in planning for the worst case scenario, attempt to make emergency preparations based on the <u>possibility</u> of a full-scale nuclear attack on this country.  If prepared to face a nuclear attack and ensuing war– family members would likely be able to survive any man-made disasters and most natural disasters.  With that in mind –

## NUCLEAR EXPLOSION

A nuclear blast is an explosion caused by a nuclear weapon with intense light and heat, a damaging pressure wave, and widespread radioactive material that contaminates air, water and ground surfaces.  A nuclear device can range from a weapon carried by an intercontinental missile to a small portable nuclear device transported by a group of individuals.

*If they want peace, nations should avoid the pin-pricks that precede cannon shots.*

*-Napoleon Bonaparte*

All nuclear devices cause deadly affects when exploded, including blinding light, intense heat (thermal radiation), initial nuclear radiation, blast fires started by the heat pulse and secondary fires caused by the destruction.

## Atomic Weapons

In an atomic bomb, the energy of the weapon is derived from nuclear <u>fission</u> - the splitting of the nucleus of elements such as plutonium or uranium into lighter nuclei. The amount of nuclear energy released by this process produces a large amount of heat and electricity. A nuclear weapon's explosive power is measured in tons of TNT. The United States is the only country to have used an atomic bomb in war -- the first (Little Boy) was dropped on Hiroshima, Japan on 06 August 1945 with a yield of fifteen KT and the second (Fat Man) was dropped on Nagasaki, Japan on 09 August 1945 with a yield of twenty KT. President Donald Trump is correct - we are not so innocent . . .

## Thermonuclear Weapons

Hydrogen bombs are nuclear weapons in which extreme explosive powers are obtained through nuclear <u>fusion</u> - the process of forming a heavier nucleus from two lighter ones. This fusion requires an incredibly high temperature achieved through the initial detonation of an atomic bomb. Similar to an atomic bomb, the explosion of a hydrogen bomb produces a blast that can destroy structures within a radius of several miles, extreme heat that can spark firestorms and intense white light that can induce blindness. Radioactive fallout can poison living creatures and contaminate air, water and soil for many years.

These weapons can be thousands of times more powerful than atomic bombs, are measured in yield equal to megatons of TNT and yet they can be made small enough to fit in a ballistic missile warhead or an artillery shell. Small thermonuclear weapons called neutron bombs are effectively used against tanks and infantry on a traditional battlefield yet won't impact nearby cities within a few miles. They work by producing minimal blast and heat but releasing high amounts of radiation.

## Air Burst

In an air burst, the fireball explodes high in the air, does not touch the earth and there is no crater in the ground. An air burst produces extremely small radioactive particles - so small they are airborne for days to years unless brought to earth by rain or snow. Only when these tiny particles are promptly brought to earth called *hot spots* and later dried and blown by the winds would these invisible particles constitute a long-term danger to humans and animals. Hot spots from an air burst are much less dangerous than fallout produced by surface or near-surface bursts of the same weapons. The main dangers from an air burst are (1) <u>blast affects</u>, (2) penetrating <u>initial nuclear radiation</u> from the fireball and (3) <u>thermal pulses</u> of intense light and heat radiation.

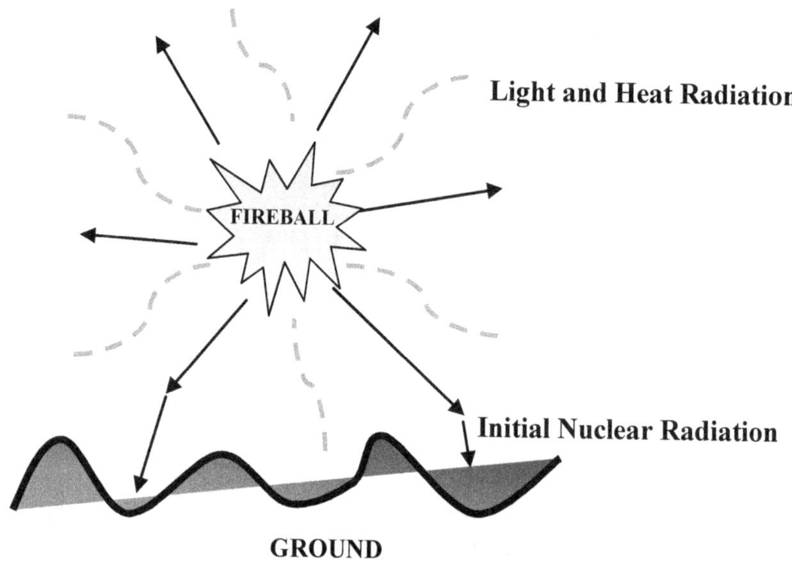


An air burst creates an electromagnetic pulse (EMP) which is a high-density electrical field similar to a stroke of lightning but is stronger, faster, and shorter than its natural-occurring cousin. An EMP can seriously damage electronic devices connected to power sources or antennas including communication systems, computers, electrical appliances or automobile and aircraft ignition systems. The damage could range from a minor interruption to the actual burnout of components. Most electronic equipment within 1,000 miles of a high-altitude nuclear detonation would be affected. Battery-powered radios with short antennas would generally <u>not</u> be affected. An EMP is unlikely to harm most people, but it could harm those with pacemakers or other implanted electronic devices.

## <u>Surface Burst</u>

In a surface burst, the fireball touches the earth and blasts a crater in the ground. Thousands of tons of earth from the crater are pulverized into trillions of particles contaminated by radioactive atoms. These particles are then carried up into a mushroom-shaped cloud miles above the earth. The radioactive particles fall out of the cloud and continuously give off invisible radiation called *fallout*. The largest and heaviest fallout particles reach the ground first in locations close to the explosion and the smaller particles are carried by the wind for thousands of miles before falling to earth. However, at any one place where fallout from a single explosion is being deposited on the ground in concentrations (hot spots), deposition will be completed within a few hours.

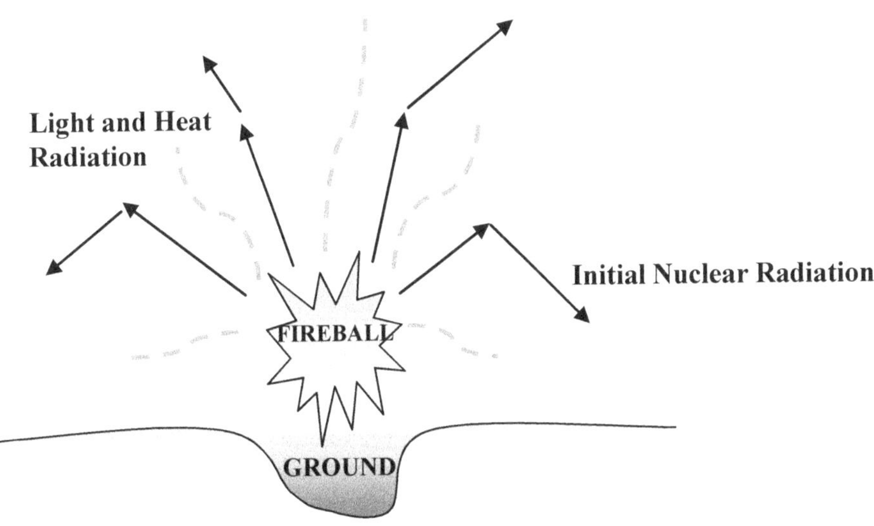


## POSSIBLE TARGETS

In general, some potential targets include:

- Airport Runways (Over 7,000 Feet In Length)
- Chemical Plants
- **Communication Centers**
- **Electrical Power Plants**
- Federal Centers Of Government (Washington DC)
- Financial Centers
- Food Producing Sites
- Industrial Centers
- **Major Airfields**
- **Major Ports**
- Manufacturing Centers
- **Military Bases**
- Military Command Centers (NORAD Etc.)
- **Missile Sites**
- Petroleum Refineries
- **POWER PROJECTION PLATFORM SITES**
- State Capitals
- Technology Centers
- **Transportation Centers**

Although a full-scale attack could destroy many missile silos and missiles, a first-strike attack is deterred in part by the fact that most missiles in silos here in the United States would be launched on warning and would be in space on trajectories toward enemy targets before their warheads could reach our silos. Populations would observe the sky lit up with an astounding brightness and would hear thunderous sounds from the initial SLBM explosions heard over most parts of the United States. Citizens one-hundred miles away from a nuclear explosion would receive their first warning by hearing it 7 ½ minutes later and these family members may have time to reach a nearby shelter before the ICBM's begin to explode over the entire country.

Additional explosions would follow to destroy surviving long runways or at a minimum, produce local fallout so heavy they could not be utilized. Homes within four or five miles of a runway at least 7,000 feet long are likely to be destroyed before residents receive warning or have time to reach blast shelters away from their homes. The homes six or seven miles away could be lightly damaged and some windows may be broken in homes over forty miles away. The vast majority of Americans would not be injured by the first explosions of a nuclear attack and only those citizens living in close proximity to primary targeted areas would be impacted. After the first assault, there would be fifteen to forty minutes before other missiles blasted secondary and tertiary sites.

There are countries in the world with a significant arsenal of large and powerful 20-megaton warheads and warheads that are smaller and more accurate in hitting the target. These smaller warheads are certainly capable of easily destroying a specific military target and in the event of a full-scale attack, *soft* targets may be destroyed by air bursts including naval vessels in seaport facilities, bombers and fighters on the ground, air base and airport facilities used by bombers, military installations and key defense factories. Many of these sites are in or near cities and neighborhoods.

The larger 20-megaton warheads could destroy typical homes up to sixteen miles from ground zero. In contrast, the smaller 1-megaton warhead could destroy most homes within a circular area having a radius of about five miles. <u>It could logically be concluded that unless the home is within twenty miles from the nearest probable target, family members need not evacuate to avoid *blast and fire dangers*. The concern for family members would focus instead on avoiding *fallout radiation.*</u>

If the nuclear attack takes place on a clear day, thermal pulses (heat radiation traveling at the speed of light) from an air burst can set fire to ignitable materials such as window curtains, upholstery, dried wood, newspapers and grass over the size of area damaged by the blast. These pulses can also cause second-degree skin burns to exposed persons and animals as far as ten miles from a one-megaton explosion. On a cloudy or smoggy day, particles in the air would absorb and scatter much of the heat radiation and the area would be less susceptible to fire.

> *I know not with what weapons World War III will be fought, but World War IV will be fought with sticks and stones.*
> - **Albert Einstein**

Unless preparations were made *in advance*, most people confined to shelters during a nuclear attack would be stressed, without food, water, clean surroundings or antibiotics to fight infections. Water from sources such as deep wells, covered reservoirs, tanks and containers would not be contaminated. Food and water in dust tight containers would not be contaminated by fallout radiation. Peeling fruits and vegetables and removing the uppermost several inches of stored grain removes essentially all fallout particles.

Family members taking refuge in shelters could work outside the shelters for an increasing number of hours each day <u>two weeks after a nuclear attack</u>. Exceptions would be in regions with extremely heavy fallout downwind of important targets attacked with a large number of weapons including missile sites and large cities. In order to begin essential tasks <u>after</u> a massive nuclear attack, survivors must be willing to receive much larger radiation doses than are normally permissible. Otherwise, too many workers would continue to stay inside a shelter and work vital to national and individual recovery would not be done. For example, food producers and truckers fearful of receiving even non-incapacitating radiation doses would not be willing to harvest, process or transport food and additional millions would die of starvation who have not adequately *prepared in advance* for such a nuclear attack.

## <u>Warning Systems</u>

In the event of a nuclear attack, a large majority of Americans including those living near ground zero of strategic targets would not receive warning in time to even reach a shelter. It is doubtful citizens living in urban areas would even hear the sirens and would probably not recognize the intent of the sirens or believe it was a legitimate warning. In the United States, the official warning system uses siren signals and radio and television announcements.

This system is not protected, however, from electromagnetic pulse affects from nuclear explosions, and if power fails, it could damage or destroy large segments of the communication system. If the system does remain intact and local authorities actually use the system, the attack warning signal is a wavering, wailing sound of sirens lasting three to five minutes or a series of short blasts of whistles or horns. If family members ever hear this signal, <u>take immediate protective action. Do not gather belongings. Do not try to telephone for information. Go promptly to the best available shelter.</u>

An additional warning system would be the Emergency Broadcast System (EBS) that would communicate (if possible) warnings on television and radio stations to the general public. In order to receive this communication, citizens would need to be watching television or listening to the radio at the time of the warning.

## PROTECTION FROM RADIATION AND FALLOUT

The Federal Emergency Management Administration (FEMA) has estimated primary targets for enemy ICBMs. The resulting fallout is displayed with the darkest colors considered as "lethal" to relatively fall-out free light-colored zones. The fallout would cover most of the United States within twelve hours after a massive attack and fallout will vary in intensity depending on the region.

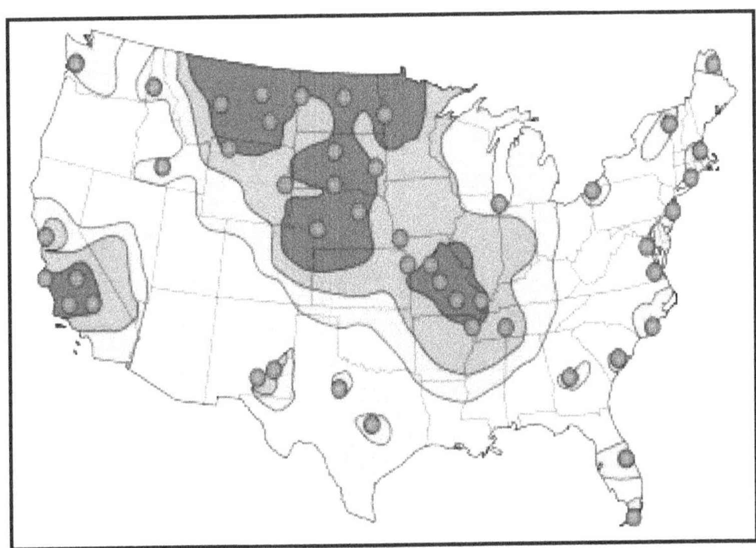

There are three factors for protecting family members from radiation and fallout:

### DISTANCE – SHIELDING - TIME

- **Distance** - the more distance between family members and the fallout particles - the better. An underground area such as a home or office building <u>basement</u> offers more protection than the first floor of a building. Flat roofs would collect fallout particles so the top floor is not a good choice nor is a floor located by an adjacent flat roof.

- **Shielding** - the heavier and denser the materials - thick walls, concrete, bricks, books and earth - between family members and the fallout particles - the better.

- **Time** - fallout radiation loses its intensity fairly rapidly and in time, the family will be able to leave the fallout shelter. Radioactive fallout poses the greatest threat to people during the <u>first two weeks</u>, by which time it has declined to about one percent of its initial radiation level.

As family members *prepare in advance* for the possibility of a nuclear explosion and the consequences, it is important to remember **DISTANCE - SHIELDING - TIME** *before*, *during* and *after* the attack.

---

**ANY PROTECTION IS BETTER THAN NONE AND THE MORE SHIELDING, DISTANCE AND TIME, THE BETTER CHANCE FAMILY MEMBERS HAVE TO SURVIVE THE DISASTER.**

---

**Evaluation**

Evaluate the region where the home and the place of refuge are located as well as homes of family members within a one-hundred mile and fifty mile radius and determine if any <u>probable</u> targets are located within those perimeters. When analyzing your susceptibility to a nuclear attack, recognize that targets in a nuclear war are broadly divided into two categories: *counterforce* targets that are <u>weapons</u> of the opponent e.g. airfields, military bases and airport runways, and *countevalue* targets that are <u>objects of value</u> to the enemy e.g. cities, industrial plants and population. For example, an enemy of the United States would consider our military bases to be a counterforce target but would consider our major cities and manufacturing plants to be countervalue targets and would become valuable to them if they were to succeed in causing our surrender.

In some cases, a target could be considered as a *counterforce* and *counter value* target. Attempt to categorize the possible targets located in your area into groups including *highest-priority*, *high-priority*, *medium-priority* and *low priority*. Recognize that not all targets will be created equal. For example, there are many military bases around the country but some would be higher priority targets because of important weapons, personnel or equipment assigned to the base.

| TARGET | Priority | Counterforce Targets | Countervalue Targets |
|---|---|---|---|
| *Airfields* | | X | |
| *Airport Runways(over 7,000 feet in length)* | | X | X |
| *Chemical Plants* | | X | X |
| *Command Centers (NORAD, PENTAGON)* | | X | X |
| *Communication Centers* | | X | X |
| *Electrical Power Plants/ Major Grids* | | | X |
| *Federal Centers (Washington DC)* | | | X |
| *Financial Centers* | | | X |
| *Food Producing Sites* | | | X |
| *Industrial Sites* | | X | X |
| *Major Cities* | | X | X |
| *Major Seaports* | | X | X |
| *Manufacturing Centers* | | X | X |
| *Military Bases* | | X | |
| *Missile Sites* | | X | |
| *Petroleum Factories* | | | X |
| *Residential Areas* | | | X |
| *State Capitols* | | | X |
| *Technology Centers* | | | X |
| *Transportation Centers* | | X | X |

Contact officials in your community to see if there are any public buildings designated as fallout shelters. If none have been designated, make your own list of potential shelters near your home, workplace and school. These places could include basements or the windowless center area of middle floors in high-rise buildings, subways and tunnels. If you live in an apartment building or high-rise complex, speak with the manager about the safest place in the building for sheltering and about providing emergency supplies for building occupants until it is safe to go out.

In the scenario below, the home and the alternate evacuation site would likely be in jeopardy due to strategic targets within the fifty and one-hundred mile radius. In the case of the home, there is an airport (7,000 feet runway) and major city within the 50-mile radius and a major seaport, strategic military base and petroleum factory within the 100-mile radius. The alternate evacuation site is within range of the military base and close to a major transportation center. Based on the proximity of targets to the home and alternate evacuation site, family members should consider constructing a high-level fallout and blast shelter at the home and/or alternate evacuation site or have an evacuation route away from the home and alternate evacuation site that takes them out of the 100-mile radius.

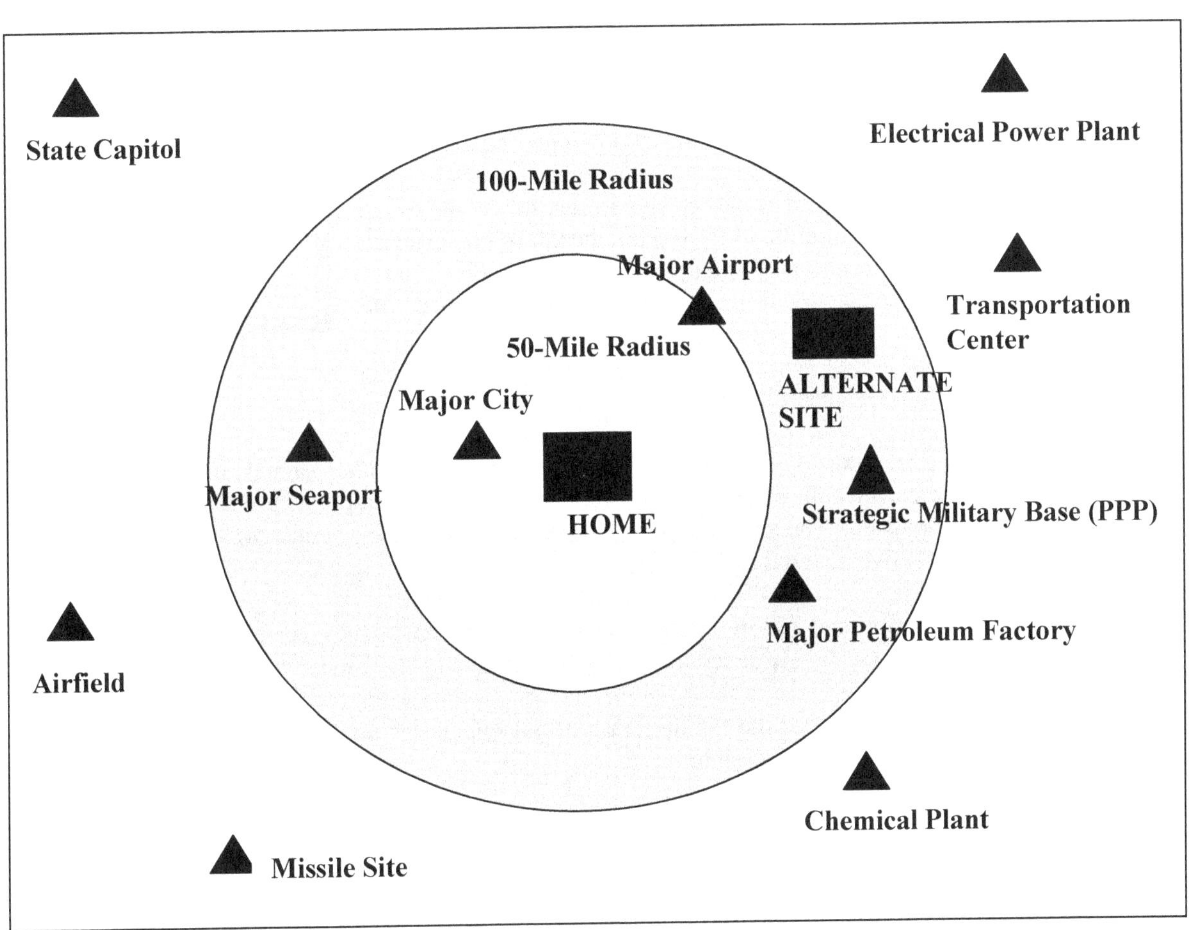


## Construction

If the family plans to construct a shelter *in advance* of any nuclear attack, there are two kinds of shelters:

(1)   *Blast* shelters are specifically constructed to offer some protection against blast pressure, initial radiation, heat and fire. But even a blast shelter cannot withstand a direct hit from a nuclear explosion. A *blast* shelter would be for families who are in the <u>near vicinity of prime or strategic targets</u>.

(2)   *Fallout* shelters can be any protected space provided the walls and roof are thick and dense enough to absorb the radiation given off by <u>fallout particles</u>. Even if building an excellent fallout shelter, it will <u>not</u> stop some gamma radiation from fallout penetrating the shielding materials and reaching occupants. The radiation dose can be reduced by designing features that include a sufficient thickness of earth or other heavy shielding material. A *fallout* shelter would be for families who are in the <u>near vicinity or within the 100-mile radius of prime or strategic targets and for families who may experience lethal fallout radiation based on the probable direction the fallout would travel from ground zero.</u>

There are many resources providing detailed instructions on the construction of shelters, including the Federal Emergency Management Administration (FEMA). As part of shelter construction, adequate emergency supplies should also be stored in the shelter.

<u>**Evacuation**</u>

Families living in highest risk or high risk areas prone to nuclear attack should have emergency supplies in the home, place of refuge and evacuation kits for an unexpected evacuation from the home due to a nuclear attack. The items should be stored in evacuation kits and loaded in the car, backpack or other type of transport if evacuating on foot.

An evacuation is <u>not favorable</u> if the family lives <u>outside</u> of a highest-risk or high-risk area and could build an expedient fallout shelter and make other survival preparations at or near the home. If transportation is not available, there are serious medical complications with family members, the profession of all or some family members' merit staying in the community (fire, police and first responders) or if the family lacks proper tools and emergency supplies, it would be more prudent to remain at the current location.

There are scenarios <u>favorable</u> for evacuation in the event of a <u>pending</u> nuclear attack. If the family lives in a highest-risk or high-risk area, evacuation is realistic if the family has transportation (car and gasoline) and the roads are open to a considerable lower-risk area. All family members should be in fairly good health or can evacuate with the assistance of others and if work performed by family members is not a profession the community will depend on during/after the attack e.g. police, fire, medical or ham operators.

> *If we don't end war –*
> *war will end us.*
>
> **-H.G. Wells**

If possible, and prior to an impending nuclear blast:

- If an attack warning is issued, make arrangements for pets, livestock and other animals under your care. Find the nearest building, preferably built of brick or concrete, and go inside and below ground if possible to avoid any radioactive material outside. The goal is to put as many walls and as much concrete, brick and soil between you and the outside radioactive material as possible.

- Listen for official information and follow instructions provided by emergency personnel. Based on what is known about the threat, you may be instructed to take shelter, go to a specific location or evacuate the area.

- If evacuating is in the best interest of the family, make arrangements for family members, pets, livestock and supplies to leave the region as soon as possible.

<u>**During a Nuclear Attack**</u>

- **Do <u>not</u> look at the flash or fireball - it can blind you.**

  o If in the home when seeing the bright light, take pets and <u>run out of rooms with windows and go to a windowless hallway or down into the basement</u>. If a shelter is close to the house but separate from it, do not leave the best cover in the home to run outdoors to reach the shelter. <u>Wait for at least two minutes after first seeing the light</u>.

  o If outdoors when seeing the bright light, get behind or under the best available cover for at least two minutes. If no blast or sound reaches you in two minutes, the explosion was over twenty-five miles away and you would not be hurt by blast affects. After two minutes, make preparations to go to the best shelter that can be reached within fifteen minutes – the probable time interval before the first ICBM's begin to explode.

- At no time after an attack begins should family members or pets look out of a window or stay near a window. Under certain atmospheric conditions, windows can shatter by a multi-megaton explosion over a hundred miles away.

- Take shelter as soon as you can, even if you are many miles from ground zero where the attack occurred - radioactive fallout can be carried by the winds for hundreds of miles.

- Remember the three protective factors:  **DISTANCE - SHIELDING – TIME**

<u>**After a Nuclear Attack**</u>

- Stay in the shelter, even if you are separated from other family members. Inside is the safest place for all people, pets and livestock in the impacted area.

- During the time with highest radiation levels, it is safest to stay inside, sheltered away from the radioactive material outside so expect to stay inside for a minimum of two to three days. Radiation levels are extremely dangerous after a nuclear detonation but the levels reduce rapidly.

- Removing the outer layer of clothing can remove up to 90% of radioactive material. Remove clothing (if practical), place contaminated clothing in a plastic bag and seal or tie the bag to keep radioactive material from spreading. Place the bag far away from humans and animals to avoid spreading radiation.

- Gently blow your nose and wipe eyelids, eyelashes and ears with a clean wet cloth.

- Family members, pets and livestock should take a shower (when possible) with soap and uncontaminated water to help remove radioactive materials. If you cannot shower, use a clean wet cloth to wipe skin that was not covered by clothing. <u>Do not scrub or scratch the skin</u>. Wash hair with shampoo or soap and water. Do <u>not</u> use conditioner because it will bind radioactive material to the hair.

- Depend on <u>local</u> fallout meter readings or on radiation measurements made by neighbors or <u>local</u> civil defense workers to determine the safety factor in their respective area. Readings from other regions may not be indicative of actual radiation measurements in the local area.

The amount of radiation fallout would vary based on the size of the nuclear device and its proximity to the ground. Family members residing in areas with highest radiation levels may be required to shelter for up to a month.

The heaviest fallout would be limited to the area at or downwind from the explosion and eighty percent of the fallout would occur during the first twenty-four hours. People in most of the areas affected could be allowed to come out of a shelter within a few days and evacuate to unaffected areas. Stay away from areas marked "radiation hazard" or "HAZMAT." <u>Recognize that radiation cannot be seen, smelled or detected by *human* senses</u>.

## PROTECTION FROM THE ELEMENTS

We have been warned for years in the last days, the entire planet would be in crisis and we should prepare ourselves for the time when we would be subject to the affects and consequences of natural disasters and manmade disasters and dangerous events. Unfortunately, it is unclear about <u>what</u> type of disasters and dangerous events will be forthcoming, <u>when</u> we should expect them and exactly <u>where</u> on earth they would take place. As we continue to observe the devastating events around the world and here at home, we are beginning to understand the significance and wisdom in the counsel of emergency preparation.

When family members address the dilemma of how best to protect themselves from disasters – I believe it comes down to <u>seven</u> general guidelines:

1. *Prepare in advance* and work hard to store a <u>minimum</u> of a **one-year supply** of needed resources, goods and supplies.

2. **Study, learn, ponder, think, analyze** and **discuss** with family members all natural disaster and manmade and dangerous events outlined in this book. Take steps to protect the home and surroundings, as well as the individual family members and complete the tasks and assignments needed to maintain the *physical, spiritual, emotional, mental* and *psychological* health of family members. <u>Remember - what you don't know - can and will hurt you during a serious disaster</u>.

3. Make the necessary arrangements in your life to **come to terms with God** - however you choose to believe in Him, however you choose to worship Him, however you choose to pray to Him - having God on your side during a disaster is a win-win situation. Only someone who is intellectually challenged (stupid) in math would think otherwise.

4.      Include **weapons and ammunition** as part of the overall emergency preparation plan to protect family members and emergency supplies.  This is a sound and sensible strategy.  Perhaps the best argument to include  weapons and ammunition in the emergency preparation arsenal is to recognize that during some short-term disasters and definitely during medium to long-term disasters – there will be many people who will not be prepared.  During desperate times - there will be desperate people - searching for emergency supplies.

5.      **NEVER NEVER NEVER** give up your weapons or ammunition to the government, politicians, military or law enforcement - **NEVER**.  Under no circumstances or for any reason - **EVER EVER EVER**.

6.      **Combine forces with other families <u>IN ADVANCE</u>** to protect homes, neighborhoods and communities from those who would harm or inflict damage on family members and property.

7.      Recognize that any of these disasters could happen and would more than likely affect you - either directly or indirectly.  Don't be naïve into believing you are immune from taking a hit.

## TEMPORAL PROTECTION

When referring to *temporal* protection, I am talking about *cannons, guns, ammunition, swords, knives, grenades, bow and arrow, slingshots, rocks* and *sticks* - in other words - <u>manmade weapons</u>.  As part of *planning in advance*, families should decide whether or not to use these types of weapons during an emergency or disaster event.

> *The strongest reason for people to retain the right to keep and bear arms is, as a last resort, to protect themselves against tyranny in their government.*
>
> **- Thomas Jefferson**

There are countless scenarios when manmade weapons could be justified and used to protect the family from groups, gangs or individuals who may elect to use lethal force to take emergency supplies during a short-term emergency or a long-term and serious disaster.  As citizens, we have the right to protect ourselves and our supplies from those who would attempt to use criminal and/or unscrupulous means to maintain or gain control of the region and/or to obtain emergency supplies for themselves during a crisis environment.

There are basically three types of groups who could potentially pose a threat to families as follows:

1.      This group comprises one individual or citizen(s) who band together in order to protect themselves and obtain emergency supplies they need in order to survive.

- **Law-abiding** citizens who have <u>not</u> prepared in advance, and due to the perception (real or unreal) they are entitled to or need emergency supplies from others in order to survive - resort to unethical, immoral and illegal means to obtain what they need to stay alive.  These citizens could be your neighbors, friends, relatives or anyone you pass on the street.

- **Gangs** who have <u>not</u> prepared in advance, and who have (in the past) continually used intimidation, lethal force, theft and other unlawful means to maintain and control their "turf" and to obtain provisions, supplies and rations they use on a daily basis.

- **Addicts** who have <u>not</u> prepared in advance, and who have (in the past) continually used theft and even lawful means to support their drug, alcohol and tobacco habit and to obtain provisions, supplies and rations they use on a daily basis.

- **Criminals** who have <u>not</u> prepared in advance, and who continually use any means necessary to obtain wanted provisions, supplies and rations.

- **Mentally Ill** citizens who have <u>not</u> prepared in advance, who may or may not have been under a doctor's care, and will take whatever steps are necessary to obtain provisions, supplies and rations they need to survive.

2.       This group comprises members of the <u>United States Armed Forces</u> (Army, Navy, Air Force, Marines and Coast Guard), National Guard and various <u>law enforcement agencies</u> assigned to federal, state or local jurisdictions.

3.       This group comprises <u>enemy combatants</u> including military forces, terrorists, or citizens from hostile countries

I believe during a majority of emergency and disaster scenarios, members of the military and law enforcement would give their own lives to protect the citizens of this country.  But I also recognize the distinct possibility these same individuals could be commanded and/or convinced by government or corporate executives to turn guns on the very citizens they have taken an oath to protect.  To make this point, consider the Egyptian uprising where military soldiers were commanded by their own superiors who were commanded by government politicians to fire on their own citizenry.

There seems to be a very fine line between (1) limitations and restrictions that must be placed on government politicians to prevent an abuse of power, (2) acceptable role military and law enforcement should play in protecting and/or defending citizens, (3) limitations placed on citizens before military or law enforcement intervention is justified and (4) retribution by military or law enforcement for illegal, unrealistic, destructive or criminal actions by citizens.

That line seems to become even more distorted when one observes the *direction* in which the guns of the military and law enforcement may be pointed and exactly *who* or *what* it is they believe is being protected or defended.  Is it the country?  Is it the Constitution?  Is it the commanders?  Is it the citizens?  Is it the governor?  Is it the members of the Senate and Congress?  Is it the President of the United States?  Or - is it themselves?

# SUMMARY

Based on the comprehensive information provided in this book, it becomes apparent how important it is to know how to avoid, suppress, or even successfully react to specific disasters and dangerous events.  It also becomes evident how critical it is to *prepare in advance* for any type of trouble.  As these upcoming disasters increase in number, severity and duration, by *planning in advance* and filling emergency pantries, families who have taken steps to *gather*, *assemble* and *store* supplies will have a better chance of survival.

No one knows the details of future disaster or dangerous events - no one knows *why*, *when*, *where*, or *how* the scenarios will take place.  But most reasonable citizens who read the newspapers, watch the television broadcasts and reports, and simply stop and look around the immediate area and observe world events recognizes there have been major changes in weather patterns and an ominous transformation in the environment, terrorist attacks, corruption in government, escalating unrest and crime, financial instability and increased health problems throughout the population.  There is an increased sense of uneasiness and apprehension in families about what the future will hold for all of us.

Remember to live each day to the fullest - stop and breathe in the sweet scent of every single rose.  Maintain a positive outlook on life while at the same time, recognize the reality of both natural disasters and manmade disasters and dangerous events occurring in the future.

By systematically, thoroughly and methodically filling emergency pantries, family members will not only have a feeling of accomplishment but will also experience a feeling of independence, self-sufficiency and relief that comes with *preparing in advance* to deal with any future emergency scenario - no matter how big - no matter how small.  Your family can be prepared.  Recognize that gathering supplies and resources for emergency pantries is a continual and on-going process.  Each family must evaluate their own unique circumstances and based on where you live, current lifestyle and other factors affecting individual situations, review the information contained in this book and make a *realistic* and *smart* decision on what would be good choices for your members.

During a disaster, families can band together to create effective and successful groups to protect all family members from criminal and dangerous outside forces.  There is <u>strength in numbers</u> and this approach will limit aggression, violence and attacks from those who would endanger families and emergency supplies.  As part of *planning in advance*, continue to work towards emergency preparation for the family but at the same time, make plans with other family groups to create an effective and strong force and coalition to protect each other and the supplies.

Carefully study and learn about *specific* types of emergencies and disasters that can occur in regions around the world and in your area, how they would affect your family, and what steps family members can take *in advance* to prepare *before*, *during* and *after* these events. By following the strategies, guidelines, tips and lists outlined in this book, families can hopefully avoid serious injuries or death if these events happen around you. In some cases, by taking preemptive measures, the family can even eliminate or reduce the impact of the disaster or catastrophe from happening in the first place.

# GEORGE WASHINGTON VISION OF FUTURE WAR IN USA

In 1777, while at Valley Forge, George Washington recorded in his journal a visitation by an angel who showed him the destiny of the United States:

"And again I heard the mysterious voice saying, 'Son of the Republic, look and learn.' At this the dark, shadowy angel placed a trumpet to his mouth and blew three distinct blasts; and taking water from the ocean, he sprinkled it upon Europe, Asia and Africa. Then my eyes beheld a fearful scene: from each of these countries arose thick, black clouds that were soon joined into one. Throughout this mass, there gleamed a dark red light by which I saw hordes of armed men, who, moving with the cloud, marched by land and sailed by sea to America. Our country was enveloped in this volume of cloud, and I saw these vast armies devastate the whole country and burn the villages, towns and cities that I beheld springing up. As my ears listened to the thundering of the cannon, clashing of swords, and the shouts and cries of millions in mortal combat, I heard the mysterious voice saying, 'Son of the Republic, look and learn.' When the voice had ceased, the dark shadowy angel placed his trumpet once more to his mouth, and blew a long and fearful blast.

Instantly, a light as of a thousand suns shone down from above me, and pierced and broke into fragments the dark cloud which enveloped America. That same moment, the angel upon whose head still shone the word "UNION" and who bore our national flag in one hand and a sword in the other, descended from the heavens attended by legions of white spirits. These immediately joined the inhabitants of America, who I perceived were well nigh overcome, but who immediately taking courage again, closed up their broken ranks and renewed the battle. Again, amid the fearful noise of the conflict, I heard the mysterious voice saying, 'Son of the Republic, look and learn.' As the voice ceased, the shadowy angel for the last time dipped water from the ocean and sprinkled it upon America. Instantly, the dark cloud rolled back, together with the armies it had brought, leaving the inhabitants of the land victorious.

Then once more I beheld the villages, towns and cities springing up where I had seen them before, while the bright angel, planting the azure standard he had brought in the midst of them, cried with a loud voice: 'While the stars remain, and the heavens send down the dew upon the earth, so long shall the Union last.' And taking from his brow the crown on which blazoned the word "UNION", he placed it upon the Standard while the people, kneeling down, said 'Amen.'

The scene instantly began to fade and dissolve, and I at last saw nothing but the rising, curling vapor I had at first beheld. This also disappearing, I found myself once more gazing upon the mysterious visitor, who, in the same voice I had heard before, said, 'Son of the Republic, what you have seen is thus interpreted: Three great perils will come upon the Republic. The most fearful is the third, but in this greatest conflict, the whole world united shall not prevail against her. Let every child of the Republic learn to live for his God, his land and the Union.' With these words, the vision vanished, and I started from my seat and felt that I had seen a vision wherein had been shown to me the birth, progress and destiny of the United States."

## EMERGENCY SUPPLIES FOR CONSIDERATION

Here is a table of items to consider in purchasing and storing emergency supplies. THIS IS NOT A COMPLETE LIST. In order to have a more comprehensive list of emergency supplies to consider for your family, additional books by Wellington on emergency preparation are available on Amazon include the following:

- A Beginners Collection of Emergency Preparation Principles - Volume 1
- A Beginners Collection of Emergency Preparation Principles - Volume 2
- Disaster Survival in a World of Crisis

- Emergency Preparation Principles for Beginners
- Prepare Today - Survive Tomorrow
- Preparing for Survival - Disaster at the Door

| OPERATION TRANSPORTATION | MEDICATION IMMUNIZATION | SANITATION FINANCIAL INSTITUTION | COMMUNICATION RECREATION |
|---|---|---|---|
| **WATER**<br><br>**FOOD**<br><br>**LIGHT**<br>Flashlights<br>Lanterns<br>Matches<br>Mirror (behind lamp)<br>Oil<br>Oil Lamps<br>Solar Battery Charger<br>Solar Garden Lights<br><br>**ELECTRICITY**<br>Solar Generator<br><br>**CLOTHING**<br>Rain Gear<br>Summer<br>Winter<br><br>**TOOLS**<br><br>**HEAT**<br>Axe<br>Bedding<br>Flint Fire Starter<br>Sleeping Bags<br>Wood<br><br>**BABY SUPPLIES**<br><br>**TRANSPORTATION**<br>Good Walking Shoes<br>Bicycle | **MEDICATION**<br>Activated Charcoal - for poisoning<br>Adhesive Tape Rolls<br>Antacids (Rolaids, Alka Seltzer)<br>Antibiotics<br>Antiseptics and Topicals<br>Bandages<br>Birth Control<br>Braces\Compress<br>Cold Pack<br>Cough Suppressants<br>Diarrhea Remedies<br>Dressings<br>Epson Salts<br>Eye Drops<br>Eye Glass Repair Kit<br>Gauze<br>Gloves (latex)<br>Heat Pack<br>Heating Pad<br>Hot Water Bottle<br>Laxatives<br>Medicine Dropper/Spoon<br>Pads<br>Scissors<br>Shampoo (lice)<br>Splints<br>Suppositories<br>Swabs<br>Thermometer<br>Throat Lozenges<br>Tongue Blades<br>Toothache Remedies<br>Tweezers<br>Wound Closures<br><br>**IMMUNIZATION**<br>Diphtheria<br>Hepatitis A<br>Hepatitis B<br>Human Papillomavirus<br>Influenza<br>Measles<br>Mumps<br>Meningococcal Meningitis<br>Pertussis (Whopping Cough)<br>Pneumococcal Pneumonia<br>Polio<br>Rubella<br>Tetanus<br>Typhoid<br>Varicella (Chickenpox)<br>Zoster (Shingles) | **SANITATION**<br>Baking Soda<br>Buckets<br>Cleaners<br>Cleaning Supplies<br>Commode/Toilet<br>Dental Supplies<br>Disinfectants<br>Feminine Supplies<br>Garbage Bags<br>Gloves<br>Insect Repellent<br>Laundry Supplies<br>Mouse Traps<br>Paper Towels<br>Personal Hygiene<br>Rags<br>Tissues<br>Toilet Paper<br>Vinegar<br><br>**FINANCIAL INSTITUTION**<br>Barter Items<br>Cash<br>Precious Gems<br>Precious Metals | **COMMUNICATION**<br>AM/FM Radio<br>Bull Horn<br>CB Radio<br>Ham Radio<br>Hidden Message Box<br>Home Signal<br>Out of State Contact<br>Paper and Pencils<br>Scanner<br>Status Letter<br>Walkie Talkie<br>Whistle<br><br>**RECREATION**<br>Books<br>Cards<br>Crafts<br>Games<br>Musical Instruments<br>Puzzles<br>Sewing Projects<br>Toys<br>Writing Materials |

> *I see in the future a crisis approaching that unnerves me and causes me to tremble for the safety of my country. Corporations have been enthroned. An era of corruption in high places will follow, and the money power of the country will endeavor to prolong its reign by working upon the prejudices of the people, until the wealth is aggregated in a few hands, and the Republic is destroyed.*
>
> **- Abraham Lincoln - prior to his assassination in 1865**

## BIBLIOGRAPHY


American Firefighters Association (AFA)
American Medical Association (AMA)
American Red Cross
Centers for Disease Control and Prevention (CDC)
Concerned Scientists Around the World
Environmental Protection Agency (EPA)
Federal Emergency Management Administration (FEMA)
Federal Energy Regulatory Commission (FERC)
McGoey, Chris; crimedoctor.com
National Agricultural Statistics Service (NASS)
National Aeronautics and Space Administration (NASA)
National Association of Police Organizations (NAPO)
National Center for Atmospheric Research (NCAR)
National Climatic Data Center (NCDC)
National Fire Protection Association (NFPA)
National Hurricane Center (NHC)
National Interagency Fire Center (NIFC)
National Oceanic/Atmospheric Administration (NOAA)
National Science Foundation (NSF)
National Weather Service (NWS)
Nuclear Regulatory Commission (NRC)
United States Department of Agriculture
United States Department of Commerce
United States Department of Defense
United States Department of Energy
United States Department of Health and Human Services
United States Department of the Interior
United States Department of Transportation
United States Forest Service
United States Geological Survey